Words for Today
2012

Notes for daily Bible reading

IBRA
International Bible Reading Association

Words

for today 2012

Edited by Nicola Slee

IBRA
International Bible Reading Association

Words for Today aims to build understanding and respect for a range of religious perspectives and approaches to living practised in the world today, and to help readers meet new challenges in their faith. Views expressed by contributors should not, however, be taken to reflect the views or policies of the Editor or the International Bible Reading Association.

The International Bible Reading Association's scheme of readings is listed on the Christian Education website at www.christianeducation.org.uk/about-ibra/2012 and the full scheme for 2011 may be downloaded in English, Spanish and French.

Editor: Nicola Slee
Cover image courtesy of iStockphoto LP

Published by:
The International Bible Reading Association
1020 Bristol Road
Selly Oak
Birmingham B29 6LB
United Kingdom
www.christianeducation.org.uk/ibra

Charity number 211542

ISBN 978-1-905893-42-3
ISSN 0140-8275

Typeset by Splash Creative Design www.splash-design.co.uk
Printed and bound in UK by Mosaic Print Management www.mosaicpm.com

Contents

Editorial

How do you read this year's cover image? It could be a scene at a nightclub or a disco, showing youthful revellers having a good time, dancing, swaying and enjoying some fireworks. Or perhaps it's an outdoor rock concert or a festival, where crowds mingle in the summer air as they listen to performers on the big stage. Or look again and see a political rally or demonstration, people taking to the streets in protest or solidarity with some campaign. The clenched fist raised in the air is then an expression of defiance and political activism, possibly even armed struggle, and the exploding flashes of light could be flares or teargas rather than fireworks.

Whether the scene is of relaxed fun and revelry or more urgent political uprising, it speaks of a contemporary world in which passion for change and engagement with youthful energies are key themes. And the image speaks of a Christian faith that is equally at home with exuberant celebration and political struggle. The Jesus whom Christians follow seemed to spend a lot of time both relaxing at parties (to the outrage of some of the strict sect) and talking about the reign of God in such a way as to fuel social and political, as well as personal, hopes in his hearers. And he didn't just talk about this coming reign, he enacted it too – in his dealings with people, healings, exorcisms and other signs of power.

As I write this editorial, recent large-scale government cuts to public services in the UK have provoked a fair amount of protest, and there have been marches, rallies and gatherings. On the international scene, we have witnessed political agitation and mass uprisings in North African and Middle Eastern countries, and currently the outcome of all this is uncertain. Mixed in with the protest has been an extraordinary hopeful energy, and some of the mass demonstrations have had the air of parties – albeit somewhat anarchic ones. Perhaps this is one manifestation of the reign of God at work in our own world and times – the spirit of freedom, longing for justice and hope that is deep in people's hearts expressing itself in the need to party and in the impulse to act publicly for the wellbeing of all.

As we read the Bible again this coming year, in the company of writers both established and new, as well as alongside many thousands of other users of these notes, my prayer is that we will find plenty of cause for celebration and know ourselves motivated to act for change in the world. As we do, may we find that we are part of that jostling, hopeful, questing throng of those who walk – and live – in the way of Christ.

Nicola Slee
Editor

Prayers

We see ourselves, O God,
people of faith and faithlessness –
dancing in the sun one day
and overwhelmed by our realities on the next,
joyfully announcing the gospel sometimes
and then trembling in our uncertainty.
We see the hope that lies among us –
and hope that we could care
and live in community with each other
and the world.

Prayer attributed to Dorothy McRae-McMahon, and used with her permission

Give us grace, O Lord, committed to Christ, to seize the present opportunity; and, empowered by your Spirit, to look to the future with expectation. Help us to love, listen and learn, to offer and proclaim, so that boys and girls, men and women, may come to the joy of your service.

Kenneth S J Hext

Jesus calls us, Jesus calls us today;
let us hear him, let us hear his true word;
let us thank him, for he gives us life.

Zambian prayer

God of celebration, God of struggle:
teach us to give ourselves wholeheartedly
both to the joy of celebration and to the pain of struggle,
so that we may know your freedom and your desire for the world
enfleshed in our midst, in our own communities and lives.

Nicola Slee

How to use a 'quiet time'

Pay attention to your body Take time to slow down, consciously relax each part of your body, and listen to your breathing for a while.

Use silence to relax and empty your mind of all that's going on around you. Know that God's loving presence encircles you, your family, your community and the world. Learn to enjoy God's presence.

Have a visual focus – a cross, a plant, interesting stones, pictures or postcards... create a prayer table on which to display them with other symbols.

Read the **Bible passage** for the day several times, perhaps using different translations, and then the notes. Allow the words to fill your mind. Try to discover their message for you and the world around you.

Listen Remember that the most important part of prayer is to hear what God is saying to us. God speaks to us through the words of scripture, the daily news, and often through people around us.

Include the world Hold the news of the day in your mind. Enter the situation of those you hear or read about and try to pray alongside them and with them.

Pray without ceasing Prayer is not only 'the quiet time' we set aside. It becomes part of the whole of life, a continuous dialogue between God and ourselves, through all that we do and think and say: a growing awareness of the loving presence of God who travels with us and never leaves us.

Acknowledgements and abbreviations

Thanks are due to the following for permission to include copyright material: Dorothy McRae-McMahon; Kenneth S J Hext; O Books; Wild Goose Publications; Liberal Judaism; Jewish Publication Society; Bible Society; Persephone Books; the Archbishops' Council of Great Britain.

Every effort has been made to gain permission for the inclusion of copyright material. The publishers would be pleased to include correct attribution of any inadvertently unattributed material in subsequent editions, on being contacted by the lawful copyright holder(s).

Bible versions quoted from have been abbreviated as follows and the publishers' permission is gratefully acknowledged:

CEV *The Bible for Today (Contemporary English Version)* Scripture quotations are from the Contemporary English Version (CEV) © American Bible Society 1991, 1995.

GNB *Good News Bible* (The Bible Societies/Collins Publishers) – Old Testament © American Bible Society 1976; New Testament © American Bible Society 1966, 1971, 1976.

NIV Scripture quotations taken from *The Holy Bible, New International Version* © 1973, 1978, 1984 by International Bible Society. Used by permission of Hodder & Stoughton Limited. All rights reserved. 'NIV' is a registered trademark of International Bible Society. UK trademark number 1448790.

NJB Taken from the *New Jerusalem Bible*, published and copyright 1985 by Darton, Longman and Todd Ltd and Doubleday & Co. Inc, and used by permission of the publishers.

NSRV *New Revised Standard Version* © 1989, Division of Christian Education of the National Council of Churches of Christ in the United States of America.

REB *Revised English Bible* © Oxford University and Cambridge University Presses 1989.

RSV *The Holy Bible, Revised Standard Version* © 1973, Division of Christian Education of the National Council of Churches of Christ in the United States of America.

Note

BCE Before the Common Era. BCE and CE are used by some writers instead of BC and AD.

Faces of the divine

Saturday 1 January

1 Creating God

Notes based on the New Jerusalem Bible by **David Ford**

David Ford is an Anglican priest working in parish ministry and school chaplaincy in the city of Leeds, in the north of England. His many theological interests include the evolving nature of the Western church as it struggles to come to terms with economic and numerical decline. Chief amongst his hobbies is beekeeping, which provides ample opportunity to reflect upon the nature of community.

Genesis 1:1-19

From absence to presence

Like God, who in creation cast aside the formless void once and for ever, so we are invited to begin this year afresh. Welcome to a new beginning!

The Bible begins with a story. This is no accident, for stories enable us to use the full wealth of our expressive capabilities: our senses and emotions, imaginations and dreams. Through stories we begin to find meaning – about God and about ourselves. And all stories are about relationships grounded in experience. The words we use simply try to voice this so that it can be shared with others. The words have no identity or meaning apart from the stories we tell through them.

It is very hard to read this story of creation as if we've never read it before. But try we must, for that is the only way to allow the Spirit to speak to us through our reading.

In the creation story we see images of contrast between divine absence and presence. God is given voice, but not form. And that voice affirms that what becomes present is 'good'. This story is more than a description of the perfection of creation. For God's decisive act of creation was also an intentional act of *involvement*. Through the act of creation, God ceases to be absent and begins to be present. God becomes a participant.

What stories in your life speak of God's creativity?

Creator God, help me to see your presence and participation in the world, and give thanks.

The power of mutual love

Numbers 6:22-27

Language is key to our attempts to express and describe the divine, but we quickly run out of words to describe what is beyond understanding, let alone description. One effect of this is that we load the divine with human attributes, which in English has led scholars to give God a predominantly male gender identity that was never intended. The resulting images of God – common throughout Western language and art – limit our understanding of the divine and may prevent others from entering into a relationship with God at all. This is precisely contrary to God's creative purposes. For the outpouring of God in creation is an act of desire. God wills us to enter into relationship with the divine.

To receive God's blessing is to be loved into relationship with God. It requires nothing of us, except our desire to accept. For many it is the very pinnacle of worship as in complete humility we welcome God's grace into our lives. The well-known and deeply loved words of Aaron's blessing offer us protection, acceptance and peace. The words reflect a God whose love of us is unconditional and unlimited, arguably like a parent's love for a child. It has taken me all my life to recognise and accept that I am loved by God like this. It is deeply humbling.

What impact might my acceptance of God's love and blessing have on God? Is a blessing received a blessing returned? Might God's creative power be strengthened by the love we return to the source of all love?

How can you demonstrate God's love for you today?

Blessed God, may you be blessed this day.

Let God be God

Isaiah 65:17-25

At school I dreaded science lessons. I don't have the kind of mind that can absorb complicated formulae or long scientific names. But when I started to study theology, I discovered a new respect for science. For every scientific discovery generates more questions than it answers. Science expands the mystery of creation. As the universe goes on expanding, so does God's love.

Despite your best personal intentions, the start of this New Year of God's creative activity may already be marred in your own community by signs of human weakness and failure. Violence and injustice, particularly against the poor, women and children, show little sign of abating. God's expanding love continues to be rejected.

Isaiah invites us to envisage a different world – a new world that God claims to be already creating! It is a world of peace and justice; a world of joy and of plenty. A world of promise, where hope is realised: 'No hurt, no harm will be done on my holy mountain' (verse 25). This is a vision for us today; a vision that the majority world desperately needs. But there is a price. For in this new heaven and new earth 'the past will not be remembered and will come no more to mind' (verse 17b).

Here is a reminder that the burden of the world's sin lies with God, not us. The suffering of the world – suffered or caused by us – is solely for God to embrace. Harbouring unkind thoughts towards those who cause us pain amounts to a refusal to let God be God: an attempt on our part to interfere with the process of restoration that God already has under way.

Consider making a renewed commitment to peace and justice this year.

Restoring God, embrace my pain and guilt, and free me to live your vision.

David Ford

Sustaining the sacred

Psalm 104:24-35

Although I live close to a city centre, there is an ancient wood within a few hundred yards of my home, where my wife and I walk our dog each day. Despite the rubbish that inevitably accumulates in cities, it is a beautiful place to watch wildlife and observe the changing seasons. A small river runs through the wood and there is a vast variety of plant life, including a lot of free food if you know what to look for. I need go no further to observe the sustaining work of God in progress.

Yet I am often in a hurry. With my mind full of the day's tasks I fail to listen to the birdsong and my eyes miss countless wonders, and my self-obsession leads me to ignore the neighbours I pass. The psalmist calls us back to notice the works of God.

In the many centuries that have passed since the Psalms were first conceived, our exploration of the world and our understanding of it have increased immeasurably. Clearly it is right no longer to think of earthquakes and volcanoes as uttering the displeasure of God. Yet we have replaced innocent ignorance with arrogant destruction of the carefully designed interdependence of creation of which the psalmist spoke. And yet God keeps creating. Such is the power of the creative process that God unleashed, the earth may be groaning under the burden of our exploitation, yet creation continues. This surely is our signal to recognise the wisdom of God and the folly of humanity. Is God's patience as unlimited as God's creativity?

Take time today to listen to the sounds of creation.

Sustaining God, help me to bring healing to your world this day.

Divine memories

Genesis 9:1-15

The ancient story of Noah is a story of his – and his family's – patience, love, trust, faithfulness and endurance. To hear it for the first time must be to journey through every human emotion imaginable, from terror in the face of destruction to the joy of salvation as the waters recede. It may be a story that resonates powerfully with aspects of your own life journey. For it is also a story of forced migration and exile.

As with many familiar Bible stories, it is sometimes helpful to read from the perspective of someone other than the main character. For instance, when this story is read from the perspective of God, different emphases emerge to show God in quite a different light from the omnipotent creator that is our dominant understanding of the divine. The story of Noah reveals God as capable of taking risks, for God places the continuance of humanity, and all creation, in Noah's hands. God chooses humility over control. God is further revealed to be a God who watches, listens and responds. For it is in response to Noah's faithfulness that God's trust and faith in humanity is restored, and the new covenant made between God and creation.

The subsequent history of the people of Israel reveals this new covenant as an insufficient guarantee of Israel's faithfulness. Even the most outspoken prophets fail to bring Israel back to God. Whilst God remembers, the people forget. And so the stage is set for God to intervene once more, taking an even greater risk with his own Son.

Which Bible story can you not afford to forget?

Risk-taking God, thank you for remembering us; help us never to lose sight of you.

Making God manifest

Isaiah 40:1-5

Only with hindsight are prophets understood. In their own time they are ignored, ridiculed, crucified. Part of the problem is that we seek truth in places, and at times, convenient to us. Yet ours is a God who delights in surprises, who challenges us to turn our world upside down. The prophets point in the right direction yet we continue to look the other way. Isaiah could not have been clearer: 'Prepare in the desert a way for Yahweh' (verse 3).

I've only been to a desert once, and then only briefly. I was struck by the awesome silence and the fearsome sense of space. Stripped of all that provides comfort or amusement, one is forced to confront oneself. And when confronted with self, one is ultimately also confronted with God. For the search for God is first a search for self. Only by unwrapping the many layers of ego that our cultures, communities, churches, even families, impress upon us, can we begin to discover who we are and what it means to be made in the image of God. As we do this, God becomes more clearly visible in the people around us. The divine becomes manifest. It is as if we are beginning to see the world through God's eyes.

This is how the kingdom is built. For as we align our nature increasingly with the divine, so we become the channels through whom God's love finds expression. It is the only means by which the world can find healing and wholeness. This divine journey of self-discovery is the purpose of life.

Where do you feel most close to God?

Desert God, reveal my true self, so that you may become manifest through me today.

David Ford

Resting is divine

Genesis 2:1-3

I'm not very good at taking a break from work. As a full-time Christian minister there is always so much more that can be done. My 'to do' list is never short of new tasks or projects. Even my holidays are taken either in significant Christian locations or at Christian events or festivals. At times I may feel guilty at the prospect of taking a holiday. At other times I genuinely don't want to, for work can be hugely fulfilling. Yet this is not what God intends for us: 'God blessed the seventh day and made it holy, because on that day he rested after all his work of creating' (verse 2).

At the beginning of this week we reflected on God's transition from absence to presence as creation came into being. Contrast that with God's intention for a seventh day of rest. This does not signal a return to absence, for the absence of God can never be holy. Rather the seventh day of rest is a blessed interruption, prior to the ongoing process of creation. It is a necessary precursor to the next stage in the building of God's kingdom. It is day packed full to the brim with godly rest!

The juxtaposition of holiness with rest is a challenging concept. Can holiness only be found in blessed interruptions? Is it only when we are at rest that we can get really close to God? Can our busyness become so overwhelming that it shuts God out? What God ordains as good we should acknowledge for ourselves and embrace. Resting is divine.

On your next day of rest, do something special for yourself!

Restful God, bring us to stillness so that we may be touched by your Spirit.

Faces of the divine

2 Divine lover

Notes based on the New Jerusalem Bible by **Alistair Ross**

Alistair Ross is a Baptist minister, pastoral theologian and therapist. He writes and researches on spirituality and psychoanalysis, and transforming moments in theology and therapy. Alistair is currently writing a book on theology for therapists. He works at Oxford University as Director of Psychodynamic Studies and is a Fellow at Kellogg College. In his spare time Alistair scrambles up mountains, with a particular love of Glencoe in Scotland, the land of his birth.

Exodus 3:13-17

'Sticks and stones may break my bones but names...'

God as divine lover takes us to the greatest heights, often when we find ourselves in the depths of despair. God reveals his/her name to a chosen and loved people simply as 'I AM', in the burning desert encounter between Moses and the one true God. Two simple words 'I AM' are ultimate statements of being, eternity and love. God's enslaved people find a new hope, a fresh destiny, and a renewed experience of being loved. God's 'I AM' means 'We are' and we shall see different dimensions of this over the next week.

Winnicott, a noted psychoanalyst, believed that to become fully human involves a baby experiencing a psychological 'I AM'. Yet this 'is a raw moment; the new individual feels infinitely exposed. Only if someone has her arms around the infant at that time can the I AM moment be endured, or ... risked' (Ann Ulanov, *Finding Space: Winnicott, God and Psychic Reality*, Louisville, KT: Westminster John Knox Press, 2001). Psychologically we live out this drama in our own lives confident we are loved, held and sustained by God. In my moments of painful loss the words 'I AM' and 'You are' hold me in God's love.

Reflect on your experience of loss and allow God's love to hold you in an 'I AM' moment.

'Truly, madly, deeply...'

Exodus 20:1-6

Shakespeare touches the pulse of human passions in *Othello*. He writes of jealousy as 'the green-ey'd monster, which doth mock the meat it feeds on' (Act 3, Scene 3). It causes so much pain in relationships and I have seen some destroyed by pathological envy and jealousy. This powerful emotion inflames us when we believe our love has been, or is being, spurned or rejected. Jealousy has an intensity that catches our breath in gasps of pain and it can lead to envy and hate, with a lingering desire to spoil. It is a monster that lurks within us and can devour us from inside.

Due to various early experiences it took me a long time to see jealousy as a positive emotion. This passage reveals an intensity of feeling and connection between God and his/her people. God experiences those 'gasps of pain' when s/he is passed over for another. God feels so passionately about us that s/he always desires the best for us. Yet this brings an obligation, as God also demands the best from us. These commandments tell us how to live life in a way that keeps us from being enslaved to ourselves and avoids bringing misery on those closest to us. Often we fail, yet in this failure we experience the faithful love of God, who restores us and calls us to follow a new pattern of living.

In a space of stillness, draw apart, calm mind and body, breathe deeply and reflect. Think for a moment on when you get jealous. Acknowledge the powerful feelings this gives rise to – both positive and negative. Allow these to linger and then lay them before God, one by one. As you breathe in, experience the passion and love of our own jealous God within you, renewing your love.

God of all Being and our Being,
we meet you in your passion.
We acknowledge our feelings,
we give them to you,
leaning again on your love and care.

Alistair Ross

Touching the untouchables

Luke 17:11-19

The young girl looked pleadingly as she asked for healing. Her skin was pockmarked and scarred. With little faith I prayed. A week later, her missionary mother rang to say her daughter's life had been changed, her anger at God had disappeared and her skin had begun to heal. They were experiencing a fresh start, as the parents too had been touched by God's healing of their daughter. When Jesus encounters people, the love of God impels him to make them whole, sometimes physically, spiritually or emotionally. In this encounter Jesus identifies the minority that see him, the healer behind the healing, as the true source of hope and love.

Unconditional love reaches out to touch those deemed by society to be different or unacceptable – even untouchable. God's radical acceptance spans gender, race, orientation, age, class or caste. Unconditional love does not require a response, yet how much richer a person becomes when they can acknowledge, with gratitude, the gift of that love. Are we among that 10% of people who respond to the unconditional love of God made known to us in and through Jesus? Will we express the gratitude of a life made whole, despite the tragedies we have faced and the mistakes we have made? Fragile faith emerges from the depths of a heart and mind that knows it has been touched by the love of God, the Divine Lover.

Who do we know that we can reach out and touch with the love of God?

God who touches and heals diseased flesh,
touch my ill-at-ease spirit in my enfleshed body
so that I may enter into the depths of your being,
recover the depths of my own being,
experience again your unconditional love
and see faith return to my barren heart once more.

'Rock-a-bye baby'

Psalm 121

Psychotherapy training often involves a course in infant observation. Over a period of twelve to twenty-four months a baby and her carers are observed. The student watches over and records the minute interactions between the baby and her mother/carer. Patterns soon emerge. Babies sleep when they are safe, secure in the knowledge that those who 'watch over' will deal with their discomforts, hungers and pains. They experience their carer as reliable, caring and loving, thus forming secure foundations for later psychological growth. Yet parenting is a skill we do not all have. We also observe anxious mothers or fathers who don't let their babies settle, continually picking them up, as if to rescue the infant from a distress which is actually their own remembered distress from the time when they were infants and did not receive the holding they needed.

Adults 'sleep like babies' when they feel safe. We have a God who neither sleeps nor slumbers (verse 4), ever watchful, ever alert to our cry. Whatever our circumstances, our comings and goings (verse 8), and our cries for help, the loving God is always available. God does not need to be roused, bleary eyed, by the wailing cry of an infant in the middle of the night. Our God is vitally interested in our well-being and safety, from the moment of our conception to the concluding moments of death, before we pass into the eternity of God.

Recall a time when you experienced being 'watched over' by God, aware of God's protection and provision.

God of our beginnings and endings,
we live in the light of your presence and love.
Help us to see you face to face
in those seeming dark, absent, and abandoned times.
Enable us to support others at such times
in the experience and knowledge of your love.

Alistair Ross

The Glencoe God

Psalm 77:11-20

I enjoy mountains, especially in Glencoe, Scotland. I love scrambling up rock faces and precarious ridges where there are no obvious paths. In good weather it is exhilarating. In wind, snow and rain it becomes daunting. As the mist descends it is easy to lose one's bearings yet still progress by following the rock. It can lead to some terrifying moments and the dawning realisation that one is simply lost.

There are many kinds of being lost. Being lost fills us with childhood anxieties and fears. The sickening moment of abandonment is one that many feel but is so painful it is pushed away. Refugees flee for their lives leaving behind all that is familiar for the lostness of a new culture and language. Many of the clients I see are simply lost and cannot see a way through or beyond their current situation.

Our God is a granite God who has been there through history, stretching back before the beginning of time. God remains strong, secure and able to lead his people back to where they belong. First with the people of Israel, now with any people of faith, God's love takes us through the most difficult and distressing of circumstances. We who were once lost, now find we are being led home to a place we can belong, in the loving being and presence of God.

Allow a quiet moment for God to strip away your surface veneer of being an all-coping adult. Recall what it feels like to be lost. Imagine what it is like to be a stranger in a new land and culture where nothing familiar remains. Let God speak to you of belonging and being.

Holy, wonderful God, allow us into your presence.
Help us see you in your glory, and to follow in your footsteps.

'Are we there yet?'

Psalm 27:7-14

Waiting is not an easy human activity and is the cause of much adult complaint, as well as coming from children on car journeys with the words, 'Are we there yet?' ten minutes into the journey. Waiting can be a serious business. Waiting to hear the outcome of medical tests or an operation leaves us anxious and afraid. Waiting to know if IVF fertilisation has been successful is agonising. Waiting for a letter about redundancy. Waiting for a text or email from someone we love and long to hear from. Waiting for God to answer our prayers. None of these is an easy or simple task.

Yet acquiring the skill to wait is an essential part of many spiritual and therapeutic traditions. Allowing oneself to 'not know' and waiting for meaning to emerge requires a stilling of the psyche, a stifling of natural curiosity and an ability to simply be in the moment. In those moments of silent waiting we so often discover who we really are for ourselves and not just for the client. In a world that rushes and is dominated by deadlines we need to hear again these words of wisdom, 'Wait for the Lord; be strong, and let your heart take courage; wait for the Lord!' (verse 14, NRSV). These words are not said into the experiences of unrest, prejudice, persecution or violence that are reality for many Christians throughout the world.

Waiting is also part of seeking – seeking for insight, meaning, love, belonging, connection, wisdom, presence and eternity. What do you seek from God that may require your waiting?

God of all hope,
allow your hope to infect our being
so that we live in the light of all you give us now
and journey expectantly to all that you will bring
in the future.

Alistair Ross

'California dreaming'

Acts 10:23-35

I stood in Grace Cathedral, San Francisco, listening to the choir; I was entranced by the worship and the coloured reflections on the floor from the stained glass windows. There was an atmosphere of welcome that touched my soul. Anyone and everyone could be at home in this place of refuge and grace. To be a stranger, a foreigner, an outsider, a spiritual casualty or a refugee and yet to be made welcome caresses the spirit and speaks of the welcome and hospitality of an all-loving God. The task for God's people is to live in community in a way that acknowledges and values difference, to become places that receive others with open arms. This is a lesson we have so often forgotten in the history of the church. The temptation to return to our tribes, where we feel safe, where everyone is like us, is one that challenges countries and faith communities alike.

As a young minister in South London I used to listen to the stories of Afro-Caribbean families who described their reception by the church in the 1950s and 1960s. My face burned with shame and all I could do was apologise and thank them for their faith and faithfulness. Yet this story can be told and retold by so many. We can never relax in expressing the accepting love and faithfulness of God.

Remember those who belong to God, but have no familiar place to belong: those who are rootless and restless, longing for welcome. Think of a name, a person known to you, who needs God's presence at this time.

God of all welcome, equip us and challenge us to embrace others.
God of all love, may we give and receive out of your Being.
Call us again to be those who touch and welcome the soul of another,
whose souls have been scarred by rejection.
May they find healing and wholeness through the love of God in us.

Faces of the divine

3 Incarnating saviour

John 3:16-21

Sacrificing

This well-known text focuses our theme for the week: the incarnation of God in a human face or, as Karl Barth put it, 'the journey of the Son of God from a far country'.

This passage conveys three related themes. First, the lifting up of the Son of Man, which makes eternal life possible. Second, God's love for the world prompted God's gift of the Son so that those who believe in him should have eternal life. Third is the theme of judgement.

If we believe in Jesus, the only Son of God, we are already part of the eternal kingdom of God. We taste eternal life in the here and now. We do not have to wait until some future world but can breathe, eat and enjoy the life of God's eternal reign where light and truth prevails now.

The grace poured out by God has no meaning in isolation from the judgement. If we have no sin, we need no forgiveness. If there is no judgement, we require no grace. Isn't this what John had in mind when using the metaphor of light and dark dualism? The light of which John speaks is the light of Jesus, the Son of God who came as one of us to show us how to live in our own particular contexts, to demonstrate love and to die in order to give us true life.

Lord God, teach us to understand fully your earthly journey amongst us in our concrete, everyday contexts.

Notes based on the New Revised Standard Version by

Aeryun Lee

Aeryun Lee is a minister of the Uniting Church in Australia, serving the Forestville congregation in Sydney. Born and educated in Seoul, South Korea, Aeryun migrated to Australia in 1989 and studied theology at the United Theological College in Sydney. She is particularly interested in cross-cultural theology and seeks to promote intercultural awareness both in the Uniting Church and wider setting of contemporary society.

Finding a human face

Philippians 2:5-11

This ancient hymn from pre-Pauline days, which Paul inserts into his letter to the Philippians, reminds me of the sacrificial act of love done by Korean women in their history, tradition and culture. The small rabbit-shaped Korean peninsula has always been, and is still today, an object of invasion by the bigger countries surrounding her. Much of Korea's history is therefore a history of bloodshed and tribulation, with frequent wars, both small and great. The majority of men were forced or volunteered into wars to protect their country, leaving the women, elderly people and children at home to take care of the households. This meant that women were in sole charge of their everyday lives and the task of bringing up the children. Their sacrificial acts of dedication to their families and children, in situations of hardship and sometimes despair, were the main force for survival in those communities. This legacy of love and sacrifice is revered by contemporary Koreans and is passed on to the contemporary generation, narrated repeatedly with pride and honour. For Christians, we might see both the men's and the women's costly and self-sacrificial acts as a form of the incarnate God at work in Korean history and experience. The process of kenosis of which the Philippian hymn speaks – the emptying out of power and prestige in order to take on the form of a 'slave' to serve those beloved by God – is embodied in the communal experience of Korean men and, most especially, women.

How do you depict Jesus who is working in your personal and communal history? Who are the person/s or community we need to serve in humility?

Let us learn more and more your humility, O God. Show us the way of emptying ourselves day by day.

Offering full life

John 10:1-10

Much of the Judea of Jesus' time consisted of poor, rocky soil, better suited for grazing than cultivation, so shepherding was a common occupation. Shepherds often worked with the same sheep for a number of years, developing a close relationship with each of their charges. G A Smith tells, in *John: World Commentary* (Nashville: Nelson, 1999) of watching shepherds in Judea and how he and his companions sometimes enjoyed their noonday rest by a Judean well to which shepherds came down with their flocks. Because the flocks mixed with each other, he wondered how each shepherd would get his own again. But after the watering and the playing were over, the shepherds went up different sides of the valley, and each called out his peculiar call; and the sheep drew out of the crowd to their own shepherd.

Once the sheep have recognised the shepherd's call and have separated themselves from the other flocks, the shepherd leads them out of the sheepfold to pasture and water. He leads rather than drives them – goes ahead to ensure that the path is safe. He repeats his call periodically to keep the sheep together, and the sheep recognise his voice and follow him. We see something similar with babies who readily accept their mother or father but reject being held by strangers.

As we bring our lives into compliance with Jesus' will, he blesses us with abundant life. That does not necessarily mean health or wealth. It means abundance, which has more to do with what is in our hearts than with what is in our hands.

How can we be more like Jesus? If we want to experience life at its fullest what would Jesus have us to do?

God of bounty, teach us how to live our lives more fully and abundantly for others, in the power of your love.

Transfiguring

Matthew 17:1-8

The Greek word for 'transfigured' is *metemorphothe*, from which we get the word metamorphosis. This text reminds us of Moses at Sinai. After his encounter with God, Moses' face shone so brightly that the people were frightened and Moses had to wear a veil over his face (Exodus 34:29-35). On the mountain, Jesus too is glorified! Glory can be defined as weightiness or importance, a mark of which is the splendour that accompanies one who has it.

Why Moses and Elijah? R T France suggests that these two men symbolise the coming of the messianic age, and their conversation with Jesus marks him out the more clearly as the Messiah who comes as the climax to their eschatological role (R T France, *The Gospel of Matthew: The New International Commentary on the New Testament*, Grand Rapids: William B Eerdmans 2007, p.648).

The truly amazing thing is how quickly the disciples will forget. Peter, James and John have seen Jesus revealed in glory, but their courage will fail them at the cross. Peter will deny Jesus three times. Perhaps there is a lesson here for us. We, too, have experienced the hand of God in our lives, but we find faith difficult when trouble looms.

God commands the disciples (and the early church, and us) to listen to Jesus. In the early church, there was no New Testament canon. Christians were faced with the question of authority. To what extent must they observe Old Testament law, especially in situations where Jesus' example gives a new twist to the old law? God answers, 'Listen to him!' We, too, are faced with serious doctrinal and ethical questions. How do we find our way in an increasingly complex world? God answers, 'Listen to him!'

God, teach us how to listen to Jesus when we are unsure of how to act or think.

Reconciling

Ephesians 2:11-22

Paul stayed in Ephesus for two to three years and it was a centre of his missionary work. From there he wrote letters to the Corinthians, Philippians and to Philemon. The strong theme of reconciliation that we find in this passage may owe something to the idea of world citizenship that was prevalent in the late first century. The Roman Empire offered an ideal of global citizenship, in which citizens could move around without let or hindrance in the pursuit of trade, commerce or security. Being a Roman citizen himself, Paul adapts this idea to speak of the more profound reality of being a member of the body of Christ. He sees the opportunity to reconcile people who are divided because of the barriers of race, religion, class and so on, through Jesus the Messiah, the king of shalom. Every road to God is open through the cross of Jesus Christ and the church is built on the only cornerstone and foundation, Jesus Christ, the one who is for all peoples. All people can be connected to God through Jesus Christ, regardless of the barriers of race, culture, religion, class and tradition. Those people who are outside of the promise can become a part of covenant with God through the cross of reconciling atonement.

For Paul, the church is the living representation of Christ, the place where Christ rules and unites the universe. Through reconciliation and unity, we overcome divisions and the church becomes God's present dwelling place, a holy space where all people enjoy justice, peace, love and harmony.

Lord, as we look around the globe, we pray for those who desperately need a safe place to live. Let us be your helping hand for them.

Aeryun Lee

Atoning

1 John 4:7-12

This text carries the core of the Christian teaching to care for one another. Many scholars agree that no one has described the origin of love and its meaning as directly or movingly as this text. Here the theological indicative becomes the foundation of a moral imperative. Because God loves us first, we ought to love one another. Needless to say, if God loves us we should love in return. This love, both for God and for humankind, will be completed one day (verse 12), even though it is now far from complete.

The love of God is exemplified most completely in Jesus' life, ministry and death; this is the heart of Christian confession. Jesus is the one who shows us most fully the nature and love of God. The one who knows God's love knows God and obeys God. This obedience is expressed in loving God and loving one another.

God's love is not abstract but is shown by God's own generous and costly giving up of the Son on the cross. Likewise, Christian love needs to be expressed, not only with powerful emotions, but most authentically through meaningful acts of love. It is the responsibility of the whole Christian community to live out the love of God in our common life together, through which others may see and experience the love of God.

Teach us, loving God, to demonstrate your love to our neighbours, through all we do and say.

Aeryun Lee

Practising love

Mark 12:28-34

The story of the scribe is found in all three synoptic gospels, but with significant differences. In Matthew 22:34-40 and Luke 10:25-28, the scribe comes as an adversary to test Jesus, whereas Mark presents him more favourably. In Luke, Jesus does not answer the scribe's question directly, but asks, 'What is written in the law? How do you read it?' (Luke 10:26). The scribe gives the answer, essentially repeating Jesus' words as found in Mark 12:30-31, but omitting verse 29. In Luke, the parable of the Good Samaritan (Luke 10:29-37) follows the encounter with the scribe, expanding greatly the concept of neighbour.

The first commandment is the 'Shema', the profession of faith made morning and night by devout Jews. The text comes from the book of Deuteronomy. The second commandment is from the book of Leviticus (19:18). Jesus' answer is significant in that he places the two commandments side by side. Love of God implies love of neighbour, because God is found at the heart of the neighbour. For the same reason, love of neighbour means love of God. God is the source of all love. It is the love of God that enables us to respond in love to God. And we do this by loving our neighbour.

Jesus was particularly associated with those people who could not be part of the mainstream, those who were pushed aside for a variety of reasons. These were the ones Jesus cultivated especially as his neighbours.

Loving God, help us to face the challenges of loving you in our neighbour, especially those most despised and neglected by our societies.

Sunday 22 January

Faces of the divine

4 Faithful companion

Notes based on the New Revised Standard Version by

Geoffrey Herbert

Geoffrey Herbert is a retired Anglican priest, now with a ministry of listening and speaking about our spiritual journeys. He is a grandfather. He occasionally writes poetry, and has an interest in studying how poets and other artists represent humanity in our life journey.

Jeremiah 31:10-17

Hoping

The title for this week, 'Faithful companion', could portray God as the one who arrives, eventually, like a St Bernard dog with some warming cognac to sustain us when we're buried under life's avalanches. That can happen (God doesn't mind being likened to a St Bernard), but the God we really find in the week's readings is far more: a companion integral with us, suffering in us (including from our lack of faithfulness), struggling and working in us for a new future.

In today's reading Rachel's weeping for her dead child moves God to compassion, as Jesus was moved 'in his guts' (e.g. Mark 1:41). Because God is God, this kind of empathy (literally 'suffering in') is total – not even like the most empathic human observer of another's distress. God occupies our space without invading us, and promises a transformation from inside, starting now. It may be quick or it may be slow: God is at work in God's time.

Hope's work: Julian of Norwich wrote 'all will be well, and every kind of thing will be well', 'every kind of compassion which one has ... is Christ in us' (Julian of Norwich *Showings*, Translation and Introduction by Edmund Colledge and James Walsh, London/New York, Paulist Press, 1978, p.149).

Think of a time when you received such empathy (compassion) from a companion. Did it bring any hope that all would be well? Was it a human sign of what God can do?

My creation, are you saved?

Romans 8:18-27

Paul has wonderful moments of seeing beyond his normal boundaries. Galatians 3:28 for example: 'There is no longer Jew or Greek, there is no longer slave or free, there is no longer male and female': it goes beyond his own culture, even beyond his own normal ways of thinking, a vision that is still being worked out in our own time.

Today's reading is another vision like that. We, and Paul, usually see salvation as for human beings – perhaps societies and cultures, but usually individuals. Now here's Paul with a vision of a saved creation! It has been groaning in birth-pains until now (verse 22). This 'now' is the time of Christ's coming. In Paul's thinking the suffering started with the disobedience of Adam and Eve: they went their own way and took the whole creation down with them. There's a great truth here. We humans have corrupted so much by our selfishness. 'Now' is the time for us to help: a huge amount depends on us for the salvation of the physical world and humanity.

Paul sees 'us', the community of the Spirit, as vital to all this. 'We' are what it's all waiting for. The Spirit longing and praying in 'us' is the very presence of the companion God who has waited all this time, has now come in Christ and is now striving to bring us to birth.

Who are these 'children of God' awaited by the creation in its agony? Are they church members? Are they a special group inside that? Are they a special group in other faiths too? Could they be none of these?

Pray for the enlightenment of the children of God and the beginning of an end to the creation's sufferings.

Geoffrey Herbert

Vulnerability gives birth to vulnerability

Luke 2:1-7

Just because we happened to be visiting at the right time, we saw the birth of our first granddaughter. We, and Helen's husband, all had our roles – eye-to-eye encourager, back-massager, water-carrier, and of course the midwife doing her bit. But it was Helen who gave birth. 'Gave' is a good word: she gave Rebecca birth as a gift. To do that meant becoming vulnerable to what was happening, letting the process take over. Actually, from conception to nativity, and afterwards, parenthood involves one vulnerability after another. Perhaps the biggest is launching the child into the world, aware of so many risks that parents can't control.

Mary's vulnerability gave birth to the vulnerability of Jesus. Within her and in him God was at risk too, in every second of life, suffering and death. Onwards from there the followers of the Way continued this chain of vulnerable people, begetting and nurturing more: gentleness from gentleness, humility from humility, patience from patience, love from love.

We all fail to be perfect links in the chain. Mary failed too, and so did the men, like Peter and Paul. These failures each increase the vulnerability of God, yet God's almightiness consists in part in making creative use of them, often in partnership with the one who has failed.

Every act of creation – a friendship, a conception, a career, a poem or painting, all costly giving – involves risk. Ponder one or two such times in your life. Did they make more good links in the chain of vulnerability? Is the risky path always the right one?

Lord, show me your kind of vulnerability. Give me the strength to be better at living it.

A good hatred

Amos 5:11-15

Amos gives violent voice to the anger of God, the God who refuses to be the friend of those who neglect the poor and have made themselves comfortable in prosperity at their expense.

God is not only the friend of the poor but also 'knows' the burdens of the oppressed with an intimate knowledge, because God is among them, identified with them, suffering their sufferings, and vehemently not the ally of the exploiting fat cats. In verse 14 God promises to be with the oppressors if they seek the good of the poor. Until then God is their enemy.

One of our daughters had a sixth-form teacher of sociology who was a committed Marxist. I asked her to bring him to meet us and interrogated him about his idea of class warfare. I said his view seemed dominated by hate. He replied that there can be a good hatred. As Amos speaks out God's hatred of injustice, I can now begin to see that teacher's point. The only difference is the hope held out in verse 15 that a 'remnant' (of the rich?) will hate evil and love good, and 'live' (verse 14).

What would this mean in the time of Amos, and in our time?

Part of most of us is caught up in the oppression of the poor and is deaf to their cries; another part is on their side and seeks justice. If this is the truth about you, hold the whole of yourself up to God's light.

Geoffrey Herbert

Silence that hears everything

Habakkuk 1:1-6

The reading for this day of holocaust memorial is a powerful protest at the silence of God while the holy city is destroyed and the people are dragged off into captivity.

Two places stand out for me as containing this terrible silence. One is the Anne Frank House in Amsterdam, where the multinational queue stands outside in near-silence that becomes total on the way through the building, deepening in the rooms whose memory is in the furniture and on the walls. The other is the beautiful synagogue in central Budapest where Adolf Eichmann had a blasphemous sub-office for his incredibly efficient deportation of almost half the Jewish population of Hungary in less than four months of 1944, mainly to Auschwitz. The guides are Jewish women who speak factually and with dignity, leaving spaces of silence as you absorb the terrible truth in their words and the things you see, some shockingly ugly, some poignantly beautiful, like visual laments.

God's silence in the Shoah (holocaust), and God's silence in the Exile are in those smaller silences: there is no answer of words or vengeance, nor even adequate healing. It has the fullness of the companion God's compassion, longing, vulnerability and loving anger that we have already visited during this week. It is like the silence in heaven in the presence of those who have been through 'the great ordeal' (Revelation 8:1; 7:14).

But God must hear our protest too.

Revisit in memory the Shoah and other holocausts: the German cities of the Second World War, Leningrad and Stalingrad, Tokyo, Hiroshima, Nagasaki, Rwanda and many smaller ones.

Watch and listen with God. Protest, if you want to, at God's silence.

Tough lover

Psalm 11

The Psalms speak as if the world is divided into the righteous and the wicked. At times they protest at the way the wicked seem to do well in life whereas the righteous come off worse.

On Wednesday we visited some ideas like this, although there Amos has another insight – that some of the wrongdoers could turn round and become a 'remnant' that will be blessed. A further step from this is to recognise that wickedness and righteousness often co-exist in the same people, including in ourselves.

Perhaps Judgement Day will be as Muslims imagine it, an angel weighing our good deeds against our bad deeds and assigning heaven or hell according to the balance. The New Testament sometimes speaks in 'balance' language. St Paul's view of grace, though, is that it frees us from the need to earn salvation, although he was quite sharp with Christians who took this to mean that it doesn't matter what you do.

In the words of the hymn, 'Amazing grace': ''Twas grace that taught my heart to fear, and grace my fears relieved.' God can meet us moving towards him, God can draw us towards him.

I'm very grateful for the times of warning, in prayer or from people who know me and love me: these have shown me where I've gone wrong and how I needed to change. And forgiveness always opens the door wide.

Read or sing 'Amazing Grace'. Note how the idea of grace is used, and see whether that fits with your experience.

Lord of grace, please carry on making me uncomfortable by your grace.

Geoffrey Herbert

Making the way

Acts 2:14-24

Joel's prophecy of the outpoured Spirit ends with a promise that whoever calls on the name of the Lord will be saved. Peter links this with the ministry, death and resurrection of Jesus to challenge sceptical hearers to look at their own lives and think again. The five thousand who had been overwhelmed by the Spirit had heard no such detailed scriptural exegesis nor any 'repent and be saved' challenge.

If we look at our church fellowships we shall probably find a good proportion of people who have not come because they heard a traditional preaching of the gospel as we normally understand it. They will be there because of some deeply moving event such as bereavement, illness, meeting someone with a vibrant faith, or having a profound spiritual experience like a mysterious presence in nature.

Our companion God doesn't ask us to run on tramlines: we each have our own faith journey, each may start in a different place and travel over different terrain. Is there one terminus to be reached where all Christians will be able to say the same thing and live by the same morality? Some Christians believe there is, some don't. Whatever our answer to this, the end-point and the way to it is the Christ in whom everything will be summed up. Can we see this happening in the lives of Christians (and non-Christians) who are very different from us?

Faithful companion God, shape us and fill us with the Spirit of Jesus.

Faces of the divine

Sunday 29 January

5 Inviting host

Notes based on the New Revised Standard Version by

Ann Perrin

Ann Perrin has been a professional double bass player for thirty years, working in orchestras in Sydney and Melbourne. She has been a lecturer at the Sydney Conservatorium of Music and has trained as a choral director. Ann is now a Minister of the Word in the Uniting Church in Australia, completing her first year in full-time ministry in the Strathfield Homebush UCA Multicentre, Sydney.

John 1:35-39

Inviting host

Are we, the people of God, inviting the host to be with us, invoking divine presence, or is it to an inviting host that we respond, offering God's hospitality to those around us? This is not an either/or situation where we are forced to choose one over the other. If we believe we are the ones giving the invitation, then the gift of Christ in our lives expects that we also become those who respond to God's invitation. Or else we will have nothing to offer.

Two things stand out in this short piece from John's Gospel, two contrasting kinds of discipleship – physical and spiritual. Although John the Baptist names Jesus with a messianic title, Lamb of God (verse 36), John's disciples merely describe him as 'rabbi' (verse 38). They follow someone who is important in the eyes of their teacher, with no inkling of his messianic purpose. This is a limited, physical kind of discipleship. But Jesus invites them to 'come and see' (verse 39). And it will be in the seeing that a deeper, spiritual following of Jesus will occur.

Where do you see God's presence in your local community and so invite others to 'come and see'?

Holy inviting God, this week bless us with eyes to see your work in our world. Bless us so that we may see how to put your work into action in our lives and offer your invitation to others.

Generous wisdom

Job 28:12-28

For the last two Advent seasons, St Ives Uniting Church in Australia has invited young composers to write music inspired by biblical texts of creation and Christmas. The minister, Douglas Purnell, said:

I am intrigued that at a time in history when the church is having difficulty having its message heard in the general culture, these young people have said to us, 'we value your questions, your stories and the historical connection between the churches and new music and this is a most exciting opportunity' ... I am fascinated at what happens when we share our stories and questions with people from outside our faith tradition, and invite them to offer them back to us through the disciplined work of their imagination. The stories can come alive in fresh ways.

Wisdom is found in God's creation of the world and in every continuing expression of genuine creativity. Wisdom is the very fabric of the universe. From creation onwards, wisdom is threaded in and through everything that exists. God's good ordering of our world can be discerned in every creative human action as well as in the divine upholding of the created cosmos. In contrast, wanton human actions that disorder God's creation are acts of foolishness and sin.

Where are the centres of creativity in your local community? How do they manifest God's wisdom?

Generous God, may we recognise your creative activity and your wisdom in our everyday acts of caring, nurturing and responding to your profound love.

Ann Perrin

Overflowing host

Exodus 16:1-16

We often think of wilderness as an empty, uninhabited place, but it is in the wilderness that Israel finds God's generosity manifested. God hears Israel's complaints and Yahweh is the key player because Yahweh is the one who overcomes the problem.

The people of Israel still hunger for their lives in Egypt; they associate glory and the power to give life with wealth, splendour and extravagance. This false glory of Egypt means that the wilderness holds very little attraction for them. But God redefines a new meaning of life for Israel.

Here is a new way of receiving 'bread'. God's care is revealed not just in the provision of food, but in the way in which daily manna is provided. There is enough for all, and double for the Sabbath. There needs to be no competition for resources, the things that sustain life. Hoarding does not work. There is enough bread where and when it is needed, but not for human greed. Bread becomes the means by which God's reliability can be trusted and neighbours can live together in trustful unity.

We witness here a sacramental action, a testimony to God's fidelity. We learn again of God's providential ordering of creation, which can redescribe wilderness as a place of life.

Where are the places of wilderness for people in your community? How is God present there?

Overflowing God, teach us to trust that our wildernesses can become places where your nurture is always available to us. May we recognise this for our lives today, for the sake of your tomorrow.

Providing enough

Psalm 23

The juxtaposition of nurture and death can be readily heard in the Howard Goodall arrangement of this psalm. Around the lilting and weaving of the beginning and end of the musical setting is heard a change of mood in the middle section, portraying the drama of evil in one's darkest valleys.

It is certainly appropriate to hear this psalm in the midst of death and dying (it is, of course, often used in funerals), but it is also a psalm of life and of God's life-giving character. The preparing of a table speaks to us of eating, drinking and seeking security in a God who is both good and merciful; the table is also a communal one that we share with others. This psalm, which is so often thought of as addressing the individual, moves us from personal assurance to community assurance. The psalmist experiences the full character of God while being reminded of past deeds. Even in the darkest places the provision of God's grace is sufficient. Our shepherd provides spiritual food, living water and a safe haven, as the Spirit of Christ walks with us.

But there is more here for the Christian who reads this psalm in the light of the gospels. Our shepherd is also the Lamb of God, who is not only the host of the Passover meal but also its very substance. So we are reminded of the Last Supper at which Jesus offers his own body and blood for our sustenance.

Providing God, you share your table with friends and enemies alike. Teach us to trust you for your generous upholding, in life as in death.

Feeding more than...

Matthew 14: 13-21

Jesus has withdrawn from the crowds, having just heard of the death of John the Baptist (Matthew 14:1-12). We find ourselves in a deserted place once more, this time with Jesus who, although desiring to be alone, shows compassion on the crowd and acts as their shepherd.

The blessing of the food in this passage reminds us of the traditional Jewish Hamotzi blessing: 'Blessed are you, O Lord our God, King of the universe, who brings forth bread from the earth.' This blessing points us back to past instances of God's providential care, as well as forward to Jesus' last Passover meal. Juxtaposed with the sumptuous nature of Herod's banquet, Jesus' simple yet miraculous feeding is all the more striking, speaking to us of God's extraordinary care through the ordinary and everyday. The feeding miracle also speaks to us of eucharist and the way in which God provides abundant spiritual food through the bread and wine of the eucharistic gathering.

Throughout the readings this week, we are seeing that God's providential care for those in need is abundant and faithful, no matter what the situation.

Feeding, nurturing God, we meet you at the eucharistic table as our host but also present in the faces of those you invite. May we be open to those whom you invite to our tables, and know your pleasure in inviting others to share with us.

Giving confidence

Philippians 4:1-7

This passage speaks to us of the peace and total well-being we receive from God. As in the other texts we have considered this week, God's character is described here, but the passage also reveals something of our own potential and destiny in Christ, through God's transformation. Paul speaks of a hope that is not only a heavenly hope but also a hope to be expressed in the activity of our lives.

God is our partner in all our human dramas of pain, hope, despair and reconciliation. Paul's claim that the Lord is near (verse 5) and will not abandon us provides us with confidence and courage for our lives. If God is near, then God can be drawn into our troubles through prayer and worship. We are enabled through God's confidence in us to move beyond our church doors to recognise where God is at work in our local communities and the wider world. It is here, and not only in church, that God's presence, mercy and grace need to be named. We are called to 'come and see' where God is at work in our local communities before we invite them to 'come and see' God within our churches.

Where will you awaken to the presence of God in your community this week?

Confidence-giving God, you have shown throughout salvation history that you come to your people again and again. Your care and nurture are ongoing. We honour you and give you thanks as our understanding of your vision of the future becomes clearer and as our confidence in you is renewed.

Ann Perrin

Life-giving host

2 Corinthians 3: 1-6

Once more we are exhorted to be the living recommendation of Christ to others: to embody the values we know are God's will for us, by living them out in God's creation. We are not to privilege the word of one person over another, but to live what is required by God. Paul writes with an extraordinary confidence in the Corinthian Christians, who constitute his letter, written on the heart, as he puts it (verse 2).

This passage witnesses to our giftedness, a giftedness that is not of our own making but which comes from God. It is God who has made us competent ministers so that we may witness to the new covenant, God's new initiative in Christ. God's gift of Christ to us enables us to be Christ's 'letters', God's ministry agents in the world for today, for the sake of God's tomorrow. Rising refreshed and renewed from our eucharistic meal, we are full of hope as we share in the work of bringing the reign of God into our lives and our communities. We are co-creators with Christ.

Out of this confidence, we invite others to 'come and see'. We witness to God's providence and wisdom, freely available in the fabric of the universe, and to God's presence, available through sacrament and human love.

Inviting host, through the witness of the peoples of Israel and the earliest disciples, you reach out to us in the power of the Holy Spirit. We pray, confident in your ongoing providential care, for the renewal of faith in our lives and in our communities.

Readings in Mark (1)

Jesus: teacher and healer 1

Notes based on the New Revised Standard Version by
Carlton Turner

Carlton Turner is a Bahamian vicar and research associate at the Queen's Foundation, Birmingham, pursuing a PhD in practical theology. His focus is Caribbean theology with particular attention to the role of carnivals, such as Junkanoo, and the ways in which they are modes of theologising. He currently serves in the Diocese of Lichfield in a team ministry in Bloxwich, Walsall, along with his wife Carla and daughter Carlyse.

Mark 1:29-39

Healer and teacher to many and to one

This week we will be concentrating on the nature of Jesus' teaching and healing ministries as he moves through the Judean countryside towards Jerusalem proclaiming the kingdom of God. Mark's narrative presents Jesus as a man of action, moving swiftly with power and success. All the healings and teachings we find in this gospel serve the purpose of ratifying Jesus' proclamation of the kingdom, which is ushered into human experience through him.

However, as the healings at Simon and Andrew's home and the proclamation throughout Galilee in today's reading suggest, there is a more nuanced and textured quality to Jesus' power at work. The impressive healing of many, both physically and spiritually, is coupled with the image of intimacy in which Jesus takes Simon's mother-in-law by the hand and lifts her up. We find Jesus' power over the crowds coupled with his escape to, and dependence upon, prayer.

During the course of the week we will be exploring this textured and paradoxical view of Jesus' power, and considering how it challenges us in our everyday discipleship.

Touch us with your power, O God, both as individuals and as a society.

What kind of ground are you?

Mark 4:1-20

Growing up in a very small island community in the Bahamas has taught me much about life. We lived in concert with the moods of the sea. We knew the land and worked hard on it. We were always indebted to its unselfishness, aware of its care for us. Those years of intimacy with both sea and land taught me much about how to live with and relate to others; how to treasure what's important in life. Now I'm older and life is not nearly as quiet. I'm faced with the responsibility of being a public figure. I often long for those days of quiet.

The parable of the sower begins with a very public Jesus whose words of wisdom are much sought after. The crowd comes to see the great teacher but hardly gets to plumb the depths of his teaching. It is in the quiet gathering afterwards, in the company of his closest friends, that we are given the secret of the kingdom of God. In this intimate space the disciples are challenged about what kind of ground their lives provide for the gospel seed. Are their lives those where the unselfish yielding of the kingdom can take place?

O intimate God, draw us into your quietness, reveal the depth of your word to our hearts, and make us fertile ground in which the kingdom may have abundant yield.

What kind of light are you?

Mark 4:21-25

My seven-month-old daughter has illuminated this passage for me in an unforgettable way. No matter where we are, be it a supermarket, a train station or even a church, she gives the most dazzling and inviting smiles to those around her, whether familiar faces or strangers. She sparks joy and happiness and brings others alive, if only for that instant. Her joy and light are unbounded.

Jesus is very clear in his teaching concerning the bushel-basket. The point of light is that it be revealed and never dimmed, whether intentionally or otherwise. Light is revealed so that it exposes darkness; it illumines truth and leads towards liberation.

The followers of Jesus are challenged to be lights unafraid to live as they are meant to live. But Jesus goes a step further in suggesting that light begets light: 'For those who have, more will be given; and from those who have nothing, even what they have will be taken away' (verse 25). For those whose lights are bushel-bound, being extinguished is close at hand.

In the end, Jesus' most impressive example of this teaching was his own act of love on the cross. The cross is still that lamp-stand that exposes darkness, illumines truth and leads to liberation.

Endeavour to share something of God's light with those you encounter today, whether by word, deed or a simple smile.

O God our light, you have created us to be living lights to lead others to you. May nothing dim our witness.

Chaotically sown

Mark 4:26-32

The parables of the growing seed and the mustard seed must have sounded strange to those listening to Jesus. Notions of work's righteousness and divine retribution that permeated first-century Palestine presupposed, in many minds, a set order, a definite pattern, and linear notions of divine movement. Yet Jesus describes the kingdom of God as anything but rigid. It is like seed scattered haphazardly that comes to life, not by human agency, but by God. It is like the mustard seed whose appearance is insignificant but through divine agency becomes a great tree providing life for birds and space for their nests. This is a dynamic kingdom. It springs to life even in the haphazardness and chaos of human experience.

For those of us with leadership positions in the church, the temptation is always to rely so much on our set plans that we suffocate the dynamism of the kingdom. Even worse, we come to a stage where we think that our plans, our efforts and our agency are the things that bring the kingdom to fruition. Jesus reminds us that God works through us, beside us, and all around us, to bring seeds to harvest, yet in a way that is beyond our fixed routines and orderly patterns. Praise God for that!

O God, grant us the faith to know that you are at work around us bringing the kingdom to harvest, and give us the wisdom not to be deluded into thinking it is by our own power and might that the kingdom comes.

Talking to demons

Mark 5:1-20

My godfather was the village drunk. He was a tall, strong man. His hair was always long and wild and he was known by his thick, sometimes plaited, beard. He lived alone and sometimes slept in the graveyard. We, the children, were afraid of him whether he was drunk or sober. Yet he was the best handyman, warden, security and trusted friend our church had. Some years after I moved away to university, he committed suicide, alone in his yard. It was during adulthood that I realised how haunted he was, how lonely he was, and how everyone saw his afflictions but never saw him as a person.

In today's story, no one understands the man's demons. No one ever really speaks to him. He has to be chained. He has to be kept in the graveyard, where he continues to harm himself but is prevented from harming others. Jesus comes along and does not try to avoid confrontation. He speaks to the man's demons, seeking their names and exorcising them. Through conversation and engagement Jesus heals the one who had absolutely no hope of restoration. There in the graveyard, the once possessed man is clothed in his right mind, having peaceful conversation with the Lord.

Healing and deliverance do not begin with aggression, assumption and labelling, but rather with conversation, honesty and compassion.

O God, give us the humility, wisdom and faith to talk to the burdened and the broken, to know their demons, and to proclaim your peace to them.

A haemorrhaging God

Mark 5:21-34

Immediately her haemorrhage stopped ... Immediately aware that power had gone forth from him, Jesus turned...

Mark 5:29 and 30

What an image! Jesus, the great healer and teacher who exorcised demons, healed myriads, and even commanded the winds and the waves to silence, now loses power. As Jesus moves with purpose to go and heal Jairus' daughter, he seems to be assailed by uncertainty and weakness. He is caught off guard, weakened by his encounter with the woman. He does not know who touched him. The one who affected lives with a touch is himself now affected by an anonymous touch of his cloak. The woman in question had been losing her blood and her life for years and finally she touches Jesus, only to find that he is radically affected by her touch and her faith.

The deeper truth of the kingdom of God, as Jesus shows us, is that God is affected by us. The incarnation destroys the notion of an impassable God who does not feel, is not vulnerable and cannot cry. This journey to Jerusalem, filled with amazing teaching and healing, ends in Jesus' blood, his life, draining away on a cross. God, like this woman, is a haemorrhaging God.

Pray for those who hurt but do not yet know that God hurts with them.

O God, thank you for being vulnerable, for bleeding, for being human.

Carlton Turner

The silenced miracle

Mark 5:35-42

Mystery and a sense of the unknown seem to pervade this healing miracle. When everyone thinks the child is dead, Jesus assures them that she is sleeping. When everyone else mourns hysterically, Jesus demands composure. But there is more. Jesus does not simply heal Jairus' daughter, he raises her from the dead! This was undoubtedly the greatest work performed by Jesus on his journey thus far in Mark's Gospel. Yet, as is distinctive of Mark's narrative, Jesus orders the witnesses to keep it all a secret. But how could they when they were amazed? How could they keep silent about the most unthinkable display of power they had ever seen?

We answer this question best if we accept the challenge of this week's reflections, that Jesus' use of power, whether through healing or teaching, was more textured and intimate than we commonly believe. Jesus seemed hardly concerned with popularity, consensus and bedazzled spectators, and more concerned with whether this girl enjoyed life again, was restored to her parents and had something to eat after being raised. Jesus' power is undergirded by love, compassion, relationship, and concern for the small stuff. Silencing the miracle was to guard against missing the entire point of the miracle, making it a matter of entertainment and not a call to transformation.

In what ways would guarding the secrets of your experience of God nourish your soul?

O God, help us to see that your kingdom comes in the small stuff too, and help us to resist proclaiming a popular God at the expense of an intimate God.

Readings in Mark (1)

Sunday 12 February

Jesus: teacher and healer 2

Notes based on the Revised English Bible by

Jim Cotter

Jim Cotter is an ordained Anglican who ministers in the parish of Aberdaron in north-west Wales to householders and to visitors. He also writes, and publishes, in partnership with the Canterbury Press, as Cairns Publications. See www.cottercairns.co.uk

Mark 1:40-45

Teaching? Healing? Of course

Jesus was a teacher. Jesus was a healer. Few would disagree. But ask what it means to be taught. To learn facts and moral spiritual statements? To be asked questions and be encouraged to think for yourself? To engage in dialogue with your ancestors of faith so that something new emerges that you've never thought of before?

And ask what it means to be healed. To be cured of an infection? To have an incurable disease but to be cared for with accurate and skilful compassion? To know that you belong to a community that does not judge you?

Keep the questions in mind in thought and prayer in the next ten days.

Now look at today's passage. A skin condition – psoriasis, warts, rashes and the like – can clear up quickly, muscular pain can vanish, symptoms of cancer can disappear between one X-ray and the next. Jesus, by his presence, his words, his touch – and here he touches those his society treats as untouchable, thus risking social contamination – triggers a release of healing energy within the other person. And it may mean that person is no longer an outcast, belonging once again, but having responsibilities again. What does it mean to be healed?

Take at least one of the questions above and ponder it for a while in your prayer.

Take your head out of the book

Mark 7:1-8

It's a cliché: everybody needs rules – for a game of football, for a public meeting, for driving a car. A rule-book can have hundreds of items. Have a look at one that affects your own life. Perhaps you've forgotten that there are so many. You've taken them to heart over the years and made them your own. You are at ease now when refereeing a match or chairing a meeting or driving to work. But remember how awkward you felt at first – ill at ease (a bit like being dis-eased).

Most religious rule books – about cleanliness, details of behaviour or belief, about the ordering of acts of worship – go back a very long way. Every so often an individual or a community becomes divided about which to keep and which to change.

The movement for reform divides opinion. Which rules are now fossils, once alive but not now? Which rules constrict rather than liberate, paralyse rather than heal? The original intentions are to prevent disorder, to prohibit the violation of things or people, and to protect the vulnerable, thus enhancing life rather than spreading a dead hand over life.

Never mind what is on your lips. What is your heart's wisdom? What is the will of the God of love who seeks justice in the public domain and intimacy in the private domain?

Ponder... be still... be silent... Let the questions go deep...
Don't force an answer but be expectant...

Examine your promises

Mark 7:9-13

Imagine that you have only six months to live. You are making your will. Your parents are still alive, but you have fallen out with them, perhaps for good reason. You know that it would make their old age more secure if you left your money to them. But your church has a restoration appeal and you could be the most generous donor (and your name would be remembered). You know you should honour your father and mother, providing for them when they become vulnerable, but surely a gift to God's house is important too. Which do you decide to do, and how?

Nobody is quite sure what 'Corban' (verse 11) means. The best guess is 'an oath to God'. Now, your law tells you that it is wicked to break an oath, even – perhaps – if it means breaking one of the commandments. It's a dilemma and you can pick away at the question for ever (especially if you're clever and a lawyer). You think it's important that your religious tradition should flourish. And suppose that tradition is clear (or you think it's clear) that certain people are 'in' and others are 'out'. And your own parents have broken at least four of the commandments to your knowledge. They've never been to church in their lives.

But Jesus is clear enough. Human need is always the trump card. Those who are isolated by blotches or sores on their skin, those who are without daily bread or nursing care, those who are elderly and weakening, they always come before any institutional claims.

Try listing the claims on your time, your energy, your skills, your money. Which should be the first three on your list? Pray about it.

Turn yourself inside out

Mark 7:14-23

Rules are all right if they are taken to heart, are heartfelt, and are lived from the heart, from the centre of your being, from the inside out. If so, they are life-enhancing. But that principle does not make it any easier for us when we are faced with genuine moral or spiritual dilemmas. Simply to expect clear answers to every question from the rule-book is to be naive, to be kept immature, and to give over your freedom to an external authority.

From the gospels we learn that we should not turn aside from an injured person even if it means breaking the Sabbath rule of rest. Or this: if your neighbour invites you for a meal to say thank you for repairing a window in her house, accept graciously whatever is put before you – even if it's a Friday in Lent or you don't like aubergines. (If your doctor has forbidden certain foods, then it is your responsibility to inform your hostess in good time, so that neither of you will feel awkward.) It is not what goes in as food that matters, but what goes out as behaviour.

Elsewhere in the gospels it is also clear that Jesus looked for households, ethnic groups and nations where there are no limits to the guest list imposed by your tradition or religion or politics. Food and table should not be used to reinforce divisions in society, nor to draw high boundaries round an in-group.

Would Jesus have preferred a rectangular table with 'head' and 'foot' or a round table where the host sits nearest the kitchen or the oven? What rules enhance life for everybody at the party?

Enlarge your heart

Mark 7:24-30

Like all of us, Jesus needed a break – for rest, for prayer, for time to reflect on his work. It is often when we take time away from our routines that new ideas, visions and challenges open up for us.

But you're distracted by a stranger in need. It's not easy to give that person your full attention, but the encounter might just trigger a significant change in your life. Maybe that is a part of the 'Jesus process' in our lives – opening ears and eyes, challenging our taken-for-granted ways, being dragged across our fixed boundaries.

In this story, it is a foreign woman who does this to Jesus himself. He doesn't run from her, and for once he loses the verbal exchange. Is it Jesus himself – or is it Mark's church – that is challenged to accept that foreigners are graced by God? If one of the meanings of 'repentance' is to change your mind, dare we ask the question, did Jesus, on this occasion, 'repent'? Never again would he call another human being 'a dog': to do so was the worst of insults.

Enter, then, a larger room, a larger house, a larger community. Shelter under a larger umbrella, huddled with strangers and supposed enemies, those whom you have been taught to despise and exclude. Resist those who want smaller, purer, well-defined churches. To follow Jesus is to keep on being enlarged: it is the only way to become completely, divinely human. No dotted lines, no statements to sign, no rule-book that excludes others from belonging – however much that rule book may need to keep power away from some.

John Dominic Crossan, in his book *The Greatest Prayer* (HarperOne, 2010), points out that the Lord's Prayer says nothing about the Bible or doctrines or churches or clergy. It is a prayer from the heart of Judaism on the lips of Christianity for the conscience of the world.

Which direction are you praying and moving in? Ponder again, slowly, the Lord's Prayer.

Clear your vision

Mark 8:22-26

We stumble along, half-seeing. If you're waiting for a second cataract operation, you see clearly through one eye while through the other your vision is blurred. People can indeed seem like trees walking. You need the touch of spittle and the energy that flows through hands – or the delicate probe of a scalpel and the insertion of a plastic lens. Thank God for both methods. Asked which you'd prefer, most of us would reply with what was most familiar in our culture. We might well have heard about the curing properties of saliva, but we might choose the travelling clinic rather than the charismatic traveller.

(It's interesting that Matthew and Luke, in their reworking of this story, omit the spittle. Because they thought it undignified for Jesus? And they reduce the two stages in the cure to one. Because two stages might imply he wasn't on divine form that day?)

Notice something else about this story. There is nothing about demon possession or about faith being needed. There is simply the technique, the stillness, and the clearing of the fog.

Also, in Mark's Gospel, after this story of the clearing of a man's eyes, the focus turns to Jesus trying to open the eyes of his disciples to the revolutionary way – and its cost – that he was calling them to. The man in the story had to 'look hard' if he was to see clearly. Each of us has to take responsibility for doing this: it's easier to rely on others, even if it means begging, and you may have a quieter life if you stay in the blur of the fog. How about you?

Pray for clearer vision.

Live wholeheartedly

Mark 10:46-52

This is one of the most vivid of the healing stories in the gospels. You can see the people involved so clearly. It is a simple task to make a short play of it. A named beggar, his shout, people telling him to be quiet, renewed shouting, Jesus stopping, people stopping, being still, expectant, Jesus saying, 'Call him', a quicker pace, 'take heart' (verse 49), a leap of hope, faith and body. Everything the man had ever hoped for was poured into one crystal clear desire: 'I want my sight back' (verse 51).

In this story it is the wholehearted desire and trust that is the trigger. No touch is needed. In the blink of an eye he can see. And he doesn't go away, but follows Jesus on the road. From being stuck in one place he moves into the unknown.

There is another sense in which eyes are being opened as this gospel progresses. First, the demons recognise that Jesus has come from God, then the disciples, now Bartimaeus. This time Jesus bids no one keep it a secret. It is clear that he is being acknowledged as God's Anointed One. But people, then and now, still have to answer the question, What kind of Messiah? And you discover that by following him, not to acclamation but to crucifixion, and not simply as a member of an audience but as a participant in the action.

You might like to look at the accounts of two earlier encounters (Mark 10:17-22, 35-40). Jesus cannot make a true disciple out of a rich man who clings to his wealth nor out of an enthusiastic follower who has delusions of grandeur. The power of money or status has to be given up. But he can make a true disciple of one who throws off his cloak and comes to him with his need. Which are you?

Imagine you are walking with Jesus those fifteen miles from Jericho to Jerusalem. What are you thinking and praying about?

Jim Cotter

Let light transform you

Mark 9:2-9

Pause, if you will, when you come to each of the sets of three dots. Ponder your own experience of darkness and light. Add your own examples.

A fierce headlamp dazzles you as it is suddenly switched on at dead of night. You shield your eyes. You are blinded for a few moments. You are bewildered...

You switch on a special lamp on a gloomy winter afternoon. It simulates summer sunlight. It cheers you up...

Your eyes sparkle. Your face lights up. You are radiant on your wedding day...

It was said of Moses that he came down the mountain after his encounter with God and did not know that his face shone...

Too much light, too soon, too suddenly, out of the dark womb into a bright room, too much reality. Unbearable...

A moment of illumination, enlightenment. Ah, now I see. No longer do I stumble in the darkness. It may be eyesight or insight that has been given. The one heals, the other teaches...

Jesus transfigured by the light of the divine, bringing that light so that others may see...

The placing of the story in Mark's Gospel shines that light towards the approaching darkness of a Friday noon...

Can the light continue to shine in the darkness, as John writes in his gospel's overture, so that the darkness can never put it out?

Sometimes the light dawns but slowly, and perhaps that is just as well. Have you ever sat still at a window or on a hillside from before first light until sunrise?

Live as the least

Mark 9:30-37

They didn't understand and they were afraid to ask. The disciples once again refused to see. If you are afraid, you shut your eyes or you look away. You can't face it.

Jesus had spoken of an unusual kingdom, he had cured the sick, he had been the means of others finding their freedom, their healing, their sa(l)ving. They thought they knew him: God's Anointed One, surely the most powerful person on earth. Understandably they wanted their share of that power.

Recall how, in the first century, honour played such an important part in the ordering of households, and assemblies and empires. The nearer you were to the top of the table the more honourable you were in your host's eyes. The other guests would notice, and your standing in the community would rise.

Jesus will have none of this. When he asks what his disciples were arguing about they are silent. Maybe some of them were struggling to understand Jesus, not finding it easy to hear talk of lives and households being turned inside out and upside down. Again and again he puts centre stage the least, the unnoticed, the nameless nobodies, the poor with no money, the slave whose face you don't see as she washes feet – and here, the child. And the child is put in the centre not because he is innocent, nor because she speaks truths that adults have long since forgotten, but because the child is the least in worldly eyes, powerless and vulnerable. Of such is the kingdom of God.

Look around your family, your church assembly, your school, your workplace. Who is regarded as the least? The youngest? The oldest? The shy? The speechless? Think and feel yourself into their shoes. Be humbled and glad if you are already wearing them. Then, once again, open your eyes and see.

Do not be afraid

Mark 10:32-34

Look back briefly at yesterday's reading, and then look forward and at least glance at verses 34-45. The two passages are like a pair of bookends, very similar. In between, Jesus is speaking about how hard it is to follow in his way. Even if it looks as if those who are not followers are having an easier time, don't reject them: they sometimes do more wonderful deeds or simpler acts of compassion than you do. Examine your own conscience and ask yourself if you have made life harder for the powerless and vulnerable. Look at the closest relationships in your life, and ask if you have been true to the demands of love. Make sure you don't have more money and possessions than you need.

All that is hard enough. But now Jesus is going to Jerusalem, leading the way. Those around him are awestruck, afraid, knowing the danger they face. Jesus' challenge to the powers that be (and that includes ourselves to the extent that we have more worldly power than others), the vested interests of rulers and colluders, emperors and governors, temple authorities and high priest, will provoke a strong reaction. But surely the all-powerful God and his Anointed One will overcome them, if need be by superior fire power or angelic army. But no. He will be betrayed, cast out, the worst of the least, crucified. The way is dangerous, risky, costly.

Ask this: Do you believe that Jesus went that way so that we don't have to, that he has taken our place so that God's displeasure may be appeased? Or do you believe that we are called to follow, to take our part in love's costly way, to participate in giving up all that the worldly way holds dear, so that what lasts will be love and not force, justice and not tyranny, compassion and not cruelty, God's presence being implanted in us by ever-available gift and grace, and God's will being done – as in heaven – so on earth?

Trees

Wednesday 22 February
(Ash Wednesday)

Trees in the Old Testament 1

Notes based on the New Revised Standard Version by

Susan Hibbins

Susan Hibbins is an Anglican, a freelance writer and editor. In her writing she seeks to apply the Christian faith to everyday life in the twenty-first century. She is especially interested in choral music, and in her spare time is secretary of a local community choir of fifty people.

Genesis 1:26-31

God's provision of the trees

From the beginning of time it was God's intention to provide for the human beings he was to make in his own image. Earlier in this creation account, God shows us the importance of trees when he ordains that, with all their potential for producing fruit, they should be the first things to appear on the dry land of the world he is calling into being. So, from the foundation of the world, trees are a symbol of God's provision of food. Trees also provide us with shade and shelter, with material for the building of homes, with branches for fuel to place on a fire.

In the Bible are trees of all kinds and in all places, delighting the eye with their beauty, and giving their fruit year after year. We see their roots reaching far into the earth, their branches soaring into the heavens. They become symbols for us of sturdiness and of flexibility, of what it means to live a life of deep-rooted faith in God. Perhaps, then, as we embark on another year's Lenten journey with Jesus on his way to the cross, trees may teach us something about our own call to become both sturdy and flexible disciples, those who are deeply rooted in the reality of God.

Dear Lord of all creation, we thank you for the trees of the world, for their beauty, and for the food they produce. Teach us by their beauty, resilience and fruitfulness how to be truer disciples.

In the shade of the oaks of Mamre

Genesis 18:1-8

One summer my husband and I visited Exmoor, and on a blisteringly hot afternoon walked through a picturesque village in the sunshine. It was a beautiful day, but the heat was intense and it was with relief that we found our way to the bank of a bubbling stream, to sit in the shade of some tall and stately trees.

There are so many aspects in these verses from Genesis, and for me the heat is the most vivid. Abraham has pitched his tent under the oak trees to gain what little shade he can and he is sheltering from the searing heat of the day in the entrance to his tent. As soon as he becomes aware of the three strangers who have come to visit, however, he insists that they should sit in the shade while he waits on them. I can imagine how Sarah felt when Abraham bustled in asking her to prepare a meal at the hottest time of day!

Here Abraham gives an example of hospitality that involves more than simply providing visitors with rest and some food. He gives up his own comfort, his own seat in the shade of the trees, to rush around in the heat while his guests rest and enjoy the shelter of the trees. And it was not a ready-meal popped into a microwave: Abraham 'ran' to find an animal to slaughter so that guests could eat. A welcome indeed!

How long is it since you invited someone for a meal? Think of people you know who are lonely, invite them, and prepare the best meal you can for them. Think ahead of how you can make them comfortable in your home, creating an atmosphere of welcome and care.

Teach us, dear God, to offer hospitality that is lavish and real.

Holy to the Lord

Leviticus 27:30-33

At many harvest festivals, churches are decorated with the fruits of the fields and the trees. Colourful displays of apples and pears adorn windowsills, while a loaf of bread shaped as a sheaf of wheat has pride of place. When I was a child we used to take our baskets of produce and tinned food to the front of the church while everybody sang 'We plough the fields and scatter'. After the service, the fruit and other food was distributed to the needy in the surrounding district. It was our way of tithing the harvest produce, in thanks that we had enough and more.

When harvest festival is over for another year, is our duty done? Helping people who need it is not a once-a-year obligation. Tithing what we have been given on a regular basis can be a conscious decision to dedicate what we have received to God, and thus to those who need our help. It is easy to attend a harvest festival service and give thanks, but not so easy to be part of a team that organises a late-night soup kitchen, or to volunteer to help at a feeding station for the homeless. Then it is not only food that we give, but love and understanding too.

The fruits of the trees are 'holy to the Lord' (verse 30). In his name, should we not give as much as we can to those who have less, and often nothing?

We thank you, Lord, for all the food that we can choose to buy, and for all the varieties of food we have to eat. Make us aware of those in our own towns and cities who have little, who struggle to find enough to eat each day. Remind us to give regularly of the plenty that you have given us.

Susan Hibbins

God's good land – for everyone

Deuteronomy 8: 1-10

The people of Israel, after forty years in the wilderness, have reached their destination. It is a land in which they will find all that they need: olive and fruit trees, sweet water to help them grow, and a land where they will lack nothing and never be hungry. God's provision has never left his people through all the years of wandering; now they will have much more than manna to eat.

We could read this passage as a description of what God has given the whole world, through all time: bread, fruit, water, and no lack of any of them, so that each person might eat enough and more. It should be the case today that everyone in the world has enough to eat. Yet still there is the obscenity of children starving to death, and the shameful amount of food that is thrown away uneaten every week while food mountains continue to pile up.

God never intended that any of his children should go hungry, day after day. The world's resources are such that each should 'eat bread without scarcity' (verse 9). It was not God's plan that one half of the world is surfeited with food while the other half starves. In essence it seems so simple to solve: that brief compassion engendered by television appeals becomes a permanent sharing of what we have, until all are fed. God's generous provision is intended for all, not for the few.

Organise an event that raises awareness of hunger worldwide. Or get political! Write to your MP asking what initiatives are planned to help the hungry nations of the world.

Teach us to share your bread with all who need it,
generous God.

Susan Hibbins

Trees

Trees in the Old Testament 2

Deuteronomy 20:19-20

Notes based on the New Revised Standard Version by

Susan Hibbins

For Susan's biography see p. 53.

Life without trees

When I lived at home with my parents, I could see from my bedroom window a young silver birch tree. It was especially beautiful in the winter, when its branches were drenched with rain because, when the sun shone behind it, each drop of moisture glistened and the whole tree became a dazzle of light. I have always loved individual trees, my too-vivid imagination considering them as friends. When I came home one day and found that the silver birch had been chopped down, I was shocked and grieved.

I'm sure our neighbour had good reasons for felling the young tree, and of course diseased and dangerous trees have to be taken down, but this passage tells us to think carefully before we damage trees for no good reason. Today, we cannot imagine felling trees because we are besieging a city and need them for fuel, or to make siege-engines with them. But still trees are felled for the wrong reasons: rain forests decimated in the pursuit of money or habitats destroyed that threaten animals' food resources and people's ways of life. The felling of all the trees on Easter Island is a cautionary tale for us today. Thankfully, we can all care for the trees immediately around us – and maybe think twice before we chop another one down.

Lord, thank you for the trees in our neighbourhood. Help us to care for them, valuing them as a treasured part of your creation.

Practical help

Deuteronomy 24: 19-22

I visit an elderly widow who is almost blind, and over the last year I have been reading aloud to her. We both enjoy these reading sessions, and I think for her the main enjoyment is in the descriptions of scenes and places that she can no longer see. My friend has very few visitors and each time I leave she begs me not to forget her. I always reassure her that I will not, adding that I will think about her during the time when I am not with her. She always responds with, 'I know, but please come again soon.'

Her words made me think about the practical help we give people. Of course it is good that we think of, and indeed pray for, people for whom we care. But for people like my friend, that is not a substitute for actually being with her and sharing an hour's reading.

In these verses from Deuteronomy, God is directing us in the same way. Leaving food in the fields, olives on the tree and grapes on the vine for 'the alien, the orphan, and the widow' (verses 19, 20, 21) is of more help than simply praying that they will be fed and their need will be answered.

It is in the practical things that we can often be of most use. Loneliness and need are all around us, at work, in our neighbourhood, even in our churches. What can we do to help?

In all my contact with others today, Lord, help me to be aware of people's needs, and then help me to find ways of helping them.

Susan Hibbins

Don't ask me!

Judges 9:8-15

Although we usually associate parables with Jesus, these verses in Judges form the earliest recorded parable in the Bible. What do they have to say to us today?

All the trees in the story, asked if they would be king over all the other trees, find excellent reasons why they should not accept the offer. This in itself seems odd: many people (or trees) would be attracted to the idea of kingship, with all its associated benefits. But none of the trees wants to change what it is or what it produces.

Are we the same sometimes? It may not be kingship (or queenship) that's on offer, but instead the opportunity to be, do and produce something completely different. Instead of embracing the chance wholeheartedly, we are reluctant. We are happy as we are; what we produce or the way we live is useful (hopefully), and we don't want to change. Even when God asks new and potentially exciting things of us, we are strangely reluctant to take the plunge. Why?

A word of caution: at the end of this passage and in desperation, having been turned down by all the beautiful, fruit-bearing species, the trees invite the bramble to be their king – a specimen that would normally be associated with choking thorns and an unwanted weed. There is the lesson: it may be easy to stay with what we know rather than trying something new, but will our fruit diminish and die?

God of change, let us never become satisfied with sameness, or proud of what we have achieved, so that we do not want to take on different challenges. Help us to be open to new possibilities to serve you and others throughout our lives.

Susan Hibbins

Under the broom tree

1 Kings 19:1-8

Elijah has reached the end of his tether. Besieged on every side, his life under threat, he flees into the wilderness, where he feels overcome by his problems. He sits under 'a solitary broom tree' (verse 4) and feels such a failure that he begs God to let him die. I imagine him leaning against the trunk of the tree and heaving a big sigh of unhappiness.

We all have times when we seek out our own 'broom trees' to sit under, where we can give way to the sense of despair that besets us. Very often life gets too much for us, and our faith is tested to the limit. There is no shame in giving in to feelings like Elijah's, and it is no judgement on our faith that we feel sometimes that we have failed.

God does not leave Elijah alone to suffer, or to die. Instead he sends an angel to minister to Elijah's physical needs and, after he has rested and eaten, he feels heartened enough to carry on. We need, too, to allow ourselves time to rest and be restored, to eat properly and look after ourselves. It may be that we need to allow other people – the 'angels' – to minister to us. This is not always easy when we think that we are the ones who should be serving others all the time. God cared for Elijah – and God cares for us too.

Lord, when I am overwhelmed by life, help me to seek a time of rest and healing, so that, renewed and strengthened, I am able to carry on in your service.

Susan Hibbins

Planted by streams of water

Psalm 1:1-6

Have you ever noticed trees that stand on riverbanks? I imagine walking alongside rivers where trees grow thickly down by the water, often seeming to stand in the river itself. Old but sturdy trees seem to thrive, the constant water around their roots ensuring that they never become dried out, even in the hottest summers.

The psalmist likens such trees to people who are steeped in God's law, or word. It is, s/he says, 'their delight' (verse 2). For myself, I have found over the years that studying the words of the Bible is a source of refreshment that only deepens the more time I spend with them. To be frank, my Bible reading was once patchy at best, but now I find that, if I miss a morning's reading, something seems to be wrong with my day.

The Bible is still the bestselling book of all time, though it is true that many copies languish unread on people's bookshelves. Just imagine the change that might happen for good if everyone who had a copy spent just fifteen minutes a day reading and meditating on God's word! I find that reading the Bible and letting the words sink into my mind and my heart has changed me – for the better, I hope. As the trees absorb the water, so we can absorb God's word, so that our souls are kept green and do not wither within us.

Increase my understanding, O Lord, so that I become aware of you in every part of my life. As trees standing by the water, may I absorb wisdom from meditating on your word all my days.

The wisdom of age

Psalm 92:12-15

In today's world, acknowledging that one will inevitably age and grow elderly seems to be something many people want to deny will ever happen to them. To 'stay young' in outlook and appearance is essential. The elderly are often shunned as a nuisance, as we pursue perpetual youth. Being with them is seen as depressing and many people do not want to look at extreme old age and think that it might happen to them. Sadly, respect for the wisdom of old age seems to be disappearing from our society.

Yet the older generation can tell us a thing or two about life. How to put down roots into something that will hold firm no matter what life might throw at us. How to bend and be flexible and survive, rather than staying stiff and unyielding and being broken. The true wisdom of a life lived with God means that old age can bring with it a serenity, a distillation of all that has been good about life's experiences, together with a calm acceptance that life has not much longer to run.

Instead of chasing after a youth that cannot last – facelifts, anti-ageing potions and a desperate determination never to slow down – perhaps we could stop for a moment, look at the trees and then into the face of an older person, and learn from them both.

Visit a lonely old person from your church and talk to them about their life.

Teach me, ageless God, to face the advancing years with courage and with hope.

The glory of God's world

Psalm 104:10-18

I work from home, and from my office window I am lucky enough to see a row of trees. Over the last three years I have come to see them as a symbol of the continuing cycle of life of which we, and all the creatures and birds, are a part. In winter their branches are bare and stand silhouetted against the early sunset; in the spring they are a haze of tender green; in summer they are full-leafed and in their prime; and when the autumn arrives their leaves change to russet, flaming orange and yellow. The birds flit in and out, seeking shelter and protection, grubs and insects. In the spring they build their nests in the branches, and I watch them flying endlessly back and forth with food for their young.

The verses from this psalm list the wonders of creation on a larger scale than my trees, and over all of them is the care of God for his world. Each creature has its home and each is provided for in relation to its needs: grass for the cattle, trees for the storks, and high mountains for the wild goats. Food is grown from the well-watered earth so that human beings receive the things they need too.

Read the rest of the psalm. I imagine the writer looking at the beauty of the world, intoxicated by its glorious creation – and thanking the God who made it.

We thank you, Lord, for everything you have made. Let us never take for granted the beauty you have scattered in our path, but be refreshed by your daily re-creation of our world.

Susan Hibbins

Trees

Trees in the Old Testament 3

Notes based on the New Revised Standard Version by

Jane Gonzalez

Jane Gonzalez is a Roman Catholic laywoman, and works as a pastoral assistant in a parish in Hertfordshire. She is also currently studying for an MA in Pastoral Theology.

Isaiah 10:33 – 11:3

Only God can make a tree

'Only God can make a tree.' This was something that my father was fond of saying. It summed up, for him, the beauty of nature and his place within it. As I have grown older and reflected more on my faith and my own humanity, it has resonated even more. There's a profound truth here about my relationship with God, my creator, and my role within that relationship as creature – blessed, redeemed, privileged among the other creatures and created things, but essentially with a place within the scheme of things. The rest of creation lets God be God. Why is it so hard for me?

Trees do nothing except be trees and in doing so give glory to God and give pause for thought to us. In the Bible, they symbolise many things – endurance, fruitfulness, hope and restoration, to name but a few. In the midst of seeming disaster, in the face of the collapse of hope for the future, in the face of extinction, a stump of a tree puts forth a shoot. Only God can make a tree. Only God can bring about restoration and renewal when all seems lost.

Can I let go of my pride and let God be God in my life? What areas of my life need pruning or cutting back?

For there is hope for a tree, if it is cut down, that it will sprout again, and that its shoots will not cease.

Job 14:7

Turning things upside down

Isaiah 41:17-20

'When the going gets tough, the tough get going' – so the song of Billy Ocean says! Well, the singer may have had the get up and go to do so, but for most of us, it isn't that easy. And often, it isn't the big traumas of life that are the toughest, but the relentless daily grind that wears us down. We might be able to find the resources to cope with the darkest days; we can celebrate the bright ones with joy, but how do we go forward when life just seems an unremitting grey?

Israel faced this problem during the arid years of exile: the task of keeping the faith, carrying on trusting and hoping in the face of absolutely nothing happening. Waiting. Isaiah brings a message of hope and consolation to those who find it hard to believe and trust. He speaks of a God who can turn the world upside down and make deserts and wildernesses bloom and flourish. Into a sparse and unforgiving environment, God will plant trees. Seven trees to be exact. Seven is the perfect number, signifying fullness and completion. Seven trees will provide materials for shelter, food and fuel, for everything that is necessary for life in abundance.

Wisdom and understanding, discernment and courage, experience and reverence and a sense of awe and wonder – these are the 'traditional' seven gifts of the Holy Spirit. Like the trees in the passage, they can be the source of life in abundance if we trust and hope and let God work in our lives.

Where are the desert areas in your life? What gift or gifts do you want the Spirit to plant within you?

[Wisdom] is a tree of life to those who lay hold of her; those who hold her fast are called happy.

Proverbs 3:18

Who is my neighbour?

Isaiah 44:13-20

I love wood. I love polishing the few pieces of good wooden furniture I have. I love the fact that wood is said to breathe. Country lore tells us that we should never cut down or prune an elder tree without first informing the tree of our intentions! This speaks of a reverence for trees and wood that we don't have for other forms of plant life. Even if most of us are not tree-huggers, we can appreciate the respect that trees engender and echo the ancient Irish monk who wrote, 'I am enriched by forest trees about me' (original source unknown). Many ancient trees are witnesses to the great events of human existence; they are the lungs of the planet and they provide for us in so many ways. We are encouraged now to use wood only from sustainable sources.

Trees are perfect in their tree-ness. They do not try to be anything other than the trees they are. Of all the created order, it is only human beings who attempt to be something other than themselves, distorting themselves, seeking to live out an image rather than a reality.

Perhaps this is the real sin of the carpenter. He makes something inappropriate, going against the nature of the tree, and against his own nature as a fellow created being. It's fine to use wood for fuel and fine to create something beautiful from it. But making an idol perverts the nature of the tree. It is an unloving act. We are asked as human beings to be in right relationship with our neighbours; we are asked to act with appropriate reverence towards the rest of God's creation. Is it time for a reappraisal of who – or what – precisely is our neighbour?

What kind of relationship does God want us to have with the rest of the created order?

Reflect on Genesis 1:28 and pray around this text, which has been the source of much harm in the created order.

God of surprises

Isaiah 55:6-13

A religious sister of my acquaintance is fond of saying that God writes straight with crooked lines. The lives and exploits of many of the major characters of the Bible seem to bear this out. David, Jacob, Peter, Sarah, the Samaritan woman, the sinful, the weak, the fallible, the cowardly – these are the ones God chooses above those who might appear to have better credentials for fulfilling his purposes and participating in the great work of redemption.

The 'God of Surprises', as Gerard Hughes calls him, has to work hard at breaking down our preconceived ideas and cosy prejudices; our tendency to make God in our own image and likeness; our desire to pack a manageable God into a bag that we just take out on Sundays (Gerard Hughes, *God of Surprises*, Darton, Longman & Todd, 1985). We need to be reminded continually that God's ways are not our ways, God's thoughts are not our thoughts.

Isaiah exhorts his contemporaries to think outside the box and to accept that what God desires will indeed be accomplished, but in God's time and as God directs. They are to expect what has become the unexpected and wait to be surprised. Isaiah's words are as relevant now as they were then. But have we got the courage to find God's meaning and message in our lives? And the willingness to be surprised?

Has my prayer life become routine and dull? Am I prepared to be surprised by the Spirit?

For great is the wisdom of the Lord!

Ecclesiasticus 15:18a

Jane Gonzalez

I have called you by name

Jeremiah 11: 14-20

As a child I used to hate telling anyone my name, and if I had to say it, I tended to say it reluctantly and softly. Perhaps it was a kind of fear of giving someone else power over me. Names imply possession and intimacy. In Genesis 2, Adam has the responsibility of naming the rest of the created order. Throughout history the naming of children has had enormous importance. In the Christian tradition, giving a Christian name implies giving a child a role model – a heroine or hero from the scriptures or Christian history, whose life and experiences may be an example to the newly baptised. Certainly, for many of the younger confirmation candidates that I prepare, the chance to pick a special name is one of the most exciting parts of the course.

In the story of ancient Israel, names are important too. A person's name often reflects his or her destiny or role; the path that the Lord wants the person to take. A name is something to live up to. In our passage, Israel has failed to live up to its calling to be a fruitful olive tree and thus has to face the consequences. Olives are tended and nurtured carefully while they are young and then left to flower and flourish, with only minimal attention from the landowner. But if they fail to crop sufficiently, then their beauty, their history, their venerable status, will not prevent them from being cut down, and their rottenness destroyed by fire.

Where are the unfruitful areas of my life? Do I really live up to my calling as a Christian?

I am like a green olive tree in the house of God.

Psalm 52:8

Jane Gonzalez

How the mighty are fallen

Ezekiel 31:1-12

One of my favourite poems is 'Ozymandias' by Shelley. It tells of a mighty king in the ancient world who thought his works and his life would last for ever, a king who said, 'look on my works, ye mighty and despair!' But all that remains now is the head and trunk of a statue in the midst of a deserted wasteland. I often wonder if Shelley had some of the powerful nations of the Bible in his mind. Certainly he had the measure of human beings whose hubris and arrogance often know no boundaries. The history of the world is littered with dynasties and rulers who think in terms of thousand-year Reichs and not in terms of right relationship with the creator.

Ezekiel utters an oracle against Egypt, citing the example of how the might of Assyria was brought low by God. God has nothing against success. God wants people to flourish and prosper. This Assyria did, like a tree blooming and growing and attaining maturity. The trouble began when, unlike a tree, the nation got ideas above its station. Trees remain trees. Human beings often seek to be more than they are created to be.

Human authority and power derive from God and, no matter how successful an enterprise, a country or an individual may seem, without a right relationship with God, disaster will ultimately come. Pride comes before a fall, as the old proverb and the old prophets say.

Where might pride trip me up in my life? How can I be humble and still celebrate the giftedness that comes from God?

Before destruction one's heart is haughty,
but humility goes before honour.

Proverbs 18:12

Behold the wood of the cross...

Ezekiel 47:7-12

Recently I visited Coventry Cathedral. It was a Friday and we participated in the weekly Litany of Reconciliation in the ruins of the old cathedral, destroyed by incendiary bombs during the Second World War. We prayed amid a diverse group of pilgrims and visitors for an end to the sin that prevents us loving and forgiving as Jesus asked us to. We stood in front of an altar on which there was a replica of the Cross of Nails, fashioned shortly after the devastation, from three medieval nails from the roof timbers, and behind which was a replica of the Charred Cross, made from smouldering beams the day after the bombs fell. Powerful symbols now, as then, of a cathedral community determined to bring healing and reconciliation where hatred and death seem often to have the upper hand. I was reminded of the ancient legend about the flowering of the cross – that the cross burst into bloom, into life, as Jesus died on it.

In our passage, Ezekiel talks of trees that will heal and nourish in the restored and renewed temple precincts. As Christians we focus on a different tree – the tree of Calvary – but herein we too can find healing and strength. The tree of life, which is the cross, restores and renews our relationship with God, 'paradise regained'. True healing of the wounds caused by war and division among the peoples of the world and in our own families and communities can be rooted only in the sacrifice of the cross, in the words of reconciliation that find their echo behind the outside altar in Coventry: 'Father, forgive'.

Who has hurt me recently? Can I forgive?

Reflect on Matthew 5:23-24.

The fruit of the righteous is a tree of life.

Proverbs 11:30

Trees

Trees in the Old Testament 4

Daniel 4:10-17

Timber!

There is a sense of shock here. Trees are usually sources of well-being and delight in so many ways, whether you are a human being, bird, or a member of the animal kingdom. Even as we hold on to this, we are led on to the brutality of the second part of the section. This tree is felled, with the ruthless efficiency of a logging team hacking its way through a rain forest. This is a sickening picture of shattered hope and promise, of the arbitrariness of so much 'clearance', which – like the rain – falls on good and bad alike.

Now, though, emerges a strange comfort, in the final lines: 'Let the stump and its roots, bound with iron and bronze, remain in the ground, in the grass of the field' (verse 15). The tree's basic core is still there – so is the hope of new life and a fresh start. I remember our woodland at Ditchingham, savaged beyond recognition by gales, regenerating into new fruitfulness. I ask God to let that encourage me to hope and trust in the power of his love to make good all that is spoilt and withered in my life.

Spend time today and throughout the week paying particular attention to the trees in your neighbourhood, praying in and through them.

Notes based on the New International Version by

Sheila Day

Sheila Day comes from Ditchingham, on the Norfolk/Suffolk border, where she has been a member of the Community of All Hallows for forty years. Trained as a musician and secretary, she has had ample scope to exercise these skills – and a few more! Currently she is joint leader of the Community, with a particular brief for the care of newcomers and enquirers to the Community.

Now for the bad news...

Daniel 4:18-27

The shock of yesterday's passage can be nothing to that which Nebuchadnezzar must have felt when confronted by Daniel with this interpretation of his dream. How much courage Daniel needed for this I know something of from my own experience. I know, too, how much easier it is to tell, and for another to hear, what they want to hear ... and I have learned the hard way that such 'kindness' leads to heartache and anger, the more so the longer the deception continues. Daniel's courage comes from the conviction that God is in this with them both. Surely he has prayed for grace to speak the awful truth non-judgementally, compassionately, and for Nebuchadnezzar to hear it in the spirit in which it is given. He is heard graciously, and Nebuchadnezzar even repents – for a while. I know that when I have been forced to 'bite the bullet' and have done so in as measured and prayerful a way as I could, it has never turned out quite as badly as I feared – or if it has, the grace to navigate the rapids has been there too!

'Perfect love casts out fear' (1 John 4:18), fear being the bogey that breeds prickles of irritation, resentment and hence more fear. On this principle, I can try doing or saying one small, kind thing each day for people who annoy me or scare me. It isn't impossible. It might encourage me – and them – to lower the defences and let God into the circle.

God, keep me grounded in the knowledge of your love, from which nothing can separate me, through which I can speak the truth, and be heard, in that same love.

Let's hear it for conifers!

Hosea 14:4-9

This passage is full of encouragement. The Blessed One blesses those who turn from their own unwisdom to the true wisdom, the varied fruit of a life that does not trust itself but knows its dependence on the One who loved it into being. So we reach the beautiful lines 'I am the pine tree who shelters you. All your fruitfulness comes from me' (verse 8, paraphrased).

Pines, and conifers in general, often do not get a good press – dark, regimented, brooding, taking the goodness from the soil. Let's enjoy and savour this line by way of contrast. We can see, too, the contrast between our occasional imaging of God as stern, inscrutable, dark, brooding – and the gentle fruitfulness depicted here. In the words of an old Celtic saying, 'there is a mother's heart in the heart of God'; and that divine mother-love is there for us all, symbolised in the flexibility and fruitfulness of this passage. We do well to remember this and to be humble enough to let God 'mother' us once in a while. We all need it.

When did you last look, long and prayerfully, at a biggish tree, or better still, lean up against one? It is worth doing, perhaps for five or ten minutes, contemplating its supportive strength, its capacity for shelter and nurture and somehow letting that communicate itself to you.

God, source of peace, strength and wisdom, be peace in my heart, strength of my will, wisdom to my mind, and inflame me with love for you and yours.

Pruned to the death

Joel 1:1-12

Oh dear! We talk and sing glibly enough during Lent about 'stripping' and self-emptying, and rightly enough. As we pray with this passage, however, am I the only person who feels that the talk and song can be a bit hollow? I look at my keeping of Lent over the years; at the poverty I profess as a Religious. Then I look at our world – or at the two-thirds of it for whom 'stripped down' means something much more like what Joel is talking about.

This is not the place for an indictment of those who are responsible for world poverty, and I'd have to point at least one finger at myself for my own thoughtless use of God's creation in so many ways. This does not get me out of hearing this passage as a wake-up call to hear and listen for the voice of the Lord urging us to repentance, and to trust in his mercy and power to bring good out of our evil.

So – as we take a long look at our stewardship of the resources we have been given, let me, let us, today perform one more unselfish action than we need, asking ourselves once more: 'do I really need this?' of some not-quite-luxury, even if it costs. And let us pray:

Lord, have mercy. Sow whatever good there is in me to help bring fruitfulness out of all that has dried up and withered in your world.

Recycle! Hearts for hardware

Micah 4:1-5

Most of us know this passage pretty well, I imagine. For me it is full of the sights, sounds and smells of Advent, not unmixed with some pre-Christmas preparation panic. It is good to have it here, out of its usual context, and to hear what it might be saying now as we approach the end and climax of Lent. Swords are turning to ploughshares, spears to pruning hooks. Weapons of destruction are exchanged for instruments of nurture and growth. Each of us is content with our own fig tree and vine; no more hankering after a whole plantation or even just our neighbour's patch. Relatedness and trust have replaced rivalry and fear. For the God acknowledged here is the Lord who created us and longs for us to listen to him as he teaches us how to embrace true peace and plenty. Each nation has its own precious identity, yet rejoices to unite in service of a common good – the God whom we know as Lord and Sustainer. Perfect love has cast out fear and ensured the well-being of every creature on the planet. Hmm!

As a member of a community, particularly one dedicated to that motley bunch known as 'All Saints/Hallows', I can, and must, look at my own living of our particular charism and rule in this light, and ask myself how my own relationships – with sisters, with the wider community, with possessions – measure up. This exercise need not be limited to nuns. How about families, workplaces, parishes? Are we factories of swords or of ploughshares? Or (more likely?) a bit of both? Which personal weapon can I dismantle today? Which God owns our 'factory'?

Lord, write your perfect law of selfless love on the vibrant tablet of our hearts, and let that shape our life together.

It isn't fair!

Jonah 3:10 – 4:11

No wonder Jonah is fed up. Despite his initial 'no!' Jonah has at least got himself to Nineveh and preached as God told him to. What happens? He is denied the smug feeling of seeing himself proved right in his eyes, even if that would have meant catastrophic losses in human terms. It begs the question: whom is he seeking to please? Who is ultimately in charge in his life? And whom do I seek to please – when I get round to seeking to please anyone apart from a few select acquaintances? Still, God may have made a fool of him, but see! God has now vindicated Jonah's obedience by growing this lovely vine to shelter him. And what then? God has destroyed it, and let poor Jonah roast in this infernal heat!

Jonah has had enough. Not unlike Elijah, though with less cause, he asks to die (another attempt to run away from God?). And God weighs in. He points out that Jonah is making a fuss over one vine that was not his handiwork but God's, and whose shelter Jonah took for granted, as a right. 'So why should I not make a fuss of this huge city – men, women, children, animals – who have as much right to life as you?' (verse 11). In other words, where is your heart, Jonah? Who is boss in your life?

When things go pear-shaped in liturgy, music or in the kitchen (three of my areas of work), can I take a deep breath and ask, in the words of an old Muslim prayer, for the Lord to enlarge my heart a little? I can look ahead and pray for the grace to cope with the surprises the day will undoubtedly throw at me, and trust God for two things: for that grace, and also for his compassionate love when I still manage – as I will – to fall short.

Speak, Lord, and give your servant ears to hear!

Yet...

Habakkuk 3:16-19

The canticle of which today's passage is part appears regularly in the scheme of psalms for Morning Prayer as we say it at Ditchingham. Always I am struck by the human fear to which Habakkuk confesses, then by his catalogue of 'what if'; and most of all, by the reiterated, 'Yet I will rejoice... I will be joyful' (verse 18).

It doesn't matter what is going on for me in terms of fear or calamity – it is little enough by global standards, even if many traditional Western religious communities, like mine, can speak with some authority on diminution, frightening rates of change if not decay, and an unknown future. As we pray this affirmation of faith, it somehow reinforces what little there is of mine. I don't think I have ever said the canticle without experiencing, deep down, a strengthening of resolve to trust and give thanks to and for the God who was, is and is to come; not to mention prayer for those for whom there are indeed no crop and no livestock to tend.

We do not have to be religious 'professionals' to make these words our own! Especially – but not only – when worried silly, when all seems lost, and all hope dimmed, we can say, very quietly, slowly, again and again, these words, probably replacing vines and fig trees with our own problems and those of others known to us. We can try to hear God saying (as he surely is) to each of us: 'I rejoice in you, too; I am glad to be your salvation.'

Jesus knew fear, of the threatened loss of everything, including his very life, most particularly in Gethsemane. He stayed with it, as he does with us. A former chaplain of the Community of All Hallows once told us that 'The courage of Jesus is ours for the asking.'

So let us ask Christ for that courage, and keep asking him, in whatever words come, and do our best to trust him for it.

Trees

Trees in the New Testament

Notes based on the *Good as New* version by

John Henson

John Henson is a writer, conference speaker and 'Inclusive Church' promoter. He is best known for *Good as New* (O Books, 2005), his radical retelling of the Christian scriptures.

Matthew 7:15-20

By their fruit you shall know them

Just as good trees produce tasty fruit and bad trees diseased fruit, so good people are nice to know and bad people give you the creeps.

Good as New, p.134

Jesus was not an academic. Some of his followers are. But if they are to be true friends of Jesus, sometimes they must forget their theological training in order to be human. Jesus was close enough to ordinary people to know their needs and to speak God's words of guidance in language they could understand. He was also close to nature. Jesus used illustrations from trees. Trees were essential sources of food in his country – olives, figs, dates, pomegranates, almonds and carob nuts. Trees were also valued as shade and shelter, and sometimes to hide in. Jesus reminds religious leaders, then and now, that being sensitive to your audience is more important than being theological.

Farmers don't waste time on trees that don't fruit well ... Save yourselves trouble by spotting a humbug.

Good as New, p.134

Jesus, help me not to say my piece, but what others long to hear.

Extending the branches

Matthew 13: 31-32

The Bright New World is like a mustard seed which a farmer plants in his field. A mustard seed is very small to look at, but it can grow into a large shrub. It becomes tall enough for birds to make their nests in.

Good As New, p.147

A mustard seed is not the smallest seed. It is quite large. There are bigger trees than mustard trees – the largest of which are only seven feet. Jesus may have chosen a mustard seed because he could show it between his thumb and forefinger to someone in the front row. The size of tree does not matter. This is not one of the 'parables of growth', indicating that something with small beginnings can become something much larger, whether individual faith or the church. The significance is in the parting shot. Though small, the mustard tree can be a nesting or resting space for the birds. Jesus and his hearers may have had uppermost in their minds the nations of the world. Or they may have been thinking about the social outcasts Jesus attracted to himself.

A big church can be exclusive; a small one can be inclusive. I am a friend of the Association of Welcoming and Affirming Baptist Churches in the USA. While most Baptists in the USA exclude gay people, there are many little mustard trees now in place giving gays a warm welcome. We could do with more mustard trees in my own country.

God, make my church a mustard tree.

Qualifying for a blessing

Matthew 21: 18-22

In the morning, on his way back to the city, Jesus felt hungry. He saw a fig tree on the side of the road. He stopped to have a look and found there were only leaves on it. Jesus said, 'You've had your last chance to produce fruit!' The fig tree looked unhealthy. Jesus' friends were intrigued. They said, 'The fig tree seems to be withering in front of our eyes!'

Good As New, pp.161–2

Matthew tells us that Jesus used a sick fig tree to perform an 'acted parable' in the tradition of the prophets. Luke decided to pass on the message in pure parable form, in case his gentile readers didn't understand the symbolism (Luke 13:6-8). What was Jesus saying?

Zechariah prophesied that in the messianic age people would invite their neighbours to come and sit under their fig trees (Zechariah 3:10). Everybody would practise hospitality – a feature of the early church Christians have since neglected. Were churches first built to save Christians from having unwanted people in their homes? At Jerusalem Jesus had his bar mitzvah at the age of twelve. But now he is not at home there. His teachings are too radical. Fewer rules and regulations and more loving of each another. How dreadful!

When people are not hospitable, they forfeit a blessing. First there is no fruit and then the tree withers.

God, make my home a fig tree.

Up a tree

Luke 19:1-10 (*Good As New*, p.225)

I live in Sycamore Street. There's a sycamore tree opposite my front window. My website is called Sycamore Seeds. My email begins with the word 'upatree'. One of my code names is 'Zacchaeus'. Keith, as we call him in *Good As New*, is my favourite New Testament character. Nobody loves him. He's undersized, unpatriotic, on the make, in fear of his life, and his only companions – apart from other quislings – are prostitutes who, like him, hired themselves to foreigners. Trembling on the branch of a tree, he cuts a comical figure.

But from that tree he had a good view of Jesus. People despised by society frequently have a sharper view of Jesus than those who crowd round him. We should listen to them. But Jesus surprised even Keith that day. Accepting Keith as he was! Asking to come to lunch! Giving him no lecture on morality! No call to repentance! (There is no suggestion, despite Keith's generosity, that he ceased to be a quisling.) Jesus not only shared a meal with him, thus sharing his sinful identity, but also ate the top quality food acquired as a result of Keith's rapacious tax demands, probably cooked by one of Keith's female 'friends'! Jesus practised 'situation ethics'. When meeting a needy, unhappy person, Jesus just did what was necessary on the spur of the moment. That's why sinners love him!

Jesus, we thank you that we do not have to be good enough or bad enough to attract your love. We just have to be ourselves.

John Henson

What happened under the fig tree?

John 1:43-51

'Nazareth!?' Nathan sneered, 'Can anything good come from that dump?'... Jesus answered, 'I saw what you were doing under the fig tree before Philip called you.'

Good As New, p.84

I imagine Nathan as a scribe. Not a Pharisee, I think, though some scribes were Pharisees. Scribes studied and copied the Hebrew scriptures. They could also write a letter for you. Nathan was intense and serious and a bit of a snob. He lived in posh Cana by the lakeside. He looked down on the peasants of Nazareth, in the hills. Philip, also from the lakeside, told Nathan about Jesus when Nathan was under a fig tree. What was he doing? And why did Jesus think it significant? Was he giving hospitality to a stranger, like a true Israelite, and keeping it quiet?

A large fig tree's branches come down to form a little den, a perfect hiding place. Maybe he was having a secret tryst with his beloved and an honest talk. Maybe he was doing a business deal and, unlike his ancestor Jacob, was unusually honest and fair with his business partner. Or maybe he was reading the scripture – the part where Jacob saw the ladder up to heaven. Maybe he was meditating and wondering how such a ladder could be set up permanently. Whatever it was, Jesus was impressed and recruited him.

Thank you, Jesus, for noticing our good points, not our faults.

In and out

Romans 11:17-24

People ... ought not to say in an arrogant way, 'You're out and we're in!'

Good As New, p.318

My cousin Jean lives in Crete, in a beautiful valley. The locals have smallholdings providing different vegetables throughout the year. The main crop is olives. I have seen Jean cutting off old branches from the olive trees along the roadsides, to serve as fuel for the winter. Olive trees only thrive as the older branches are cut off and the newer ones allowed to flourish.

Paul uses olive trees to attempt to explain the mystery of the constant dying away of God's people, and regrowth from unexpected sources. His answer is not to propound a rigid doctrine of predestination but rather to wonder at God's skill at continuing life.

The Western churches have become old and tired and need a new lease of life. But the same is true of their daughter churches in the former missionary fields, for these also now have a history behind them. They are already getting stuck in their ways. Newer and older churches benefit from mutual grafting. Even more they need grafts from unexpected places. The gentile outsiders renewed God's people in Paul's day. Perhaps today, for renewal we need to look to secular culture, which in many ways is more lively in thought and more compassionate and understanding of human nature than the churches.

Help me, God, to be aware of the wideness of your operations, and to be more keen to learn than to teach.

John Henson

A better future

Revelation 22:1-7

I would prefer it if the Book of Revelation were not in the Bible. I have Martin Luther on my side. The Eastern churches also ascribe a lesser status to Revelation. For me Revelation contradicts in essential elements the teaching of Jesus. Whereas Jesus condemned the instinct for vengeance, Revelation seems to inflame it. The Jesus who rode on the donkey of peace, in Revelation appears on a warhorse. Too much concentration on Revelation has led to the emergence of many weird sects, chiefly distinguished by their lack of love. The book should certainly not be recom-mended to the new recruit.

I have to acknowledge that Revelation has inspired many people, particularly by its language of worship, which Handel – amongst others – has made immortal use of. And there is the vision of the New Jerusalem, which has inspired social reformers, the Labour Party, and the Women's Institute. Even here, however, there is a craving after prosperity, which today we are coming to recognise as an expression of greed. That tree with twelve fruits instead of one! We can't wait to have it! And our energy problems solved at a stroke! Free and perpetual lighting!

But the healing of the nations, surely meaning not just a worldwide health service, but also the end of strife and enmity, ugly prejudices and racist posturing… That would be good!

Jesus, our true Word, teach us to bring all scripture under your judgement.

Trees

The tree of shame is made the tree of glory

Notes based on the New Revised Standard Version, and Hebrew and Greek texts, by

Brenda Lealman

Brenda Lealman has been an RE adviser and school inspector, with a special interest in the place of spirituality in education. She is also a published poet and a former chair of the Creative Arts Retreat Movement (CARM). She has travelled widely, including staying in ashrams in India and as guest lecturer at a theological college in the Canadian Arctic. She is retired and lives on the North York Moors.

Genesis 2:4b-9, 15-17

The garden of delight

The Chilean miners trapped underground for two months in 2010 emerged out of the earth into the Atacama Desert, into life. Many lifted their arms in thanksgiving. In the Genesis story, a human (Hebrew, *adam*, humankind, not a 'proper name') emerges out of the still-desert earth, shaped by God out of the dust (Hebrew, *adamah*). God gives to the human being breath, life. God gives the human a garden, an enclosure, a paradisal space, lush with plants and fruiting trees. A river and blessings pour through the garden: a garden of delight (in Hebrew, *eden* means 'delight').

Human beings are meant for delight: wondering delight in the abundance of gifts and beauty. And somewhere in the centre of the garden is mystery, two mysterious trees: the tree of life and the tree of the knowledge of good and evil. The human being is told not to eat the fruit of the latter tree. The boundary around the mystery, God the source of everything, is not to be crossed.

In imagination, walk in the garden of delight. Five readings this week are metaphorical narratives or 'myths': they communicate deep truths, and require an imaginative response.

Something goes wrong

Genesis 3:1-13

'Where are you?' God calls out to humankind (verse 9). But the man and woman are hiding amongst the trees of the garden. They are no longer wide open to God's presence, uncalculating, spontaneous. A serpent has appeared in the garden of delight, has talked the woman into eating the forbidden fruit of the tree of the knowledge of good and evil; the fruit looks attractive, good. The woman in turn talks the man into doing the same.

What has gone wrong? It is impossible for us to know exactly what was in the writer's mind but here are some suggestions. Disobedience? 'You shall not eat' (Genesis 2:17). God is lawgiver. The humans have disobeyed him. Power-seeking? 'You will be like God' (verse 5). Humans put themselves in the place where God should be. Inertia? 'Your eyes will be opened' (verse 5). Take the easy way: follow the agenda of others; don't bother to search and draw on your own depths. Coming to self-consciousness? 'knowing good and evil' (verse 5). The emergence of consciousness; the dualism of self and world, self and God; the rise of the judgemental self. Here, the emphasis is not on sin but on inevitability: as humans we grow away from the sense of undifferentiated unity (which is perhaps what the garden of delight is about), into a world of separate selves, divisions, competitiveness and the consequences.

Father God, may I honour you, others, our planet, and always seek to affirm, not to undermine.

Exile east of the garden of delight

Genesis 3:22-24

Human beings are curious – they long to discover, learn, explore. And that is good. But now that they have knowledge, are they going to become a danger to themselves, to the order of the world they inhabit? Will they snatch the secret of eternal life from the tree of life? Instead of standing in awe before the mystery at the heart of life, do we humans want to invade it, seize its power, analyse and possess it?

The garden of delight is lost. The human journey must continue east of Eden; and there is no going back. The garden is out of bounds. The way to the tree of life is guarded by cherubim (winged sphinxes), and by a terrifying sword that flames and turns, that slices humanity off from uncomplicated goodness, unselfconscious delight in the presence of God.

In the church of Santa Maria del Carmine, in Florence, is a fresco painted by Masaccio in about 1427; it illustrates the expulsion from the Garden of Eden. The woman howls with pain. The man hides his face. It is an almost overwhelming depiction of anguish, loss and desolation. This is the human condition in exile east of Eden: sorrow, conflict, competition, grief, greed, suffering – all those crooked ways of the crooked human heart.

Is there a place for lament, for challenging, questioning God? See Psalms 10, 42, 69, 73, 88.

In your prayer, use one of the psalms listed above and read it slowly and reflectively.

Return from exile: tree of curse and grace

Galatians 3:6-14

Paul reprimands the Galatians (members of a Christian community in Galatia, now central Turkey). When they first became Christians, their lives were transformed in the Holy Spirit; now they are being led astray by Christian Jewish agitators who are telling them that Gentiles must accept the Jewish law (be circumcised) before becoming Christians. It's as though the Galatian Christians are moving back into the enslavement of exile east of Eden. Behind Paul's message is this question: how do we move from exile, or 'life in Adam' (often used by Paul to describe the human condition of being under the dominion of sin) into new life?

Paul writes from his experience: by God's grace, dying with Christ and being raised by him, Paul experienced an inner death and birth into new life. He uses Abraham as the exemplar of being given new life through grace, apart from works of the law, even before he was circumcised. Paul's point is that the way out of exile is through the abolition of living according to requirements, of measuring up, of judging how well we do: this is the curse of life under law. Curse is the opposite of blessing: the curse of exile as opposed to the blessings of the garden. It is likely that Jesus was killed by crucifixion in a deliberate attempt by the high priest to put him under God's curse: 'Anyone hung on a tree is under God's curse' (Deuteronomy 21:23). Anyone cursed by God could only be an impostor, not the Messiah. But for Paul, because Jesus became a curse by hanging on the tree, in his death the curse of the law was exhausted. By grace we are returned from exile.

'Return' is the word used in Hebrew for 'repentance'. Often the word suggests 'return from exile', re-orientation of one's life, a fresh start.

Recall, with thanks, a moment of grace when you received the gift of a fresh start.

Return from exile: the tree of crucifixion

1 Peter 2:18-25

This is a circular letter written to churches in five provinces of what is now Turkey. There is no agreement about when, where or why 1 Peter was written, nor about who wrote it. It is often dated after the death of St Peter in 64 BCE. Suffering is frequently referred to, and it could come from the time of persecution of Christians under Nero (54–68 CE), Domitian (81–96 CE), or Trajan (98–117 CE). Or the references could be to local harassment of Christians. The recipients of the letter are called 'exiles': could this have symbolic significance, or does it mean that they are transient workers?

Whatever may be the case, the members of these communities need encouragement. Perhaps many of them were slaves with no hopes of ever obtaining their freedom but who found inspiration in their Christian meetings. Peter doesn't tell them to struggle against the authorities but to go quietly about their work, to put up with unjust punishment and to follow Christ's 'example', in Greek, *hupogrammos*, which means 'the under writing'. Teachers would write out the letters of the alphabet on wax tablets and schoolboys copied these letters in the space below.

Recall from your own childhood the struggles, the attention and risks involved in that sort of copying. Imitating Christ is not going to be easy. For powerless people, their experience of life must so often have seemed at odds with the power they had been told is in Christ. And Peter doesn't lead them into a comfort zone, but tells them that their way into life is through the wood of the cross, the tree on which Jesus hung. It is through Jesus' death, through suffering and pain, that the exile is subverted from within, that we are liberated; and liberation brings the risks and enormous possibilities of new life.

Reflect on some suffering in your own life, which, despite the pain, astonishingly brought blessing. Thank God for this.

Another garden of delight: another tree

Song of Solomon 2:1-7

Soon, I'm going out to plant a tree, a common hawthorn, in a small woodland down the valley. The tree isn't in memory of anyone: it's my thank offering for everything that is, a celebration of life. That is what the Song of Solomon is – a celebration of life, of everything. It is a beautiful, haunting work, drama rather than poem. The voice of a man teasing, playful; of a woman searching, longing. Figures wander the streets, leap over hills; the lover knocks on a door, vanishes. Settings change: an enclosed garden, a walled city, a woodland glade. All fleeting, fragmentary. A feast of sounds, of bird song; fragrance, of vine blossoms and pine resin; textures of skin; colours of crocuses, narcissi and lilies. The man's body is 'ivory work, encrusted with sapphires' (5:14), 'his lips are lilies, distilling liquid myrrh' (5:13). The woman's eyes are doves (1:15). These are metaphors struggling to articulate delight.

In 2:1-7, the lovers' trysting place is a green woodland glade filled with wild flowers, cedars, cypresses and pines that make a canopy over them (1:16b-17). The radiance of the natural world reveals the lovers' own radiance. The man metamorphoses into an apple tree, the woman feeds on his fruit, sits in his shade. There is no jealousy, no pride, no disobedience here, just delight. Another garden of delight.

Centuries later, in 1784 CE, someone in New England wrote a poem in which Christ is transformed into an apple tree: 'The tree of life my soul hath seen, / Laden with fruit and always green: / The trees of nature fruitless be, / Compared with Christ the apple tree' (in *A Collection of Divine Hymns, or Spiritual Songs,* ed. E Smith, 2010). Christ is the tree of life.

In imagination, using if you wish any of the arts – painting, writing, music, fabric art, dance – create out of your experience your own garden of delight, and give thanks for it.

Jesus' entry into Jerusalem

Matthew 21:1-11

Imagine Jerusalem at the beginning of the week leading up to the Jewish Passover, with two processions taking place. One of them is a military procession escorting Pontius Pilate, Roman governor of Judaea, arriving to reinforce, for the duration of the festival, the Roman troops permanently stationed in the city's fortress. There is drumming; sounds of marching – foot soldiers, horses; helmets, weapons; banners. This is the might of the Roman Empire, of the emperor (Tiberius, at this time, about 30 CE) elevated with divine titles such as 'son of god'.

The other procession consists of a raggedy group of peasants and a wandering preacher, Jesus of Nazareth. Jesus sits on a donkey: hardly a triumphal entry. But crowds of people greet him, cut branches from the trees and spread them on the road; others spread out their cloaks. Does this procession display some humour? An intended, dangerous parody of the imperial procession? Is Jesus protesting against a political system of oppression? Protesting against the temple as the centre of Jewish power and wealth and in collaboration with the Romans, against a religious system that legitimised oppression, exclusivity? The text indicates that Jesus is indirectly making a claim to messiahship: 'your king' (verse 5); and that some people are acknowledging his kingship despite or because of his lack of imperial trappings.

The events of Holy Week invite us to choose. Which of these processions will you cheer on, and why?

Pray for the courage, and the humour, to be part of Jesus' raggle-taggle procession rather than belonging to the pomp and show of the world's might.

IBRA International Appeal

Imagine the only book you have to help you read the Bible is in French (or if you're a French speaker, try Tagalog!). Maybe you can understand bits of it, but imagine your joy when you discover someone has translated it into English for you!

Hundreds of thousands of people around the world experience similar joy when they discover the IBRA books and readings lists have been translated into their language. And this is all through the generosity of IBRA readers.

Each year, the IBRA International Fund provides funds for local groups to translate, print and distribute IBRA Bible notes and reading lists. Last year more than 68 000 people in eleven different countries received copies of the IBRA books which had been translated, printed and distributed by IBRA partners. The reading list was also translated into French, Spanish, Telugu (India), Tokelau (Samaoa) and several Congolese languages, enabling 250 000 people to receive them in a language useful to them.

The funds are given exclusively by IBRA readers like you, who give generously towards the fund, raising over £20 000 each year. With your gift, more people will be able to experience the joy of reading the Bible using notes or a list of readings in a familiar language.

Please consider either giving for the first time, or increasing your donation this year. You can donate using the envelope which is part of the leaflet insert that came with this book, or add your donation to your order for next year's books.

Thank you!

International Bible Reading Association
1020 Bristol Road
Selly Oak
Birmingham
B29 6LB
Tel. 0121 472 4242

IBRA
International Bible Reading Association

Readings in Mark (2)

Holy Week

Notes based on the New Revised Standard Version by

Lori Sbordone-Rizzo

Lori Sbordone-Rizzo works as an itinerant teacher with at-risk young people and adults in economically poor communities in New York City. She prays to love God and see the revolution in her lifetime. In 2012, she is hoping to be teaching more scripture, less mathematics and grammar.

Mark 14:17-21

Time's up

He's tried to warn them: 'We're going to Jerusalem, where I will be mocked, betrayed, beaten and killed.' Unable to make any sense of this, James and John respond by requesting the seats to his left and right when he is glorified. Jesus replies, 'Are you able to drink the cup that I drink?' The boys nod like bobble-head dolls, 'Sure Jesus, no problem' (Mark 10:35-9). It turns out that the 'seats' they're asking about are reserved for two thieves, and the cup is crucifixion.

On the night before it all went down, Jesus makes it plain. He holds up a loaf of bread, says, 'this is my body' (verse 22) and breaks it. I wonder if Jesus can feel the nails against his palms as he speaks these words; if this gesture with the bread is his way of coming to terms with what's about to unfold.

Can I drink that cup? Hell no! Except I believe with my whole heart that God always equips the one he calls. Jesus has one requirement for discipleship: 'Take up [your] cross' (Mark 8:4). Crucifixion isn't just something we watch Jesus do. In some way, we all must walk this path. We walk forward in faith, knowing it is God alone who is holding us up.

Lord Jesus, give me courage to walk with you this week.

Poured out

Mark 14:32-52

At supper, Jesus passed around a cup of blessing, a new covenant between God and humanity. In order to make good that promise, he must raise a very different cup to his lips – one containing the full measure of God's wrath for our sin. We watch as it does its terrible work, draining Jesus of his authority and reducing him to some discarded prophet. Where is the man who commanded the sea and fed the multitudes, who walked on water and made a legion of demons tremble? Now he is the one who trembles, who throws himself on the ground and begs for mercy.

All Jesus has left is his relationship with his Father. It's what makes him unique. Other rabbis performed 'deeds of power' but only Jesus dared to address God as 'Abba' (verse 36). Abba is intensely familiar. It is what Isaac called Abraham when his father laid wood on his shoulders and the two walked to the place of sacrifice. 'Abba, I am afraid, but I trust you because you are my Abba.'

At Gethsemane, Jesus the Son of Man is a regular Joe, one who has no control over his demons and who, like us, is scared to death by darkness. We scream, 'Abba, help!' and sometimes it seems like God comes running, and sometimes it seems like nobody's home. We fear we have been abandoned, but we keep screaming, just in case.

God, I believe you are there, mainly because I don't know how to live without you. I would love some assurance that you are near but, more than this, I need the courage to love you through the trials you put before me, because I cannot lose my life and you as well. Please, Abba, I beg your mercy.

 Lori Sbordone-Rizzo

Things we do in the dark

Mark 14:53-72

'Even though I must die with you, I will not deny you', (Matthew 26:35) bragged Peter. He was so sure of himself. People who are sure of themselves think they have 'no need of a physician' (Mark 2:17).

But give Peter credit. When Jesus was arrested, the others scattered; Peter followed at a distance, all the way into the Chief Priest's courtyard, joining the guards at their fire. Then a servant girl recognises his face. Peter calls her a liar and runs into the darkness. She follows, and now she has a witness who corroborates her story (which, by the way, is better than the testimony the Sanhedrin has managed to manufacture against Jesus). The police have Peter surrounded. He is a husband and a father. The next word out of his mouth could put him on a cross. Is it a sin for a father to save his life when speaking the truth will only give Caiaphas another innocent victim? I know how I would want my father to answer that question.

How do we even know this story? Only Peter could have told it. Our leaders rarely admit a mistake, and then only if they are caught. No one heard Peter swear he had nothing to do with Jesus, except his accusers. What sort of leadership style is this, where you admit to betraying your rabbi and wind up as the rock of the church? One where the king reigns from a cross, and the marks of his authority are not armies, but scars.

God, you know all my secrets. Please find a way to use me anyway.

Lori Sbordone-Rizzo

Authority: true and false

Mark 15:1-15

When Pilate moved into the governor's headquarters, he decorated the walls with bronze shields bearing the name of Emperor Tiberius. Jewish people responded by leaving their jobs and gathering at Pilate's gate, imploring him to remove the blasphemy. Pilate refused. Jewish leaders sent a letter to Tiberius, informing him of Pilate's actions and begging him to take action. Immediately, Tiberius commanded Pilate to remove the shields, publicly upbraiding him for his insensitivity. If he gave the Jewish community another reason to riot, job security would be the least of his worries.

Mark gives the impression that Pilate didn't want to sentence Jesus to death. The young rabbi's claims to be king may have been seditious, but more likely metaphorical: this bloody heap of a man is no threat to Roman dominion. Pilate gives Jesus a chance to clear himself but, to his great astonishment, Jesus refuses. You can almost see him, rubbing the sleep out of his eyes and shouting at his prisoner, 'Do you want to die?' He plays the Barabbas card, trusting that popular wisdom will not choose a murderer over an idealist, but the crowd screams for the rabbi's death. Pilate has surmised that Jesus is simply the loser in some all-night theological debate at the temple. He's been dragged into this mess because the Jews do not have the authority to execute blasphemers. Except that his authority itself is a lie. In truth, he has no authority. Pilate will do as the crowd demands because, if he doesn't, he risks Tiberius' wrath. As the pathetic governor caves under the threats of a dominated people, the true king awaits his crown. The world is upside down.

Lord Jesus, give me a voice to pray for justice, even amidst a crowd shouting 'Crucify!'

Lori Sbordone-Rizzo

Ugly

Mark 15:16-24

See what we did to the king of glory? Psychiatrists affirm that we are all capable of torture. I know no reason to doubt it, but what's wrong here goes deeper than the hand on the whip. How blind must we be to chain God to a post and beat him within an inch of his life? We humans pride ourselves as the pinnacle of creation; the ones fashioned after God's own image. Yet when our creator came to live amongst us, we nailed him to a tree and left him to bleed to death. Torture is abominable, whoever the victim, but we treated the best person the earth has ever known to our very worst behaviour. I am sorry, but that's just scary-ugly.

There are no messianic secrets here, no parables you need special ears to understand. Here is love laid open. Here is the one who commanded life into the body of Jairus' daughter, baring his back to a cat-o'-nine tails. Here is the secret revealed. God in Christ is taking in all our ugliness, like the herd of swine took in all Legion's demons, but rather than driving him off a cliff, Jesus will pick up his cross and walk out the Father's will. The Messiah is the one who rises from this beating with no hatred, who prays for the soldiers to the very end. It is for this reason one of them will confess, 'Truly this man was God's Son!' (Mark 15:39). With his own eyes he has seen love divine.

Lord Jesus, your love for us is as deep as our lowest moments, and higher than I can imagine.

Bound together

Mark 15:25-39

The cross is scandalous. If you don't believe this, try explaining our faith to a child. How do you explain that Jesus' own father required this? The obedient son is completely alone. He cries out to his father, 'Why have you forsaken me?' (verse 34) but Jehovah does not rush in and gather his Son into his arms. He turns his back, as if he has joined those who walk off in disgust at the utter failure of Jesus' life. It's so grim, the darkness at noon is comfort.

God had to comprehend our worst in order to bring us to our best. I understand this, but every Holy Week I still ask if all the suffering was necessary. In the end, there are two possibilities: either God is a sadist or God truly loves his beloved, and the cross was unavoidable. Love requires all; 'save yourself' (verse 30) is not an option. If Jesus acts on his own behalf, we are all lost, but he is bound together with his father in love for each other and for us, and this love makes it possible for him to lift the cup of suffering and endure its staggering consequences.

Sometimes events in my life are staggering, causing me to question everything. I wonder if God loves me at all, but I do know that I love him. We are bound together in love, and as our Saviour commands, '[W]hat God has joined together, let no one separate' (Mark 10:9). Somehow, God will make this beautiful, as the cross is beautiful beyond understanding. All I know is that my heart is fixed.

On this day of all days, I thank you God for all you did to bind my heart to yours.

Lori Sbordone-Rizzo

Time out of time

Mark 15:40-47

On Holy Saturday, I bake my mother's Easter Pie. It's a miraculous contradiction, befitting the resurrection; the traditional Neapolitan 'grain pie' without the grain – something that made sense to my family and nobody else. The pie has three elements: crust, custard, cream.

Crust: Sift 375 grams flour, 100 grams sugar, 1½ teaspoons baking powder. Pour into a food processor and add 3 eggs, 113 grams butter and milk (or limoncello) as needed until the dough forms a sticky ball. Turn onto a floured board, knead and divide into four parts. Cover with wax paper and rest in refrigerator for 1 hour.

Custard: Thoroughly mix 6 egg yolks, 300 grams sugar, 735 grams milk, 1 teaspoon vanilla essence and a handful of flour. Pour into a saucepan and cook on low, stirring constantly until the mixture coats your spoon. Cool.

Cream: Mix in order, beating after each addition, 18 eggs, 900 grams best-quality ricotta cheese, 200 grams sugar, vanilla essence, zest of a lemon and orange. Finally, beat 6 egg whites to stiff peaks.

To assemble: Roll pastry into four circles. Use three to cover the bottoms of three regular cake-pans. Cut the fourth circle into strips. Mix cream and custard together, then quickly fold in whites. Pour into the pans and top with strips to form a lattice. Paint crust with an egg-yolk wash. Bake at 170°C/335°F for 1 hour until the top is golden brown and the filling firm.

My mother has been gone twenty years. This pie is how I bring some of her goodness back. I am not strong enough to roll away the stone but, like the women at the end of Mark's Gospel, I wait in hope.

Help us, God, to reach into your story and bring some of its goodness to people who are weary and long for your appearing.

Lori Sbordone-Rizzo

1 Corinthians

The wisdom of God

Sunday 8 April
(Easter Day)

Notes based on the New Revised Standard Version by

Chris Bedding

The Reverend Chris Bedding is an Anglican priest in the Diocese of Perth, Western Australia. He is also an actor, director, musician and comedian. His passions are ministry amongst people in the first third of life, dynamic liturgy and advocacy for the oppressed.

1 Corinthians 15:50-58

Life after life

It's arrived! Purple penance and red rage gave way to yesterday's bleak emptiness, and now we bask in the white-gold glow of resurrection. Death has been swallowed up and has no sting! Victory is ours! But victory for what? Human brokenness desires permanency after a death. The powerful are rewarded with statues and portraits, with buildings, streets, stars and creatures named in their honour. For more ordinary folk, the pre-planned funeral and the meticulous drafting of a will continue their influence even as the body perishes. Some shrewdly find ways to haunt the psyche of their descendants for many generations. We want to live for ever.

Yet when we are caught in the beam of resurrection faith, we discover no glittering prize of infinite celebrity. We will all be changed. Our petty assumptions will be challenged and our controlling wounds healed. When the perishable, mortal body puts on the imperishable and immortal – our lives will not be continuations, but transformations.

The nature of life in this entirely new reality is the subject of the early chapters of 1 Corinthians. How do we live in community while caught between the perishable and imperishable?

Victorious God,
you conquered death and evil's power
and life burst forth from brokenness and decay.
Dispel our desire for immortality
and grow in our hearts a yearning for transformation.

Please do not leave your brain at the door

1 Corinthians 1: 1-17

Paul can't stop addressing the Corinthians as *adelphoi* (brothers and sisters) throughout this letter. He urges them to be united in the same mind and purpose. He emphasises that it is through God that they have been called into fellowship with Christ. He reminds them that they belong not to Apollos, Cephas or even Paul, but to Christ. Like a frustrated schoolmaster, he pounds this vital information into their heads, lest they forget that their personal and communal identity is entirely caught up in the resurrected and glorified Jesus.

You can, we're told, pick your friends but not your family. We are born into a particular social and economic milieu and we can't escape it. Even with a complete identity change, the imprints of our origin remain. Likewise, when we are born by water and the spirit, the indelible mark remains. Whether it suits us or not, we are inextricably bound to the church and called to be in unity with our fellow Christians.

Does this mean that we are reduced to simpering niceness in an effort to get on? Must we submit mindlessly to central authority to preserve institutional integrity? Or do we require everyone else to conform to our neat ideologies? No. It means that we put aside our agendas and prejudices in order to seek the mind of Christ together.

Mother, life-bearer, source of all wholeness,
all that we are is bound up in you,
all that you are is printed on our soul:
confront your church with truth and confound our conflict.
Reveal the concealed, and unite us in our quest for
authenticity,
in the name of the provocative Christ.

Line dancing

1 Corinthians 1: 18 – 2:5

Many of us have an inherent distrust in dichotomies. Us/them, right/left, saved/unsaved – who among us has not seen the damage done by such divisive behaviour and judgemental language? Paul's distinction between those who are perishing and those who are being saved might strike us as yet another demarcation line through humanity. Even though we know we are on the correct side of the line, it troubles us that the 'perishing' are, in fact, our neighbours and family. We have no desire to exclude them from God's foolishness and weakness made known to us in the scandal of the cross. We want to draw them in.

Becoming a part of the Christian community, however, is not to draw a line between oneself and the rest of humanity. Rather, it leads to the abolition of destructive boundaries. The few wealthy believers in Corinth had to share the love-feast with the workers and peasants. Paul comes not as a learned Pharisee, but in weakness and fear. The gospel subverts and inverts status. To be a Christian, therefore, is not to take on an exalted position within society or culture. Rather, it is to be in solidarity with those who are neither wise, nor powerful, nor noble.

Human wisdom urges us to delineate and distinguish, to sift and separate. We seek points of difference, brand recognition, an edge over our competitors. God calls us to gather, include and share. Foolishness, indeed.

God who breaks the bow,
break down the barriers on which status feeds.
God who shatters the spear,
smash pseudo-nobility and the power of rank.
God who burns the shields with fire,
purge the borders that wealth and affluence create.
End exclusion. Incite us to embrace.

Being a fool is hard work

1 Corinthians 2: 6-16

There is rarely praise for those who speak God's wisdom, secret and hidden. The wisdom of this age advocates a constant state of readiness for war. The spiritual person who speaks of non-violence and reconciliation is the object of ridicule. The wisdom of this age demands constant, conspicuous consumption. The wisdom decreed before the ages, which declares that the earth's resources be distributed with equity, is sidelined. Often, we remain silent in the face of human foolishness, because we know that we will be labelled fools if we speak God's wisdom.

Once again, Paul outlines an ideal using a contrasting image. Just as only a human can understand the human spirit, so only God's Spirit can understand God. The unspiritual, unwise, cannot know the wisdom of God. But we can. Is it because we are somehow a better class of people, the landed gentry of the spiritual world? Is it because we are born into privilege, with wisdom in our mouths like a silver spoon? Not at all. The only reason for our wisdom, the only justification for our prophetic voice, is the mind of Christ.

To speak God's wisdom in contrast to human 'wisdom' takes courage. To pray for the mind of Christ seems to us an audacious request. The witness of martyrs and prophets, and the faithfulness of the saints, is inspiring, but seemingly impossible to emulate. Though whoever claimed it would be easy?

Come, Spirit of life
and pour your wisdom into our minds,
uniting us with Christ.
Make us imitators of Christ
and inspire the prophetic voice.
Help us laugh in the face of ridicule and
make us eloquent in the face of injustice.
Give us the courage of Christ, in whose name we pray.

The kids are hungry

1 Corinthians 3: 1-9

Nobody likes to be called stupid or childish, but this doesn't stop Paul! He has just written most eloquently about the Corinthians' identity as people of the Spirit. Now he points out that they are such a pack of argumentative whingers that he can't even offer them the fullness of the gospel. Their arguments and envy, factions and petty loyalties are constricting the flow of food. Their behaviour is causing them to be underfed and they are starving.

A favourite cutting criticism of contemporary church life is to claim 'I'm not being fed'. Dull preachers, banal liturgies and turgid music all contribute to a sense of emptiness in the spiritual stomach. But are we even ready to feast on solid food? Are we truly ready to grow into God's house, God's field? Many of us harbour a secret desire to continue with quarrelling and jealousy. We like the soothing therapy of church life – but to put aside human inclinations and embrace the life of the Spirit is a bridge too far.

Paul's message is harshly clear. Neither he nor Apollos is the source of the gospel. In the same way for us, no stream of theological thought or particular aesthetic is the source of good news. Believers who desire solid food must constantly re-embrace the reality that they are God's servants, and it is God who gives the growth.

God of all that is good,
fill us with solid food when all we want is slop.
End our malnourishment
and enable us to gorge ourselves on your abundance.
Help us to grow fit and strong
that through us the presence of Christ may be known,
for it is in his name that we pray.

In culpable hands

1 Corinthians 3: 10-23

Playwrights and architects deserve both our awe and our sympathy. They write or draw with such expertise, crafting a vision with subtle nuance. Then they hand over their work to actors and directors, builders and plumbers – knowing that the finished product may differ radically from their dream. So, too, for the Christian in life and ministry. Children are baptised and we pray that they will finish the race and keep the faith, but we can neither know nor control their future. The initiative planted today may wither when we move on. Our best intentions may bear no fruit.

Paul seems resigned to this reality. He has built the foundations knowing that others will build upon them. His not-so-subtle warning reads like a last-ditch effort to protect his legacy. He is not alone in this desire. Who among us does not dream of leaving our mark, whether out of selfish desire, or selfless concern for our descendants? Paul himself has left a substantial mark, though one wonders what he would think of those who attribute their inspiration to him today!

The building analogy is continued, but now with a subversive, shocking twist. Having compared the ekklesia to a building in general, he now says that they are, in fact, God's temple. Paul is undermining the sacred centrality of temple worship. No more sacrifice, no more tribal identity markers, no more unjust religious power and corrupt leadership. To serve and worship God no longer requires an edifice in Jerusalem, but a gathered community who share in God's madness.

Jesus, empty our hands.
Help us to release responsibility
but not accountability.
Give us hope for tomorrow
grounded not in our success but in your wisdom.
Empty our hands, Jesus,
and put us to work as agents of change.

Chris Bedding

Wise guys need not apply

1 Corinthians 4: 1-13

Would you choose to be a servant? Some do – the burgeoning global hospitality industry holds a certain glamour for those who enjoy travel and exotic locations. Service has long been a stepping-stone on the way to higher incomes in the affluent West. But most servitude around the world is the result of poverty and lack of opportunity. The affluent are kept fed, cleaned and entertained by those who have no other choice.

Yet we are to think of Paul and the other apostles as servants and stewards. The church in Corinth is the royalty, and the apostles are the slaves. This is God's absurdity at work once again. The marginalised are lifted high and entrusted with the message of salvation. The Corinthians engage in regal intrigue and petty political conflict. Paul's message is clear – the path to wholeness lies in weakness and disrepute. Jesus was exalted through blood and murder, yet in this violence lay the end of evil's power. So too, for Christians, the path to resurrection will at times be terrifying and painful.

For millennia, Christians have taken audacious risks and kindled hope in the midst of despair. They, too, exchanged God's 'foolish' wisdom for the world's 'wise' foolishness. The church has been at its best when it seemed to the world most aberrant. Paul and the apostles became fools for the sake of Christ. For whom are you a fool?

Observe someone who serves you – good, bad or indifferent. Reflect on the things you learn about apostolic ministry by watching a real servant in action.

Do we have the guts, O God,
to ask that you make us weak?
Will we dare to ask that others detest us?
Can we embody the preposterous news that the forgotten matter?
Shame our wisdom and make us holy fools,
like the Christ through whom we pray.

1 Corinthians

Disorder in Corinth

Notes based on the New Revised Standard Version by

Barrington Litchmore

Barrington Oliver Litchmore is an ordained Presbyter of the Methodist Church in the Caribbean and the Americas. He is currently serving as the Superintendent Minister of a rural circuit of the Jamaica District. Barrington also serves as the chair of four Methodist school boards and chaplain of one high school located within the circuit. He is married to Wendy Pamela.

1 Corinthians 4:14-21

The father speaks

Paul's first letter to the Corinthian church is evidently addressed to a disorderly community. As intimated in the first chapter, he expresses discomfort concerning loyalty to personalities, namely, Paul, Apollos, Cephas, and even Jesus Christ. His plea for unity in this context is rooted in the reconciliatory message of the cross. However, the realities of human disorder require human intervention as well as divine response. Paul's maturity in the faith and the vastness of his pastoral resources are vital tools in addressing the various levels of disorder existing within the church.

In today's passage, Paul speaks confidently as a father recognising the paucity of the relationships present within the church community. There is much relevance in Paul's admonition to Caribbean communities where major concerns are often expressed regarding the absence of the father figure in the home, the school and the church. The disordered lives of many male youths are often blamed upon this absence. As we explore the theme of disorder, in the week ahead, we will see that other, more positive, pastoral influences are all significant in the quest for restoration of order and a sense of civility in the life of the Christian community.

What renewed and intentional focus may be necessary in your own context to enable mentors or leaders to work with children and young people in laying good foundations for later life?

Reflect upon the formation, stimulation and revitalisation of men's groups within the church and the community, and pray for them.

Ostracise or restore?

1 Corinthians 5: 1-13

Paul's sense of indignation seems stirred at two levels: first, by the extent of the immoral practices demonstrated by an individual within the community and, second, by the threat that these practices present for the wellbeing of the community. Negative reactions are often raised against an entire community because of the failings of a particular minority. Certain communities in Jamaica are often stigmatised for the high incidences of crime and violence committed by a comparatively small group. The reading suggests that such persons ought to be ostracised in order to safeguard the reputation of the community.

At the time of writing, the Jamaican press has reported a gruesome attack on five young men by others armed with guns. A curfew was imposed in the area in order to apprehend the offenders and so that they might be ostracised from 'civilised society'. Regrettably, the resources needed for rehabilitation and restoration are often not forthcoming. Even more regrettable is that, in our context, the voices of ostracism often sound louder than those of restoration.

The church is always encouraged to embrace a spirit of reconciliation and restoration within its ranks (Matthew 5:23) and to be the initiators of such a process within the wider community. It is the mandate of national church councils to emphasise the need, and provide the space, for restoration. Paul argues in another context that the transgressor ought to be restored in a spirit of gentleness (Galatians 6:1).

Lord, forgive us for the times when we agree with the authorities in ostracising the offenders without even reflecting upon the possibility of restoration. Help us to be involved in the ministry of restoration within our community.

Barrington Litchmore

Who is to judge?

1 Corinthians 6: 1-8

Paul's outrage at the believers' practice of seeking redress within the pagan justice system is understandable. He is well aware of the extent of the disregard that this system had for the church. The practice of settling disputes externally could only serve to breed disrespect within the community, and to destroy the goodwill that ought to emerge from the practice of love, forgiveness and justice.

Inevitably, instances will arise within the church community where the law of the land may need to be called upon and prevail. Illegal occupancy of church lands is one such issue confronting several branches of the church within the Caribbean. However, the church's standards of internal justice are tested against the standards of the teachings of Jesus, particularly as enunciated in the Sermon on the Mount (Matthew 5:38-42). Here, justice is not merely concerned with restoration but is qualified by the immeasurable grace that characterises the nature of the relationship Christ shares with us. In the matter of grievances, as in other expressions of human relationship, Christ's spirit and teachings ought to influence the final court of reference and appeal.

Is our community overwhelmed with 'unsolved' and 'untried' cases among the membership? It is vital that such issues be dealt with expeditiously in order to preserve order and to stimulate growth within the community.

Lord, help us to harness the relevant human resources within our various communities, in order that we may promote peace with a strong sense of justice.

Examining the disordered self

1 Corinthians 6: 9-20

As a result of conversion and baptism, the individual ought to witness to his or her spiritual cleansing by lifestyle as well as words. Any involvement in immoral practices will certainly be contrary to such a conviction.

Growth and confidence in faith are often influenced by the virtues taught within the home during the formative years. Parents and other persons of influence within the lives of children and young people should strive to remain focused and intentional in the performance of their responsibilities and in the passing on of right belief. Ultimately, however, individuals must take responsibility for their own decisions, recognising the freedom that is ours to claim as we mature.

In an era where the practice of one's faith seems to be increasingly regarded as a personal and private experience, freedom may be easily misinterpreted, resulting in irresponsible and selfish behaviour. Freedom ought to be determined by the person's understanding of the gift and the demands of Christ. The entire being ought to be progressively influenced by the very nature of Christ, so that one is formed in one's actions and decisions by Christ himself. In this way, personal and corporate accountability become a vital force for good within the community of faith.

God of all grace, may you continually inspire within us the spirit of accountability toward you, ourselves and the communities to which we belong.

Marriages and motives

1 Corinthians 7: 1-16

As Paul reflects upon the varying and complex dimensions of marriage relationships within the church, his directives assume a pastoral and pragmatic approach. He is conscious of the voluntary nature of these relationships and therefore refrains from being overly directive. He is also careful not to invoke the authority of Jesus, emphasising that he speaks only of his own personal opinion.

Paul's discourse on marriage relationships, calling attention to the potential for Christian witness as well as positive reasons for celibacy, is significant for its sensitivity to its time and context. However, we read Paul's advice in a very different time and context, in which our understanding of sexuality is very different, and in a church in which we continue to wrestle with the variety of human sexuality and the ethics of sex.

The Caribbean church in general continues to maintain and practise the traditional approach to marriage, understanding it as a relationship that is solemnised ecclesially, and/or legally, between two persons of the opposite sex. This approach, however, often denies the church from responding to significant pastoral opportunities regarding same-sex relationships and other non-formalised relationships. There are many women, for instance, who struggle with their faith and the reluctance of their male partners to solemnise their relationship. In such situations, the church is challenged to re-examine the relevancy and sufficiency of its traditional pastoral resources.

How can the church become more aware of the diversity of sexual relationships and provide safer spaces for those who experience marginalisation within wider society?

Lord, teach us to care for all who search for love and acceptance in the variety of human relationships.

Barrington Litchmore

Marriages and encumbrances

1 Corinthians 7: 25-40

Here again, Paul admits that he is expressing his private opinion. On this occasion, he is concerned with the unmarried and with widows and their state of preparedness for the end of the age. According to Paul, it would be advisable for these groups to preserve their present status, thereby averting any additional crisis that would naturally accompany the end times.

Even though Paul's expectation of an imminent eschatological crisis was proved wrong, his advice can still hold relevance to our times, in relation to the preparation for, and the outworkings of, marriage. Emphases upon the legal aspects of property ownership, the care and custody of children and divorce settlements, for example, have sometimes gained undesirable prominence in relationships, leading to the demise of some marriages. Premarital counselling that explores such areas as traditional myths, sexual intimacy, family planning, handling of finances, gender roles, religious affiliation, and so on, is vital for the understanding of the marriage relationship, as well as exploration of what commitment to the marriage vows entails. The essence of marriage, characterised by mutual agape love, ought to be promoted and encouraged in our time, no less than Paul's.

Lord, may our church embrace its mission to prepare couples adequately for marriage. May we lead persons experiencing crisis in their relationships to the sources of healing and reconciliation.

Practising sensitivity

1 Corinthians 8: 1-13

Much controversy was involved in the subject of the consumption of foods offered to idols. One group, comprising the intellectuals and moral sympathisers, held the view that idols were non-existent. Thus, for them, it was an absurd practice to refuse meats that had been formally consecrated to idols. Paul seemingly shared this opinion, but certainly not their spirit. He believed in the right of Christians to exercise independent judgement. He therefore cautioned against the exercise of freedom claimed by some, which might overwhelm the sensitive conscience of those who thought differently. The liberty that some claimed through faith in Jesus Christ had indeed become a stumbling block to the weaker members.

The Caribbean church continues to wrestle with doctrinal, moral and ethical issues, including gambling, capital punishment, abortion and homosexuality. The voice of a powerful minority, the 'liberated', which often influences decision making, does not always provide the real answers for persons who are genuinely seeking. Denominations that emphasise doctrinal differences and their 'exalted spirituality' also contribute to the erection of 'stumbling blocks.' Being sensitive to 'the weak' requires continued reflection on the distinction between the exercise of liberty and the command to love one's neighbour. Whenever these two tensions conflict, then love ought to prevail.

How do you identify with the group described as the 'liberated'? What are some of the stumbling blocks you may have erected toward others? In what ways do you identify with the 'weak'?

Teach us, O God, to use our liberty for the greater liberty of all, not for our own pleasure and ease.

1 Corinthians

Sunday 22 April

Baptism and the Lord's Supper

Notes based on the New Revised Standard Version by

Andy Lyons

Andy Lyons is a Methodist presbyter currently serving in the Bromsgrove and Redditch Circuit. He trained at the Queen's Foundation, having previously been professionally involved in community development and equal opportunities work. He is keenly interested in liturgical theology and liturgical renewal, and the question of what might unite Christians in worship across denominational, age, gender, ethnicity, sexual identity and orientation and disability divisions.

1 Corinthians 9:1-14

Me, myself, I

We live in an age where my right to self-determination dominates political and social thought, and where freedom of choice seems to be applied to all areas of cultural and social life. We live in an age where I, as a consumer, have the right, at least if I have enough money, to buy whatever makes me happy, makes me look young...

At first sight Paul seems to be arguing solely for his own rights based on his account of how important he is. But at verse 13 Paul tells us that he does not insist on his rights. Through rhetoric he shows up those who in the previous chapter insist on their rights. As we go through the week's readings we will see how Paul calls for the giving up of individual and small-group rights for the sake of the Christian community and the gospel.

What do we insist on as our right? It is easy to identify the 'awkward squad' in our churches who insist on certain ways of doing things. Reflect, however, on what you think is so important that it must be preserved or done in certain ways.

Who am I?

1 Corinthians 9: 15-27

In a service I took recently I sat down on some steps to talk with the children. Afterwards I was amazed at how much this was noticed and appreciated. I would like to say it was a deliberate strategy! What I had done was to communicate face to face. Paul tells us how he becomes all things for all people. His concern is pastoral. He meets people where they are. Such an approach can also be seen in Jesus, who was regularly criticised for eating and drinking with sinners and tax collectors.

But there is a cost to such an approach. The athlete follows a well-disciplined life to achieve the prize of victory. Many people cultivate a particular self-image, working very hard, sometimes at great financial cost, to project the right impression. Most of us simply find a skin, a persona, with which we are comfortable and which we would rather not alter. But how easy do we find it to shed our image, if necessary? When we enter into places outside our comfort zone, can we adapt – not to become acceptable and liked, not to be something we are not, but in order to relate to and serve others, so that we might show that God is for all?

No doubt all of us have met others who humble themselves in order to be for others. We might think of aid workers, nurses, personal care assistants and so on – they know the value of every human life and give freely of themselves. But their actions do something more. Their service creates a community and enables others to learn to serve also.

Generous God, you give of your very self through Jesus Christ. We give thanks 'that he emptied himself, taking the form of a slave' (Philippians 2:7). Give us grace to be for others.

Andy Lyons

Who we are

1 Corinthians 10: 1-13

The city of Corinth was a cosmopolitan place and the people of the church at Corinth were a mixed bag of Jews and Gentiles. Paul tells them they need to learn from the history of the people of God. The people of God benefited from God's saving action when they journeyed through the wilderness; and yet because some complained all suffered. We are not merely individuals – we are members of families, of communities, of society, and of the church. When we think of ourselves only as individuals, and/or only as people of the current generation, we misunderstand who we are.

In the funeral service we say words to the effect that as the deceased has passed from this world, the trials and tribulations of this world are over. All of us are tested and challenged in many ways through life. How we respond to these challenges affects those to whom we are bound. Complaining about our lives, and disobedience to the ways of God, lead to destruction, not just for us, but for many.

Paul points out that it is idolatry and immorality that cause destruction. These occur when the wisdom of God, that is Christ the rock, is not heeded. Some in the Corinthian church seemed to believe that they were especially blessed with spiritual gifts. But testing comes to all – both strong and weak.

In our churches, what are the signs of pride and what do we complain about? If things are not great, do we believe that God will give us strength? How do we seek God rather than idolatrous substitutes? Most importantly, do we know the ancient biblical stories and reflect on what these might teach us?

O God, One in Three and Three in One, teach us to know that we are joined together with you and each other in all things in life.

Community rules!

1 Corinthians 10:14 – 11:1

Now the fundamental principle is declared. Christian people belong to a new community that is formed by the death of Jesus. The ritual action they perform together is the sharing in one bread and one communal cup. Other communities have other communal practices that unite them; Christian people have the Lord's Supper.

The particular issue that Paul confronts is the eating of meat that has been sacrificed to idols. This is not a problem for most of us. But many in the church want hard and fast rules by which to live and to prove we are loyal members of the community. Rules, however, have to be imposed on others. But Paul is not interested in setting rules – rather, he seeks for us to act in ways that are our own voluntary decisions, so that we behave in ways that are beneficial for others. We are challenged to give up our own rights for the sake of others. The strong and the rich are challenged particularly to give up their rights.

The giving up of our rights is predicated on the basis that the Lord's Supper is the remembrance of Christ's own act of self-giving. The rule of the community is the giving up of self for others, for community rules!

Who rules the church (both denominational and at local level)? How much power do we exercise in determining what happens on Sundays and in the rest of the life of the church? If you recognise that you hold power, that you exercise influence, is what you want for the benefit of others or yourself? If Christ gives up his all for us to know God, what are we called to give up?

Gracious God, you are for all. You create, redeem and sustain the whole created order. Enable us to be gracious for others.

Gender identity and roles – and more beside

1 Corinthians 11: 2-16

At first sight we may want to pass over this passage quickly, arguing that it is contextual theology that has no relevance in our modern era. Paul's discussion relates to the role of men and women in public worship. His reasoning is influenced by his reading of creation, social customs and propriety, and by the new role women have in the community to pray and prophesy. His valuing of women in the assembly may well be greater than it appears at first sight. The argument and potential interpretation are complicated.

But something else is going on here. The particular issue is gender roles and identity. But the discussion is illustrative of a wider issue. The issue concerns which traditions the church should hold fast to (verse 2) and which customs are changeable (verse 16) in the conduct of public worship. Today different denominations hold different traditions. As a Methodist I know that what we sometimes claim to be a Methodist tradition is not what John Wesley would have claimed as tradition! In recent years the desire to make the gospel relevant has led to the development of new ways of worship. Many questions can be asked about the relationship of our worship to tradition.

Given Paul's stress on the Lord's Supper as the focus of church unity, one question, among many, is how often the Lord's Supper should be celebrated. Questions also emerge here about hierarchy, as well as women's roles in the church. In our own time we face other issues of discrimination of practice. Finally we are confronted with the challenge of judging for ourselves – as long as we remember that 'all things come from God' (verse 12).

O God of all wisdom, grant to us the gift of discernment to know what is vital, what is true, what is your way.

The rule of the community!

1 Corinthians 11: 17-34

There is one absolute rule that Paul will not let the Corinthians relativise. When they come to share the Lord's Supper there must be no division of the community. Paul urges them to discern the body, which is both Christ's and the church's. The rule of the community is to be united, to be as one, around the table of the Lord. Over the course of Christian history we have not managed to stay together around the Lord's table and our theological splits over remembering and celebrating Christ's saving acts are still the cause of much heartache.

Recently I was due to take a service of Holy Communion at a church and then discovered that some of the congregation would not be present because they would be in the hall doing café church. Whilst there were good intentions behind this move – the attempt to offer a new and exciting way to worship, recognising that many find the traditional communion alien – I believe that there is no reason good enough to split a local community like this. The very essence of the faith, the gathering to remember and celebrate our Lord's sacrifice, is lost as we gather apart from each other.

What are the rules of our communities? I don't mean the formal church mission statement, but what is said and done and acted out that sets the real ethos of your community. Identifying the unwritten rules, the assumptions and behaviours that shape a community, requires a discerning eye. And, having identified them, how do they support or contradict your mission statement – or indeed Paul's rule of unity?

Hospitable God, may our churches be places of unity, of generosity, of welcome. May we recognise each unique and wonderful member of your body.

Group dynamics!

1 Corinthians 12: 1-11

A group with a mission, a task or a purpose is most effective when the group contains people with a variety of skills that complement each other. Groups that don't work well are those containing people with the same skills, or where one or two people think that their skills are more important than those of everyone else. Paul recognises that God has skilled the Corinthian church through the gifts God has granted to each of its members.

The divisions that have separated the church are of course based on many complicated historical disputes. Overcoming these is a long and slow process. But the gifts God gives are for serving the same Lord, and for a common purpose or good. In recent years, church growth strategies have emerged that suggest we should aim to build churches of people with similar ideas and interests. But God appears to be interested in the notion of different people coming together to serve God. Much theological writing in recent years has focused on the idea that God's own self is unity and diversity held together – God as One and God as Three. Is God's way of unity and diversity something we can foster?

We will all know of churches that have split for a multitude of reasons. I serve a church that lost several members some years back to another church, because they had an experience of charismatic gifting. The community could not find a way to enable all to live, worship and work together for God's purposes. In the week before I wrote this, the German Chancellor said that Germany had failed in its attempt to become a multiracial society.

How can we live and work as Christian people who foster the ideal that in Christ all are one?

O God of each and all, teach me to know that the other whom you create and gift is also your child.

Andy Lyons

1 Corinthians

Gifts of the Spirit

Notes based on the New International Version by
Sibyl Ruth

Sibyl Ruth is a Quaker. She lives in Birmingham with her husband and teenage daughter. Sibyl is a freelance writer and also does voluntary work supporting people who are survivors of violence and abuse.

1 Corinthians 12:12-31

Good gifts

My mother loved getting ready for our birthdays, for Christmas. Our presents would be laid out on the living room sofa. But as I grew older I got dissatisfied. I knew I should be grateful, of course. But I'd not received quite what I wanted. Perhaps my brother had been given something better. Or I'd have this sense of something missing...

Now I like the idea that everything – including one's physical self – is a gift. But at heart I'm still the same discontented person. Worse maybe. I get fed up with my middle-aged body. My teeth need dental work. There's this niggling pain in my shoulder. I remind myself that I've been fortunate. Everything functions.

And then there's the 'body of the church'. Often I think – yes, I know there is 'that of God' in all of us. But could we be less argumentative? Not so timid? More spontaneous? How about showing greater self-discipline?

But then I go and sit in Meeting for Worship. We are all here. In the same place. At the right time. And I am truly thankful.

What gifts have we received? Do we find them easy to accept?

Meditate on, and try to feel thankfulness for, what you have received.

Familiarity

1 Corinthians 13: 1-13

Occasionally a biblical text becomes so familiar I stop being able to hear it. Like a song that's played on the radio too often. My mind will drift away.

This passage is one my head teachers chose for school assemblies. These men were probably decent, conscientious people. But to me they were remote and authoritarian. Not only did they seem 'without love', they appeared to lack basic human warmth. Even then, their choice seemed ironic. They stood on stage in front of us – as good as admitting they were no more than 'clanging cymbals', 'resounding gongs' (verse 1).

Years later I was asked to read these verses at a funeral. The person who had died had had real difficulty in showing loving-kindness. It was only my sense of obligation that made me agree to the request.

Only 1 Corinthians had changed. Or possibly I had. Now that bald statement 'without love I am nothing' (verse 2 – loosely) seems unbearably bleak. Because love is an emotion we can't will into being, which lies beyond our control. It's shaped at our lives' very beginning by the love that we do, or don't, receive from others. However hard we try, committed relationships may end. Friends test our affection to the limit. We might excel in the outside world, yet fail with those whom we want to keep close.

But the idea of a future when we shall see more clearly – know better – brings consolation.

Is there some 'inspirational' text that you think you know, but haven't actually read for years? Make time to take a fresh look it.

Sit with your chosen text and reflect on the changing ways you come to it.

Writing, speaking, listening

1 Corinthians 14: 1-12

Paul is a writer. He knows that using the best words at the appropriate time can make a huge difference. When a person speaks obscurely or 'into the air' (verse 9), energy is wasted. An opportunity has been missed.

I spend part of my working life with emerging authors, helping them to develop. I read their manuscripts. I reflect on what they're aiming to say. Has the writer thought about audience, whom they're addressing? Inspiration is all very well. But authors can lose themselves in a private world of emotion. What will help them to reconnect with others?

We tend to think that speaking is easier – more natural – than writing. But although anybody can minister in a Meeting for Worship, some of us never do. People are afraid that nerves will make them inarticulate. But although we might all long to have 'the tongues of angels' (1 Corinthians 13:1), Quakers are advised that the greatest qualities they can bring to ministry are 'faithfulness and sincerity' (*Quaker Faith and Practice*, 2.55).

And once a week I'm a volunteer on a phone line. The callers are women and men who are survivors of sexual violence and abuse. They need to talk about what's happened, how it continues to affect them. But what they've experienced verges on the unspeakable. So the calls contain many silences, hesitations.

I believe that the ability to wait attentively is also a 'gift of the Spirit'. Careful listening may bring 'strengthening, encouragement, comfort' (verse 3).

Today contains opportunities to use words that 'build each other up' (verse 12 loosely). What will you say?

Reflect on the power of words and of silence.

Sibyl Ruth

Sharing a vision

1 Corinthians 15: 1-11

I had to complete a questionnaire while applying for temporary work. The questions involved a scenario where I'd be managing new recruits. I would train the group and keep them focused on a project lasting a few months. But problems multiplied. People fell out with each other, disagreed how the job should be done, became disaffected. I had to sort everything – and everyone. One available option was to call the team together, and go over some of the basics.

Paul faced similar challenges. Except the situation was a real one, and he had less support. His project had no closing date, and he was far away from his team. Paul did his best to manage the Corinthians, by reminding them what it was they originally signed up for. (I have sympathy for the people in Corinth. Being part of a developing religious movement would be more demanding – less straightforward – than they'd anticipated.)

Recently I was on the Steering Group of a Quaker organisation. We had a big decision to make. The strain of not knowing how to make it was creating some unease. There were no apostles to advise us, but a grant-making trust gave us some money for a consultant. The consultant got us to focus on our core values and beliefs. This made us realise we had more in common than we'd thought. Suddenly the way ahead was not so difficult.

How much do you know about the values and beliefs of the people around you?

Uphold anyone you know who needs to make an important decision.

Preaching – and privilege

1 Corinthians 15: 12-34

The negative associations of the verb 'to preach' are as strong as the positive ones. My dictionary refers to giving advice 'in an offensive, tedious or obtrusive manner' (*Chambers English Dictionary*, seventh edn, 1990). To me this suggests ambivalence. Part of us reckons we should let ourselves be persuaded. Another part resists.

But for the preacher it is straightforward. They have a duty. And, like the Ancient Mariner, they must make it hard for their audience to edge away. Coleridge's 'Rime of the Ancient Mariner' is one of my favourite poems. It concerns an unfortunate wedding guest buttonholed on the way to the celebration by somebody who will not be put off.

Paul would have sensed the Corinthians might be fidgety, resistant. So he raises the stakes. Doubt is not an option. It would be like removing a load-bearing wall. The whole church would come down. He throws in some chiding and exhortation too. 'How can some of you say...? Come back to your senses!' (verse 12 loosely)

But my inner dissenter has a way of siding with those who can't tread the party line. Recently I read Edmund Gosse's autobiography *Father and Son*. Philip Gosse believed in the literal truth of Genesis, and did everything possible to ensure his child would do the same. Yet the book ends by showing how Edmund 'as respectfully, as he could, without parade or remonstrance ... took a human being's privilege to fashion his inner life for himself' (*Father and Son*, London, Penguin Classics, 1988, p.251).

What old influences have you discarded? Who has helped you to 'fashion your inner life'?

Think about your own struggles between conviction and dissent and uphold all who preach.

Teachers and traditions

1 Corinthians 15: 35-49

Reading 1 Corinthians is like eavesdropping on a phone conversation. We keep getting hints of what's happening at the other end. It seems those pesky Corinthians are asking all manner of questions. So Paul, in didactic mode, decides to issue a rebuke. 'How foolish!'

I'd call this Method A. It was a tactic favoured by one of my old history teachers. The aim is to stop further interruptions so Paul can go on with his discourse. But someone using Method B – like my economics tutor – would say, 'Interesting point.' He'd allow the group to go off at a tangent and see where it led. If I look back I can see I learned more from the man who taught me economics.

But Paul is a brilliant lecturer. And he can vary his approach. Here he's about to say, 'Listen, I tell you a mystery ... we will all be changed' (verse 51), or in the words of the King James Version, 'Behold, I show you a mystery.' Paul sounds like a science teacher demonstrating an experiment. Or Professor Snape at Hogwarts?

Johannes Brahms used Luther's translation of this text in his *German Requiem*. It's not a conventional Requiem, as Brahms deliberately avoids texts that name Christ. To me this suggests that, although the power of our teachers has limits, their efforts are not in vain. Even the work of freethinkers may affirm the value of Christian traditions.

Which teachers have taught you the most? How did they do this?

Acknowledge the diverse communities of those who teach and those who learn.

So long, farewell

1 Corinthians 16: 1-13

Endings aren't easy to get right. In a Meeting for Worship we may have to awake from a gathered silence. Or wrap up our thoughts on some deep piece of ministry. It can be tricky to shift from the sublime to the everyday, but an Elder will shake hands with their neighbour, and then we're on to announcements. Typically these combine nagging with nurturing. Please could we put our names on the coffee rota? Is there anyone we should remember in our prayers? Thank you to everybody who organised last week's social... Even in an age of email, there is something vital about this exchange of information at the Meeting's end.

On the telephone helpline, goodbyes are often awkward. Even painful. In some conversations, there will be a sense of moving forward. A disclosure – or a decision – has been made. However, at other times a caller gets interrupted and says, 'I have to go now.' Or just hangs up.

Frequently it's unclear how the caller will handle the challenges ahead. We have no idea if a person will choose to ring again. Often I finish by saying, 'Take care.'

I suspect that Paul and I wouldn't have got on well. Yet when it comes to goodbyes our emotions are similar. I can identify with those parting words. 'Be on your guard; stand firm in the faith; be people of courage; be strong' (loosely, verse 13).

Each day is full of endings. Which of them are also beginnings?

Uphold anyone you know facing their own endings or beginnings.

Jerusalem

Sunday 6 May

Jerusalem: City of David

2 Samuel 6:12-15

Symbol of peace and sign of conflict

When King David conquered the Jebusite stronghold, he brought the Ark of the Covenant there. In what's presented as a triumphant homecoming, David sacrificed animals and danced before the Ark 'with abandon' (verse 14). For his people it symbolised God's presence and protection. Solomon built a temple to contain it and, ever since, Jerusalem has remained at the heart of Judaism, even when conquered and ruled by other nations, even when the temple was destroyed, rebuilt and destroyed again.

Jerusalem contains the holy places of Jews, Christians and Muslims. It is a place of pilgrimage – and also at the volatile centre of world politics. Palestinian Christians write: 'Jerusalem is the heart of our reality ... it continues to be emptied of its Palestinian citizens, Christians and Muslims ... Jerusalem, city of reconciliation, has become a city of discrimination and exclusion, a source of struggle rather than peace' (The Kairos Palestine Document, 2009, see www.oikoumene.org/gr/resources/documents/other-ecumenical-bodies/kairos-palestine-document.html).

Yet, beyond the stones of the old city and the concrete of the new, rises the vision of the eternal and heavenly city, celebrated from the Psalms to Revelation – embodying human hopes, at the centre of our faith.

Can we find in these Bible passages signs of the New Jerusalem, the City of God where all shall live at peace?

Pray for the peace of Jerusalem.

Notes based on the Revised English Version by

Jan Sutch Pickard

Jan Sutch Pickard is a poet and storyteller living on the Isle of Mull, and a former Warden of the Abbey in Iona. In the last few years she has served twice with the Ecumenical Accompaniment Programme in Palestine and Israel, based in small West Bank villages but with a chance to spend time in Jerusalem and reflect on its divisions. A Methodist local preacher, she leads worship for the Church of Scotland on Mull.

Holy ground?

2 Chronicles 6: 12-21

King Solomon prays in the great edifice he has built, in the city to which his father David brought the Ark of God's Covenant. The Ark is now in the heart of the temple, in the heart of the city. Does that mean God is there?

Solomon believes this is the very place to worship God – amid the assembled people, on a special platform he had made with only the most precious materials. But does that guarantee God is there?

Solomon's prayer returns to God's promise – of strong rulers for Israel, as long as the descendants of David obey God's law. So power and success for a nation is only one half of the covenant?

Solomon asks 'But can God indeed dwell with mortals on earth?' (verse 18) That is the question! Can we confine God in our buildings and co-opt God into our power-games? Right now, Arab homes are being demolished in Jerusalem to build Israeli settlements, and to make a 'City of David' theme park. Jerusalem is a place of controversy and strife, not peace. Injustice is being done by the Israeli government in the name of God.

Solomon's prayer, offered in God's name, asks a question relevant to the politics of the Middle East, and (close to home) to our own much-loved church buildings: 'Heaven itself ... cannot contain you ... how much less this house that I have built!' (verse 18).

God, you are holy, and you are everywhere. When we are aware that we stand in your presence, we are standing on holy ground. Help us to understand that we cannot confine you in one place, or keep you to ourselves; that the true holy places are where all your children are welcome. We confess that our divisions and injustice have no place in your kingdom of love. Hear from heaven your dwelling and, when you hear, forgive.

Common ground for all humanity?

Psalm 22

Is this psalm about Jerusalem? Other psalms, such as 122, rejoice in 'a city built solidly' (Psalm 122:3), express hopes of peace and prosperity. Or we hear her children yearning for a city from which they have been exiled, with only God to comfort them. But where is the city here? And where is God? The first half of the psalm is a cry of despair. The words strike home. Where have we heard 'My God, my God, why have you forsaken me?'

These are Jesus' words on the cross, a lament from his people's tradition expressing his own desolation. When the psalm was first composed, it was a prayer of great honesty, out of the depths of human suffering. It has spoken to and for many people, before and after the time of Christ. It is read during the stripping of Iona Abbey on Maundy Thursday. As everything of beauty and meaning is taken away or covered up, and the candles are put out, the reader of the psalm struggles to follow the words in the darkness, so that the affirmation of God's presence and saving power, which come in the second half, can barely be heard.

It must have felt like this when Jerusalem was invaded and the temple destroyed; when Jesus was nailed to the cross, outside the city wall. And still today, not just in Jerusalem, suffering people – losing health, family, home, jobs, land – wonder whether God has abandoned them. And we may wonder at the faith of those who can still praise God.

Loving God, I feel your presence, around me and within me. I remember a time when I was afraid you were not there. Thank you for hearing my cry. Thank you for being there, accompanying me through times of darkness and distress. I remember there are other people (in the news, or in your neighbourhood or family – name them) who may be asking right now 'God, where are you?' I remember Jesus, who came to share our human lives, in this world: Immanuel – God with us. Thank you.

Jan Sutch Pickard

Ground Zero

2 Kings 25:8-21

How terribly precise the timing is: 'In the fifth month, on the seventh day of the month' (verse 8), on that day Solomon's temple was destroyed. The armies of Nebuchadnezzar overran Judea, captured and blinded its king, entered Jerusalem and pillaged and burned the temple. Its priests were carried away and killed. Most of the population of Jerusalem was taken into exile. For devout Jews the Babylonian attack seemed the vengeance of a God they had offended – by idol worship – in this same city.

This was not the last time Jerusalem was attacked; the temple that was rebuilt was destroyed again, centuries later. In a broken world, such experiences are not unique. Yet the way this date is recorded is reminiscent of how the date 9/11 is imprinted on the consciousness of people round the world today. It records an event, an atrocity, and a moment when people's perception of the world and their place in it changed for ever.

What are the 'significant dates' in your own life? (Banks often ask us to register such a date as a password, something that proves our identity.) Take a moment to remember one of these, its shock or sadness – or indeed its joy. How did it change your life? Did it change you?

What is most important is not what happens to us (or when), but how we deal with such experiences, and through them continue to grow as God's children.

God of space and time, God of the here and now, you have stayed with us through suffering and joy; help us to stay with you, walk in your way, whatever happens, today and every day.

Grounds for sorrow or joy?

Ezra 3:8-13

The trumpets sound again, echoing from the pale stones of Jerusalem. The nation taken into exile by Nebuchadnezzar of Babylon was set free as King Cyrus of Persia rose to power. He sent the Jewish people back, with dignity, to Jerusalem to 'build the house of the Lord the God of Israel' (Ezra 1:3). Surely, grounds for rejoicing? The book of Ezra lists the families who returned, with all their roles in temple worship – though there had been no temple for a long time.

First, on the site of Solomon's temple, in the open air, they built an altar, then began to offer sacrifices and to observe the festivals. The day came when they began to rebuild. As the foundations were laid, the trumpets sounded and the people sang one of the psalms they had remembered throughout their exile.

At this point, we are told, people reacted differently to what was happening: some (remembering what had been lost) wept and wailed, others shouted for joy. It was hard to distinguish between the waves of sound. But this was not contradictory or strange.

When, in 1940, Coventry was devastated by bombs, the cathedral burned with the city. The decision to rebuild the cathedral, taken the morning after its destruction, wasn't an act of defiance but a sign of hope. The cathedral's ministry of Peace and Reconciliation has provided spiritual and practical support in areas of conflict round the world. In Coventry the place of living worship and the place of remembering are both holy ground.

God of consolation, and encouragement,
we thank you for the power of memory to move us,
and for the power of hope to help us move on.

Jan Sutch Pickard

Going over the ground

Nehemiah 2: 11-18

Nehemiah – diplomat, community organiser and civil engineer – took on the task of surveying the broken walls of Jerusalem. Exiled, he used his influence as a valued servant of King Artaxerxes to get permission for this mission. To demoralised survivors in the ruined city he didn't at first explain his purpose but went out by night, inspecting the damage. Then he reminded the people of their plight, challenging them to change it: 'Come, let us rebuild the wall of Jerusalem and suffer derision no more' (verse 17). Recognising that Nehemiah knew what he was talking about, most responded positively, getting down to work. When others jeered, he replied that this was God's work.

Like the story of the Iona Community, which came into being during the depression as unemployed men and ministers in training worked side by side to rebuild a long-ruined abbey in the Hebrides, this is not just a story of a monument restored, but a story about the rebuilding of community.

For the Iona Community, 74 years on, it is still clear that work and worship are one. For Nehemiah, the task he undertook, in all its practical details, was – as much as any priest serving in the former temple – his way of serving God.

Look at your life now. What do you see that needs to be done? Where do you feel 'the gracious hand of God' on you? What is your practical response?

Look at your hands, see the touch and the tenderness,
God's own for the world
Look at your feet, see the path and the direction,
God's own for the world
Look at your heart, see the fire and the love,
God's own for the world
Look at the cross, see God's Son and our Saviour
God's own for the world
This is God's world
And we will serve God in it.

Present on Earth, Wild Goose Resource Group, 2004
(see also www.ionabooks.com)

Jan Sutch Pickard — Jerusalem

Ground of faith

Zechariah 1:16-17

Jerome, translating the Bible into Latin, described Zechariah as 'the most obscure book'. Scholars have found it hard to interpret its prophecies, set down after the Babylonian Exile, some referring to what was going on at the time and some to a far future. These verses aren't obscure, though: a message of encouragement to returning exiles continuing the task of rebuilding, a reminder that God has 'returned to Jerusalem with compassion' (verse 16).

Several of this week's readings, and the books from which they are taken, emphasise the importance of sustained effort – otherwise how could the walls of Jerusalem have been rebuilt? Underlying this there needs to be a well-founded faith. We know that, while we have the skills for a job, if we lose a sense of why we are doing it – the worth of our hard work – we can 'burn out'. For the Jews, Jerusalem and the temple were God's project, 'the city of his choice' (verse 17), on which they were called to work. This gave them a reason to go on – 'comfort' in the active sense.

A German hymn translated by John Wesley begins, 'Now I have found that ground wherein/ Sure my soul's anchor may remain' (words by Johann A Rothe, translated from German to English by John Wesley, *Hymns and Sacred Poems*, 1740). Jews, from the times of the Exile to today, find that 'ground' in Jerusalem. For Christians it is also a place of pilgrimage. But the city is not an end in itself. It turns our eyes to God. God's love, in Christ, is the ground of our being.

Great God, Ground of our being, your love gives our lives meaning. Help us to see your presence in every great city and in the small places: village shops, classrooms, hospital wards, our homes. Help us to live our daily lives with hope, faith and compassion. In a world of inequality and injustice, may we find and help build the true Jerusalem: the heavenly city, the place of your presence, here and now.

Sunday 13 May

Jerusalem

Jerusalem: the Holy City

Notes based on the New Revised Standard Version by

Paul Nicholson

Paul Nicholson, SJ, is a Roman Catholic priest belonging to the Society of Jesus (the Jesuits). He is currently Director of Novices in the Jesuit novitiate in Birmingham, England, responsible for the first two years of training for men from Britain, Ireland, Holland, Flanders, Latvia and South Africa. Since his ordination in 1988, Paul has worked chiefly in the fields of spirituality and/or social justice. Between 1999 and 2006 he was Director of the Loyola Hall spirituality centre outside Liverpool.

Luke 2:27-32

The love of great cities

A traditional tag, distinguishing the founders of religious orders, claims: 'Benedict loved the countryside, Francis the market towns; but Ignatius (founder of the Jesuits) loved the great cities.' And he loved no city more than Jerusalem. Indeed, given the chance, he had intended to live his life there, serving the pilgrims who then, as now, thronged its streets. Although this was not to be his fate, he retained to the end of his life a concern for the city where Christ carried out much of his ministry, was executed and, after his resurrection, returned to his Father.

Already, for Jesus, Jerusalem was the holy city. For those who follow him, it is no less so. This week's prayer moves around the city and its outskirts, deepening a sense of its significance for those who find a foundation of their faith there. We start with the story of Jesus, as an infant, being presented at the temple that stood at the city's heart. Maybe, in reading the passage, the memory of a baptism or christening that you have attended will further your appreciation of what it might have felt like to be in that sacred place, that city, at that time.

Called apart or called together?

Luke 2:41-51

In this scene, Luke shows us Jesus at the age when, in his culture, he is expected to make the faith of Israel his own. In later generations that would be the eve of his bar mitzvah, his becoming a 'son of the Law'. We are invited to picture the temple, the holy sanctuary at the heart of the holy city. We see that moment when Jesus' awareness of the call his Father has for him crystallises. Nothing can be allowed to come between him and the living out of this call, not even his closest family relationships.

To be holy literally means to be 'set apart' for the service of God. In my office I have a print of a painting by Simone Martini of the finding in the temple. It shows Mary, seated, looking distraught. A worried Joseph gestures towards her. Meanwhile, Jesus, every inch the surly adolescent, stands with his arms folded across his chest and a petulant expression on his face. Although here in the temple he may have discovered something of his vocation, his particular call from his Father, he still has something to learn, the artist suggests, in the field of social skills.

What does holiness look like to you? How do you find a balance between the call to let God be first in your life, and the real demands of all your other relationships?

Father, you call us to be holy as you yourself are holy. Give the help we need to recognise the meaning of that call in the everyday details of our lives and in our relationships with those through whom we hear your calling.

Bathed in holiness

John 5:1-18

The temple was not the only holy site in Jerusalem. This pool, variously known as Beth-zatha, Bethsaida, or Bethesda, was also recognised as a site of God's activity. Here God's healing touch could be felt, just as today many would feel it at the shrine of Lourdes, and other such healing shrines. Yet Jesus seems to invite us into a wider view, not restricted to a particular place or procedure. Whenever and wherever he is encountered, healing is the result. And this healing is not just of body, but takes in whatever might stand between me and God.

Few who go to Lourdes receive a cure there that the authorities, with their careful investigations, will recognise as miraculous. Many return conscious of having received a degree of healing, whether of body, soul or spirit, not least through the loving concern of other pilgrims whom they meet there. In this way the work of God spreads, from one person to another, from one holy place out into the world, as the waters of a pool bring life to its surroundings.

In your prayer today, you might start by thinking of your own 'holy places'. Where are they, and what impact have they had on your life? Then consider how this influence has spread out into the rest of your life, into your relationships and your sense of how God works with you in the world.

Think of a city that is in the news headlines today, and pray for the needs of its people.

Paul Nicholson — Jerusalem

Footprints of faith

Luke 24:44-53

Even today, on the Mount of Olives overlooking the old city of Jerusalem, a guide will show you the stone from which Jesus supposedly ascended to his Father, complete with his footprints. Ignatius Loyola was so taken with this when he visited the site that he bartered his nail-scissors for a second look, so he could be sure of the direction Jesus was facing when he left this earth. Few today would be so credulous. Yet the underlying instinct recognises the importance of Jesus' humanity, and of the physical settings of his life and death. Jerusalem was, then as now, not only a focus of God's activity, but also a city in a land of occupation, of racial conflict, and of sporadic violence. How might this have helped shape Jesus' message? What memories of the city would he be taking with him as he returned to the Father who had sent him?

As I reflect upon these questions I become more aware of how particular places and situations have shaped my own faith. Growing up in London in the 1960s and '70s I have a Roman Catholic faith deeply influenced both by the experience of Irish immigration of the previous century, and by the struggle to move beyond that inheritance to become part of mainstream British culture.

Whether your own background is urban, suburban or rural, how has it influenced your relationship with God?

Lord Jesus,
your human existence was shaped by small-town life in
  Nazareth,
and the lure of the big city, Jerusalem.
Make us aware of how our own lives have been moulded
by those places to which you have guided us,
and in which we have encountered you.

Jerusalem — Paul Nicholson

Now what?

Acts 1:10-14

Jesus' last words before his return to his Father in Matthew's Gospel are a sending-out of the disciples to spread his word throughout the world. Luke presents a similar speech, but adds the detail that they should stay in Jerusalem until they 'have been clothed with power from on high' (Luke 24:49) by the Spirit. So here we see them returning to the same room where they have been staying, and gathering in prayer to wait.

In this telling of the story, Jerusalem has not been superseded. It remains the holy city, the source from which God's life-giving word will flow into the world. The faith of each one of the hundreds of millions of Christians in the world today can be traced back to that group gathered together in prayer. My own faith, and yours, finds its fountain-head there.

In your own prayer today, you might like to trace the way in which that faith has reached you in the intervening centuries. Beginning in Jerusalem, disciples carried the word through the Roman Empire, and it gradually spread throughout the entire globe.

What do you know of where your own faith came from, and of those responsible for bringing it to you? How have you become a link in that same chain, passing the faith on into the future?

Today I give thanks for all those whose loving witness brought Christian faith to me.

Pray for the peace of Jerusalem

Acts 3:1-10

Before its destruction in 70 CE, the temple, at the heart of Jerusalem, remained a focus of prayer for the early Christian community. And it seems that, then as now, places of worship drew those in need, who hoped to receive something from the people who came to pray.

Notice how, in the course of this story, it's not just the lame beggar's health that is restored. His whole role changes. He begins as a supplicant, entirely dependent on the generosity of passers-by. He ends as a fellow-worshipper, joining Peter and John as they enter the temple, and praising God with them. It is perhaps his evident faith, as much as his renewed physical wellbeing, that makes such a deep impact on the crowd around him.

The second part of the name Jerusalem, 'salem', is related to the Hebrew word 'shalom', normally translated as 'peace', making Jerusalem the 'city of peace'. In fact the concept is a much broader one, encompassing the whole of a right relationship with God, with the world around, and with other human beings. It is this right relationship that the former beggar in this story enjoys by the end of this passage.

Can you recall times when you have enjoyed something of this gift of shalom?

Lord, you called the peace-makers blessed.
Help us to know that same peace in our own lives,
and bring it to others through our witness in the world.

Paul Nicholson

At home in the new Jerusalem

Revelation 21: 1-17

A fluffy cloud, a person of indeterminate gender in a white nightgown, and a harp. These are the familiar cartoon elements associated with heaven. The biblical view of the life that we are to enjoy after this one could hardly be more different. A new, renewed, heaven and earth, different from, but standing in a recognisable continuity with, all that we know and value here and now. A new, renewed, city, not as an abstract ideal, but having much in common with the Jerusalem known by the prophets and by Jesus.

The promise is that all that is good in our present world will be taken up, transformed, and given back to us. If my life has been shaped by my environment and the society within which I live, it will continue to be so shaped. Yet there is one key difference. 'See, the home of God is among mortals' (verse 3). Nothing, in this new Jerusalem, will separate me from God. No pain, no suffering, no doubt and no persecution will ever get in the way again. Certainly, it's not easy to imagine such a state – which is perhaps why we restrict ourselves to fluffy clouds and harps. Yet, we are assured, 'these words are trustworthy and true' (verse 5).

What would it be to live, for today at least, in this hope of heaven, of the renewed city of God?

How might you imagine the 'new heaven and new earth', the 'new Jerusalem' (verses 1-2)? Pray for an enlarged vision.

Readings in 1 Samuel

Sunday 20 May

The calling of Samuel

Notes based on *Tanakh: The Holy Scriptures* by

Pete Tobias

Pete Tobias is Rabbi of the Liberal Synagogue, Elstree, in Hertfordshire. His latest book, the first of a children's series, *The Secret of the £5 Etrog*, was published in 2010. Pete features regularly on BBC Radio 2 and is a devoted fan of Watford Football Club!

1 Samuel 1:1-20

The diary of a Jewish mother

Imagine if Hannah had kept a record of her experiences. What a wonderful picture of biblical Israel we would have, seen through the eyes of the mother of the prophet who guided it through one of its most formative and challenging times. Here are extracts from Hannah's imaginary diary.

'Every year we come to this place, to bring our offerings to the Eternal One of Israel. This is Shiloh, the home of the Ark of the Covenant, brought from the wilderness by my ancestors. It contains the power of YHWH, who scatters all enemies before him.

But none of this means anything to me. What care I for the history of Israel or the miracles that God wrought for them? It matters nothing if this God cannot grant me a child! Once again we come to this place, and I pray, believing my words will be heard. So strong is my belief – and my desire to have a child – that I promise I will give my firstborn into the service of YHWH here at Shiloh.

As I make this promise, the old priest Eli approaches me. He thinks I am intoxicated, but I tell him my anguish. He sends me on my way with words of comfort, and my soul fills with hope.'

Like Hannah, we should never doubt that God might fulfil our hopes.

'Children are a gift from the Eternal One; the fruit of the womb is God's reward' (Psalm 127:3). Pray for all who long for a child.

A promise kept

1 Samuel 1:21 – 2:11, 18-21

'And now we return to Shiloh. My heart is filled with joy, for I am bringing with me the son that God gave to me in answer to my prayer last time I was in this place. But there is sadness also, for I must keep my promise, and deliver him to Eli the priest so that he can serve God as I promised.

'And my soul moves me to utter words of gratitude to the same God before whom I pleaded in this place. How swift we are to make requests and demands of God; how slow to give thanks and fulfil our promises to him! But I shall give my thanks and I shall keep my promise. And every time that I visit my son in this place, I shall bring him a robe as a gift; a token of my love, that he may remember me.

'And the kindly priest who sent me from here with words of hope now gives God's blessing to my husband and me. And again, the God of Shiloh goes with us and blesses us, bringing us the family for which I have always yearned. And my life is fulfilled by each of them – though still I think often of my beloved firstborn, Samuel.'

Let us always remember to be grateful for the blessings we have been given.

We praise you O God, source of goodness, to whom our thanks are due.

Daily Liturgy, *Siddur Lev Chadash*, Union of Liberal and Progressive Synagogues, 1995

My son, the prophet

1 Samuel 3:1 – 4:1a

'Praised be the God of Israel who dwells in Shiloh! For my son, my firstborn Samuel, whom God gave to me when he heard my prayer, has been chosen by the almighty as a prophet! Eli the priest told me of an incident when God spoke to my little boy in the depth of the night, and how Samuel had thought it was Eli who was speaking. But it was the voice of the God of Israel, telling my son that he was going to bring some terrible punishment on Eli and his family. I feel sorry for Eli and his family, of course, but what mother could not feel joy when her son is spoken to directly by YHWH!

'And my Samuel's fame has spread all through the land! Of course, not all prophets are loved and respected. Prophets criticise the way people behave, and judge their actions on God's behalf. No one likes to be told they're doing wrong. But I know that if my Samuel says he heard God speaking to him, then that makes him a true prophet in Israel. And that makes me the proudest mother in Israel!'

The spirit of prophecy is the voice of God that struggles to be heard within us all. The challenge for us is to listen in order to hear God speaking.

Would that all God's people were prophets
and that the spirit of the Eternal One was
upon them!

Numbers 11:29

 Pete Tobias

Losing my religion

1 Samuel 4:1b-18

'Can I ever go to Shiloh again? The Ark of the Covenant, the very presence of Israel's God, is gone from that place, captured by the Philistines in battle. Eli and his family of priests are no more. My son has returned to his home in Ramah. But there is no celebration, no joy in this homecoming. I see the weight of responsibility settle on my son's shoulders, I sense his weariness and his sadness.

'But in his eyes I see also hope. I see the same hope that God inspired in me when I prayed for this child of mine to be born. I remind him of this, and I believe he draws strength from my experience, which is his also.

'"Eli is dead," he says in a sombre voice. "And now it is for you to lead Israel," I reply. He shakes his head. "But the Ark is taken." "There are powers in the Ark that we cannot comprehend," I tell my son. "But the courage to believe in God's power is in each of us." He nods.'

In times of despair, will you be one of those who bring hope?

There are times of faith, and there are times of doubt and despair in the histories of peoples and the lives of individuals. Faith has always been a venture, a pilgrimage, a struggle ... But God, holding a candle, looks for all who wander, all who search.

Siddur Lev Chadash, Union of Liberal and Progressive Synagogues, 1995, p.219

Love your neighbour

1 Samuel 5:1-12

'Israel is defeated and without its Ark, but the God of Israel wreaks his revenge on the Philistines who have captured it. My son the prophet hears this news in his home in Ramah, and the hope in his eyes burns ever brighter. As a mother, I delight in the improvement in my son's mood. As an Israelite, I should feel joy that our cursed enemies, who humiliated us on the battlefield at Aphek, are suffering. But as a human being I feel unease – I cannot celebrate reports of Philistine pain; I feel the cries of mothers weeping for their children.

'I share my concern with my child. I am dismayed by the fierceness of his response, which suggests that neither he, nor the God whose words he receives, has compassion for their enemies. I try to reason with Samuel, explaining to him my belief that there can never be peace in our lives if we forever repeat the cycle of hatred by delighting in our enemies' misfortune. He fixes me with a sad expression and tells me that he also has such visions, but that there is no place for them in our cruel and violent world. "Perhaps in a future time," he shrugs. "We are all responsible for shaping the future," is my reply.'

Reflect and pray on the following biblical texts. 'You shall not stand by idle while your neighbour's blood is being shed' (Leviticus 19:16). 'Have we not all one Maker? Has not one God created us?' (Malachi 2:10)

As you love yourself

1 Samuel 6:19 – 7:17

'"Sometimes the actions of our God are hard to fathom." Those were Samuel's words to me when he struggled to hear the Eternal One. He tells me he misses Shiloh: he could sense God's presence there more easily. But he says he will build an altar here in Ramah, and seek God in his home.

'I cannot fathom it. The Philistines, punished by our God, have sent the Ark of the Covenant back to the Israelites. But many Israelites have perished, punished for approaching the divine presence. Who or what is this God, causing such pain and administering such punishment?

'My son has established a stone to acknowledge how God has helped us. But God has not only helped; he has punished us also. My people may want to celebrate victory over their enemy, but I am angry at the suffering – of our enemies and of our own people. How can God want this? And how can we thank him for letting it happen? I rage at my son and my God, but they both stand silent and impassive, like the stone.'

There are times when our world seems to speak only of God's silence. Is our faith strong enough to cope with that?

I believe in the sun, even when it does not shine.
I believe in love, even when I do not feel it.
I believe in God, even though God is silent.

Written on a cellar in Cologne during the Second World War

Give us a king!

1 Samuel 8:4-22

'The faith of the Israelites in their God is waning. The elders have told him that they want a king to rule over them – this wounds Samuel, who has served only God since the earliest days when I took him to Shiloh.

My son knows that the world is changing. The people wish to place their trust in human beings, even though they have seen God's power. My son is perplexed; he seems to wear a permanent frown on his brow. He fears for a people who believe that they can shape their own destiny without a sense of God guiding their hands and hearts. He explains that God has told him to choose a king as the people request. He does not understand this, but he has faith that God will guide the thoughts and actions of Israel's king-to-be. I pray that he is right.'

It is better to take refuge in God than to rely on human beings.
It is better to take refuge in God than to rely on princes.

Psalm 118:8-9

We are children of a time that has sought to dethrone You. We have witnessed the power of mortals to create and worship the work of their hands. Strange then to see the emptiness Your absence has brought upon us! Scarcely do we tremble before You. O, but we tremble at ourselves and our works, and fear the days to come!

Machzor Ru'ach Chadashah, Liberal Judaism, 2003, p.119

Sunday 27 May
(Pentecost)

Readings in 1 Samuel

King Saul

Notes based on the Hebrew text by
Pete Tobias

For Pete's biography see page 143.

1 Samuel 9:1-21

Am I not a Benjaminite?

With the decision to appoint a king, Israelite history took an irrevocable turn. It introduces us to Saul, one of the most tragic figures of the Bible. Saul is racked with insecurity, while his relationship with Samuel is filled with contradiction. Samuel appears only briefly, to chastise, criticise or threaten. David, son of Jesse, waits invisibly in the wings.

'Ah that Saul! A troubled man. He should never have been chosen as king. He was too flawed. And so alone.

'I only saw Israel's first king once. He cut a dashing figure. If rulers needed looks to command the respect and loyalty of their subjects, then Saul was ideal. Perhaps even God thought Saul looked the part – or maybe the almighty was trying to prove a point: that humans are easily fooled by superficial characteristics and fail to understand the human soul.

'Samuel understood Saul. After all, Samuel had been told by God that Saul was going to be king. Saul's sense of inadequacy came from within – a doubt that began as soon as Samuel told him he was destined to be king. Saul protested that his tribal roots made him unworthy for such rank. And that was only the beginning...'

Can your faith help you overcome a sense of not being able to fulfil a task that is demanded of you?

When doubt, anxiety or pain hinders our efforts to commune with you, grant that our prayers may find their answer in firmer courage, deeper insight and greater fortitude.

Machzor Ru'ach Chadashah, Liberal Judaism, 2003, p.376

Is Saul also among the prophets?

1 Samuel 9:22 – 10:16

'If there was a moment in my son's life when he doubted the wisdom of the almighty's advice, it was when he had to give the reluctant ruler instructions that would lead to his becoming king. After the events, Samuel complained to me that the whole performance of Saul appearing to prophesy simultaneously elevated the position of the king and diminished the role of the prophet in the eyes of the people.

'"The role of a king is to gather armies, to lead the people in battle against their enemies, and offer them protection and security," he said. "The role of a prophet is to remind the king of that obligation, and of his duty to uphold the laws of the God of Israel. If a king prophesied, he would not protect the people properly. And if a prophet became too involved in everyday matters of state, he could not truly represent the will of God."

'"But the two of you need each other," I said gently, sensing my son's agitation. "And you need to respect each other's abilities." "Saul does not even respect his own ability," was the reply. And my heart went out to both these troubled men.'

Have there ever been times when, like Saul, you have felt yourself unworthy of a role that is assigned to you?

You are not required to complete the task, but neither are you at liberty to abstain from it.

Pirkei Avot

No, Saul is among the baggage

1 Samuel 10: 17-27

'O Saul, you poor troubled man, how I felt for you when my son explained what happened the day you were declared king of Israel. How did you feel when my son led you through another performance, eventually revealing you from your hiding place among the baggage?

'Why did you hide, Saul? Did you think that you might not be found? Do you not know that when God has called you, you cannot ignore the call? My son Samuel knew this, even when he was only three years old! But you, Saul, feared the call of the almighty. Did you sense my son's disappointment when the people demanded a king? I do not believe that Samuel wanted you to fail, though he complained to me often enough that he wished you had not been chosen.

'Little wonder, then, that there were those who did not believe you could rule Israel. You knew of their opposition, but you kept silent. What fears were there in that silence, Saul? Were these the seeds of self-doubt that would destroy you?'

Have you ever 'hidden among the baggage' when called upon to act? Did your faith help you overcome your fear?

Eternal God, where can I go from Your spirit? Where can I flee from Your presence? If I ascend to the heavens, You are there! If I make my home in the lowest depths, behold, You are there.'

Psalm 139:7-8

Shall Saul reign over us?

1 Samuel 11

'And then came the turning point, Saul. The moment came and you grasped it – was it good fortune, or did God send Nahash the Ammonite to unite the Israelite people behind you? You had no need to consult my son – did you imagine that he might seek to dissuade you, reinforce your uncertainty and doubt?

'It seems that God spoke directly to Saul that day, as though to show my son Samuel that his time of leading Israel might be over. Certainly the people of Israel saw Saul in a new light and were pleased to confirm him as their king, finally acknowledging his rule at Gilgal. Samuel reported to me that wonderful celebration that took place there, sacrifices of thanksgiving for the defeat of Nahash and the Ammonites.

'My Samuel was never the same after that. It was as though a part of him passed to you, Saul, the part that connected him to the God of Israel. But you were never the same either, O flawed king. Or rather, you were briefly different: for a while you became a real king and led your people. But I knew, as did Samuel, that this would not last; your self-doubt and insecurity would return. And I think you knew it too.'

Have you ever felt that you have overreached yourself? Can your faith support you in such moments?

Excessive confidence throws us off our guard, whereas fear teaches precaution.

Herod I, in Josephus, *Wars* I.19.4

See this great thing

1 Samuel 12

'I never had my son marked down for a showman. But when he took his leave – temporarily at least – from leading the Israelites, he put on a performance to rival that of Moses on Mount Nebo – or even at Horeb!

'Needless to say, I was not permitted to be present at what everyone assumed was Samuel's 'retirement' – the moment where he 'officially' handed over the leadership of Israel to its king, Saul. But I heard reports about it, and I challenged my son the next time he came to Ramah.

'"Nice speech," I said. "But why the magic show?" "To remind the people of God's power," he shrugged. "And of your ability to invoke it – a privilege not granted to kings," was my reply. "Another example of your determination to undermine Saul, your revenge on the people for having rejected you and asked for a king."

'My son stormed from my presence. I never saw him again. But I knew in that moment that Samuel would find a way to bring Saul's reign to an end. And from that moment I felt more pain for Saul's impending departure than that of my firstborn son.'

How do we cope when members of our family behave in ways that disappoint us?

When we call to mind the duties and affections of family life, how greatly are all blessings enriched, all cares and sorrows softened. May the hearts of parents and children always be turned to one another.

Siddur Lev Chadash, Union of Liberal and Progressive Synagogues, 1995, p.348

Your kingdom will not endure

1 Samuel 13: 5-15a

'And Israel's nemesis returned. The Philistines, once devastated by the Ark of the Covenant, rose again to threaten the security my Samuel had established, and Saul had secured with his military prowess. But my son had already despaired of the king he had installed, so when the call came for him to bless the Israelite troops before battle, he ignored it.

'Whose sin was greater? My Samuel for not responding to the call to perform the sacrifice before battle? Or Saul for making the offering without a man of God present?

'History will judge, but once again I feel the finger of blame pointing at my son. And my heart fears for Saul. How did you feel, O faltering ruler, being told that God would take your kingdom from you? Or perhaps, dear Saul, it is more true to say that being asked to rule Israel was what took God from you…

'Already there is talk of a new king for Israel being sought, and I know my Samuel will be at the heart of this search. May this king enjoy the love and support of Israel's God that was so cruelly denied to you, Saul. And may you, troubled king, find peace.'

May we learn to find God in our failures as well as our achievements.

Each of us has regrets that others cannot know.
And so, we pray: …if we are discouraged, give us hope.

Machzor Ru'ach Chadashah, Liberal Judaism, 2003, p.53

Nothing can hinder the eternal one

1 Samuel 14:1-23

'And so my life reaches its end. As I look back on the days I have known, reports of Saul and Jonathan's triumph over the Philistines reach Ramah. What do the tales of military victory matter to me as I reflect upon my days? My son knows also that this victory is a hollow one, that ultimately Saul will not prevail.

'But my thoughts are not concerned with such matters. I must prepare to meet the God to whom I prayed so many years ago at Shiloh, who answered my prayer to open my womb and to whom I gave my firstborn son in return for his goodness.

'The stories of nations and kings will be written in the chronicles of history by those who experience and outlive them. But the tales of our lives, our successes and our failures, our hopes and our dreams, will live in the actions of our children, of those whom we have influenced and taught and loved.

'May my son Samuel be remembered for the good he did, the judgements he brought and the changes he effected. And let the final words of his mother Hannah be words of gratitude to the almighty for his guidance, protection and love.'

May the sense of God's presence in our lives give meaning and purpose to our days.

Our Creator and Sovereign, have compassion on us and on our children.

Machzor Ru'ach Chadashah, Liberal Judaism, 1995, p.73

Readings in 1 Samuel

David

Notes based on *The Message* by

Jenny Warbrick

Jenny Warbrick lives in Birmingham, UK, and is a freelance educational trainer and writer. She is an enthusiastic member of her local Anglican church and is married with two teenage children.

1 Samuel 14:24-46

Restoring perspective

Although no doubt familiar with the stories of Samuel's call and David versus Goliath from childhood, we may be less familiar with the whole book of Samuel. I heartily recommend it. It is a real page-turner, full of drama and suspense and flawed human characters like us. The recurrent theme is of faithfulness to God being rewarded with success, and disobedience leading to disaster.

Jonathan's audacious plan to trick the Philistines, his trust in God's unconventional methods, and the sweet taste of honey, contrast strikingly with the fear of aged King Saul: Saul, with his blinkered and inconsistent approach to God, and his sour mood. Saul's desire for vengeance against his enemies outweighs his reason. By ordering the army to fight on an empty stomach, he traps himself into requiring the necessity of executing his own son for sampling the local honey (although Jonathan is saved by the soldiers). Ironically, he is more outraged at the soldiers gorging themselves on ritually unclean meat than by the prospect of his son's death!

Saul has got his priorities wrong. His attempts at prayer are too little, too late. Can you relate to this? Regular prayer restores perspective. Allowing God to filter our preoccupations and anxieties enables us to see what really matters.

Lord Jesus, help us to be disciplined in prayer, like you.

Positive impulses

1 Samuel 15:7-23

This story casts Saul in a bad light. Remember he didn't offer himself as a royal candidate. He was spotted by Samuel whilst finding his father's lost donkeys! Saul must have been very surprised to be anointed king of Israel. He had a challenging task in overcoming inter-tribal jealousy to unify the new nation. Nonetheless, Saul had charisma and created a successful army that defeated the Ammonites. By this stage in the story, time has passed. Has Saul become complacent, with a tendency to trust his own judgement more than God's?

God's instructions for taking revenge on the Amalekites seem very harsh. Complete destruction of an entire community, including innocent children and livestock, is an atrocity. But we must appreciate the Hebrew scriptures' concept of 'Holy War'. Spoils of war were not to be used for personal gain, but destroyed and so dedicated to God. Saul's capture of King Agag as a trophy is an arrogant gesture, and using the enemy's best sheep and cattle for sacrifice shows a distinct lack of gratitude. Saul's act of disobedience enrages God, who rejects him as king.

Sometimes we may come under strange or challenging impulses that unsettle us and it is not always easy to discriminate between our own inner impulses and the prompting of God. We are perhaps inclined to doubt our instincts, yet following a sudden urge to contact someone out of the blue may be for them a real lifeline in a time of crisis. Trust God's judgement and you may be surprised where such impulses lead.

Think of a situation where you felt called to do something unexpected or difficult and consider the consequences for everyone involved. Thank God for anything positive that came out of it.

We can be so sure that every detail in our lives of love for God is worked into something good.

Romans 8:28

Worth more than you think

1 Samuel 16:1-23

Poor Samuel isn't allowed to mope. He is grieving for Saul, whom he will never see again, but God has already planned his next mission. He is to find and anoint the next king and his journey will take him to Bethlehem. Micah's prophecy (Micah 5:2), so often heard in Christmas services, springs to mind, and reminds us that Jesus was to share the same obscure birthplace.

Samuel fears Saul's wrath, as unpredictable moods now plague the king after his rejection by God. At Jesse's house, Samuel is presented with a beauty parade of his seven sons. He selects the most obvious candidate, but in marked contrast to Saul's disobedience in the previous reading, Samuel allows room for God and defers to God's surprising decision.

David's entry is reminiscent of the Cinderella story. His own father calls him the 'runt' of the litter (verse 11), and he is clearly the last person anyone would expect to become king. But as soon as he sees him, Samuel knows he is the chosen one, and he anoints David immediately, before the amazed and perhaps resentful brothers can object. 'Men and women look at the face; God looks into the heart' (verse 7). In our celebrity-obsessed culture it is good to be reminded that God's criteria for judgement are not the same as the world's. God knows our true worth and God has a unique task in mind for us too.

Pray for discernment so that you will know what God is calling only you to do at this time.

Nothing is ever wasted

1 Samuel 17: 31-50

The triumph of shepherd boy David over the military giant Goliath is one of the most memorable stories in the Old Testament. Everyone clearly thought David was mad, especially Saul, who has grown fond of this lad who can alleviate his bad moods with his lyre playing. After the comical scene where David staggers about in armour, clearly more inhibited than protected, his determination to face the towering enemy with nothing more than a simple sling and five stones must have seemed suicidal. But David has more than these weapons to protect him. He has selfless courage, loyalty to his master, and an unshakeable faith in God's ability to protect him, however dangerous the situation. His experience as a shepherd-boy has prepared him for this very moment. He is a superb shot and has taken on wild animals and won! He has no doubt that, with God on his side, he will be victorious. And it only takes one carefully judged aim to prove him right.

How can this be relevant for us? Well, first, nothing we do is ever wasted. The experience we accumulate in a lifetime, however strange and apparently irrelevant, will come in useful at some point. And even if not used directly, it will have contributed to our development as people, forming our character and core qualities. Even illness or trauma can enable us to empathise with and support others. Second, armed with faith in God, there is no challenge we cannot face.

God our Father, guide and protect us as we seek to live out a Christian life in a challenging world, and help us to use our wisdom and experience for the good of others.

Jenny Warbrick

The road to self-destruction

1 Samuel
17:55 – 18:16

David's humility is remarkable. Appearing heroically before King Saul with proof of Philistine defeat in his hands, he could be forgiven for feeling elated. But David is far from proud and acutely aware of his lowly origins. He identifies himself only as the son of a loyal servant of the king. Perhaps he feels unworthy of his prize. Who ever heard of a shepherd marrying a princess? David continues to impress. He is both fearless and successful in every military task set, and patient with Saul's deepening depressive moods, even when his life is threatened.

Diametrically opposed to the humble, trusting and loving David stands Saul: proud, suspicious, jealous and full of hatred. It is sad to watch their relationship deteriorate. From liking him very much, Saul's insecurity about his throne leads him to fear David. Public adulation of the victor (verse 7) haunts the king. Saul's awareness of how much David is loved by God, as well as by his son Jonathan, and admired by the people, only exacerbates his insane jealousy and leads him to plot the death of his most faithful servant. What a tragedy!

We don't really have control over how others see us. We can be surprised equally by others' admiration or dislike. It is hard to deal with strong feelings either way. But what is certain is that our jealousy of others is pointless and destructive – of relationships and ultimately of ourselves.

Loving God, help us to be sensitive to the feelings of others, especially when celebrating success. Help us to be genuinely glad for the success of others, without being jealous of them.

Jenny Warbrick

Challenging times

1 Samuel 19:1-18

Saul's mood is as changeable as the weather. One minute he wants to kill David, the next he swears not to hurt him, and the next again he is throwing spears at him in attempted murder. His own daughter, clearly terrified of her father, deceives him in order to aid her husband's escape. Saul needs to be referred to a psychiatrist! What kind of a recommendation is being empowered by God's Spirit, when David is treated like this? It's like being the fall guy in a bad movie, perpetually on the run and in fear of his life.

But God shapes David's character through such testing times. Despite every challenge, he remains devoted to Saul and faithful to God. There isn't a single complaint or a hint of resentment. He becomes resourceful and resilient, and in exile will develop the leadership skills needed to fulfil God's plan for his life. That's quite a hard act to follow.

When we find ourselves in a situation where we are doing our absolute best and it just isn't working, it can be very discouraging. We can feel that God has abandoned us. Maybe it will end in tears and we'll find it hard to understand why we had to experience it. But we will have gained something valuable, even if it is to recognise our limitations. We will be wiser, more self-aware and more suited to whatever God has got planned for us next.

O God, our protector, you have our best interests at heart. When we come up against challenges, help us to be resilient, like David, and trust that you will always be with us.

Jenny Warbrick

Sacrificial friendship

1 Samuel 20:1-23

After much negative focus on Saul and his mission to destroy David, it is refreshing to hear of the enduring friendship between Jonathan and David. The close bond between these two, sealed with a covenant before God, is poignant when compared with Saul's hatred and persecution of David. Jonathan's love and commitment are in no doubt. 'He loved David more than his own soul' (verse 17). David is in need of such reassurance. There is a sense of panic and despair in David's voice that we haven't heard before. The complex plan they devise to warn David of Saul's intentions involves huge trust and the risk of death. Reaffirmation of their oath cements their mutual dependence.

Oh, to have a friendship like that! Stories of personal heroism and sacrifice in emergencies or war are remarkably common, and fill one with admiration and wonder. We are unlikely to be put in a position where we have to risk death for one of our friends, though we perhaps could imagine dying for a family member.

Yet we can offer sacrificial friendship in more ordinary and mundane ways – for example, by making time to talk and meet regularly, so that we can be woven into the fabric of someone's life, through good times and bad; by supporting them practically through illness or bereavement; by praying for them. The rewards of giving will far outweigh the sacrifice and we may well find ourselves on the receiving end one day.

Take time to pray for each of your friends by name. Give thanks for them and their special qualities, and think how you can best provide sacrificial friendship for them.

Sunday 10 June

Readings in 1 Samuel

The death of Saul

Notes based on the Hebrew Bible and the New Revised Standard Version by

Renato Lings

Kjeld Renato Lings is a Danish translator/interpreter. He holds a PhD in theology from the University of Exeter (UK). Renato currently lives and works in his native Denmark.

1 Samuel 20:24-42

Covenants and blessings

In the Hebrew Bible, some personal relationships are noteworthy for their intensity and durability. The bond between Ruth and Naomi is for life (Ruth 1:16-17). It is blessed by God and the community (Ruth 2:12; 4:14-15). David and Jonathan establish a lifelong covenant invoking the name of YHWH, God of Israel. Their mutual loyalty reaches beyond death to include their descendants (1 Samuel 20:15).

King Saul, father of Jonathan, is unable to celebrate his son's commitment to David. Faced with David's successes and his own failures, Saul reacts with depression, jealousy, rage and attempted murder. He grossly insults his own son.

Like Saul, some Christians today fail to accept the deep commitment of their children to same-sex partners. Instead of celebrating, they may react with disbelief, grief or anger if their daughter or son shares with them the news of a covenant established with a very special female or male friend.

We may learn important lessons from the bond between Ruth and Naomi. Thanks to this committed relationship, Ruth the foreigner became ancestress of David, king of Israel. Responding to the news of Jonathan's untimely death, David exclaimed that the greatest love he ever experienced was that of Jonathan (2 Samuel 1:26).

Are you able to celebrate lifelong commitment between two people, even two women or two men?

God of all creation, open our eyes to the blessing of committed, loving relationships.

Strategic madness and dishonesty

1 Samuel 21:1 – 22:5

As his rule degenerates into outright tyranny, King Saul treats David as his number one enemy. David becomes a fugitive fleeing the wrath of Saul; finding food in unexpected places and under false pretences; anxious to acquire weapons; going into exile; faking madness in a dangerous situation; becoming the focal point of a growing rebel force.

David's temporary show of madness brings to mind the performance of Hamlet, prince of Denmark, who faced similar pressures. This ancient Danish legendary figure was selected by William Shakespeare for one of his most powerful works. Both David and Hamlet pretended to be mad as a strategy for survival.

Whenever I meditate on Shakespeare's Hamlet, I am struck by the ways in which he acts, thinks and speaks like a gay man. In many countries today, lesbian and gay people hide behind straight masks. They feel compelled to speak and act in certain ways to avoid hostility from their surroundings. Many marry an opposite-sex partner. Like David and Hamlet, their life situation does not reflect their true personalities.

A lifestyle based on pretence is emotionally draining and psychologically damaging. The healthiest lesbian and gay people are those who challenge prejudice and oppression. Like the rebels joining David, they associate with groups of human beings with whom they can stop pretending and be authentic.

Do you encourage truthfulness in your family and church community?

Spirit of truth, bless all your children who yearn to lead honest lives.

The arbitrariness of the death penalty

1 Samuel 22:6-23

At this stage King Saul's paranoia is growing. Rather than seeking the way of peace and doing the will of God, he becomes obsessed with power and perceives any unauthorised activity in his territory as a threat. As he accuses the priests of Nob of treason, they tell him the truth: they helped David, thinking that he was still in Saul's service. Yet Saul decides to have them killed. By letting the words of a single witness count as sufficient evidence, Saul clearly violates the laws of Israel (Numbers 35:30; Deuteronomy 17:6 and 19:15).

Saul's descent into despotism has modern parallels. Dictatorships tolerate no opposition. They suspend civil rights and have people arrested, tortured and perhaps executed on mere suspicion. Dictators take the powers of investigator, police, prosecutor, judge and executioner in their own hands.

The existence of the death penalty gives all tyrants a dangerous tool that they are prone to use. Wherever the death penalty is accepted, it may lead to miscarriages of justice. Periodically, it emerges in the US media that someone convicted did not receive due process and that evidence of their crime was insufficient. If we justify the use of the death penalty, we risk lending indirect moral support to despotic regimes that disregard the fundamental rights of their own citizens.

Is your church community aware of the dangers inherent in the death penalty?

God of life, let the seed of justice take root in our hearts.

Renato Lings

Overcoming evil with good

1 Samuel 24

Imagine that your worst enemy (Saul) is out to get you with a group of armed men. At a certain moment he goes into a cave to relieve himself discreetly. He does not know that you (David) and your followers are hiding deep inside the same cave. In this situation he unwittingly makes himself vulnerable to you. Your followers try to convince you to take him prisoner. Yet you decide to let him go unharmed because he once received a divine blessing. A moment later you step outside and tell him what has just happened. He acknowledges that you have repaid evil (persecution) with good (mercy).

Jesus teaches his disciples to pray for their enemies (Matthew 5:44). Paul tells his readers to bless those who persecute them (Romans 12:14). And 1 Peter 3:9 encourages Christians not to repay abuse for abuse but to say a blessing. Thanks to such New Testament references, we may tend to think that this principle has Christian origins. Yet the Hebrew Bible provides us with a striking example as David puts it into practice.

Most people, including myself, find the very idea of praying for their enemies an extremely difficult thing to do. Perhaps we have not realised how pivotal the biblical teaching of repaying evil with good is if we are to bring about real change in people's lives – and in our own.

Are you able to put this principle into practice?

God of mercy, thank you for repaying human evil with divine good.

Renato Lings

A second chance

1 Samuel 26

For the second time, King Saul has mobilised an army to catch fugitive David. In a daring move, David enters Saul's camp in the middle of the night. He is able to approach the sleeping Saul at arm's length. Yet again David has so much respect for Saul that he spares his life and removes only two significant objects. Subsequently David lets Saul know what has happened. Once again Saul seems to repent of his murderous intent.

David's ability to give Saul a second chance is extraordinary. Few people anywhere would be able to muster such resilience in the face of adversity. David does not seek revenge but fairness and justice. He may be at the receiving end of Saul's persecution, but what really matters to David is the fact that Saul was divinely chosen to be anointed king of Israel.

I am reminded of the unjust persecution of lesbian and gay people at the hands of authorities that call themselves Christian. Some people in authority believe they have a divine mandate to deal harshly with their fellow believers. This is happening today. Through no fault of their own, lesbian and gay people are treated like David at the hands of Saul. Yet many do not give up hope. They continue to believe in a God of justice and give Christianity a second chance.

Are you able to give someone who failed you a second chance?

Loving God, touch the hearts of today's persecutors and persecuted.

Obsessed with fear

1 Samuel 28:3-25

King Saul is becoming caught in the deadly spiral of his own unfortunate actions. Soon after persecuting and expelling all mediums and wizards from the land of Israel, he is seized by fear in the face of an imminent war with the Philistines. At this time he tracks down the only woman medium left and visits her in disguise at night to seek her help and advice. As she discovers his identity she is terrified but still agrees to call the spirit of Samuel, who has died recently. Samuel offers Saul no hope. He predicts the death of Saul and his sons on the battlefield.

Towards the end of his self-contradictory, erratic life, Saul is entirely unblessed. He trusts no one and even goes looking for help to the very people he has tried to eliminate. In several significant ways, the tragedy of Saul resembles the fate of Shakespeare's tyrant Macbeth. Like Saul, the latter seeks the advice of witches when things go terribly wrong.

One tragedy in the recent life of my own country, Denmark, is its current obsession with terrorism and the concomitant spirit of fear and suspicion. It has hurled us into unwinnable wars in Iraq and Afghanistan. It has made our government adopt xenophobic policies within our borders. As we push for 'democratic values' abroad, we are consistently undermining them at home.

Does your church community promote understanding, trust and love?

God of all nations, lead us out of our fears.

Battling against humiliation

1 Samuel 31

In Saul's final battle against the Philistines, his three sons are killed. He is badly wounded and unable to flee. So he asks his armour bearer to kill him for a specific reason: he is afraid that the 'uncircumcised' Philistines are approaching to literally 'penetrate' him and 'make a sport of him' (verse 4).

Saul's armour bearer refuses to obey the order and so Saul kills himself. Subsequently the Philistines make a triumphant display of the mutilated bodies of Saul and his sons. The corpses are stealthily retrieved at night by a group of Israelites from Jabesh-Gilead and brought back to be buried with dignity.

This may be the only episode in the Hebrew Bible in which a man speaks openly of the potential disgrace of sexual humiliation at the hands of a victorious enemy. On the battlefields of antiquity, the harsh procedure of male–male anal rape was a tangible way of reducing the vanquished party to slave status.

As I write, a similarly repulsive situation occurs daily in certain all-male prisons, including in so-called Christian countries. New inmates may be subjected to sexual abuse, often in the form of anal rape at the hands of 'senior' prisoners. In this very graphic manner a hierarchy is established and reinforced. This is not a matter of erotic attraction. The underlying impulse is the desire to assert male power.

Does your community provide any help to people who have suffered sexual abuse?

God of the oppressed, have mercy on all victims of rape.

Fathers

Fathers and children

Job 1:1-5

Father God?

'Pray "Our Father,"' said Jesus. 'If God is Father, then the father is God,' feminist theologians reply. As a father, I look to God to shape my 'fathering', and seek to reflect, in my 'fathering', something of God. But I know God is also *not* a father – God is mother, and lover, and friend, and stranger, and so many other metaphors that give us but a glimpse of the divine in the language and images of earth.

So how do the biblical texts portray fathers – earthly, ordinary, imperfect fathers? What images of God might we glimpse, and perhaps question, in those texts? And how might we respond, and be transformed – we fathers, yes, but also we mothers, lovers, friends, neighbours – we children, both of human parents and of God?

Job's pious, yet anxious, early morning prayers for his children do not, it turns out, protect them from life's tragedies. So Job cries out to God in righteous outrage. This world is not fair! And eventually, in the midst of a whirlwind, Job sees the vastness and complexity of the universe, he sees God eye-to-eye, and he is awestruck.

Dare we pray not for safety, but for awe and wonder for ourselves and our children?

Notes based on the New Revised Standard Version, by

Al Barrett

Al Barrett is a dad and a husband. He lives, and works as a parish priest, on a large urban 'outer estate' in east Birmingham, England. He also manages to do some reading, writing and odd bits of teaching on topics in feminist theology, child theology, liturgy, and community regeneration. Among his recent publications, he contributed to *Presiding Like a Woman* (Nicola Slee and Stephen Burns, SPCK, 2010).

Other people's children

Genesis 21:1-14

God made Abraham and Sarah a promise, a child – but because God takes God's own good time, Abraham and Sarah set about sorting it out for themselves. Abraham and Hagar conceive Ishmael – and then, of course, Sarah's promised child comes along! Suddenly, there is competition. Family inheritances, and God's promises, are at stake. Suddenly, the village 'isn't big enough for the both of us', as they used to say in those old Westerns.

As a parent, it's so easy to see my own child as a priceless treasure and other people's children as 'problems'. The English newspaper headline writers who demonise young people as 'wild animals' surely don't have their own children in mind? And when it comes to getting your child into the preferred school, it's every parent for themselves, isn't it?

But if God is for 'us', God is not necessarily against 'them'. That is the hard lesson that the children of Abraham, and we Christians as late-comers to the family, are still learning. God does not play 'zero–sum' ('I win, you lose') games. God keeps his promise to Abraham and Sarah, *and* provides for Hagar and Ishmael, journeying with them through the wilderness of Beer-sheba. All children are God's children. God calls us to joyful responsibility, not just for 'our own', but for all God's family.

Look for an opportunity this week to express love and generosity to someone else's children – especially those of parents who are quite unlike you – it might be risky!

Abba, Amma, bless 'those' children – you know who they are – and bless their parents too, with what they need to survive, and more.

Means to an end?

Psalm 127:3-5

My two-year-old son, Rafi, constantly surprises me with his imagination, his sense of fun, his capacity to learn: 'He can name six dinosaurs!' I proudly tell the world.

But Rafi is not some kind of not-so-secret weapon in my personal status games, his achievements 'gold stars' for my own 'parenting star chart'. My delight in his discoveries is misplaced when it becomes pride: those discoveries are not returns on my investment – they are pure gifts of God to him, which he, gratuitously, happens to share with me. And he is no means to my competitive adult ends, some kind of commodity I have produced and cultivated: he is pure gift to me: a gift unearned and undeserved, to be received with awe and gratitude at his otherness, and responded to and released with loving care.

In many parts of our world, children remain a vital life-line for their parents, saving the elderly and infirm from destitution. Our indifference to the poorest in our world lays heavy burdens on young shoulders, turns gifts into necessities.

But God gives gifts in many forms: I have friends for whom poetry, wisdom, hospitality, music, vision, are divine gifts, the awkwardness and otherness of which they wrestle with determinedly, and which they share with great generosity and humility.

What gifts has God given us? How can we treasure them, while holding them lightly? How can we share them with our neighbours – even our enemies?

Explore ways of supporting campaigns for the care of the world's most vulnerable children (e.g. www.unicef.org).

Abba, Amma, thank you for the wonderful, mysterious gifts you give me. Help me to hold them lightly and to share them bravely.

Stuck with our mistakes?

Genesis 27:30-40

My son can pull the wool over my eyes already. A 'trickster' like Jacob, he knows that saying 'No' when the truth is 'Yes' (and vice versa) can make his life easier, or happier, at least for a while. 'Have you washed your hands?' (Pause) 'Um... Yes, Daddy...'

Parents of two or more children have to deal with this all the time: learning to 'read' them, to spot the evasions of the truth, the manipulations of the situation (and of their siblings), is clearly an acquired skill. And all the books tell us that consistent parenting is essential, for building up mutual trust and establishing clear boundaries.

So what happens when we get it wrong, when the words are out of our mouth and we realise we've made a mistake? Is there no turning back? Are the courses of all our lives then irreparably fixed? Well, as it turns out, Esau finds a generosity of heart to forgive Jacob (Genesis 34) and, fatherly blessing or not, he, like his brother, enjoys life in abundance (Genesis 36). But the descendants of Esau-Edom and of Jacob-Israel are never, in the Hebrew Scriptures, the best of friends.

We are, in many ways, the inheritors of our parents' blessings, as well as their mistakes. But the stream of God's blessing does eventually burst its banks – the wounded Son, our Brother, does return to us, breathing forgiveness and peace, and inviting us to re–say our denials as affirmations of love.

Amma, Abba, gently unpick my mistakes, bless me with your healing love, and give me the courage to join you in remaking the world.

Not quite in on the action

Judges 13:1-24

Dads don't get a great press these days – not in our neighbourhood, anyway. Some are nowhere to be seen. Some are still around, but hardly active on the parenting front. Some get angry, sometimes violent.

Manoah's story stirs an awareness inside me that perhaps all we dads share: something about not quite being in on the heart of the action, however hard we might try. It's a blessing, of course, not being 'the child-bearer' – not going through the monthly bleeding, the swelling of pregnancy, the pain of labour and its after-effects; but it's also a bit of a curse. 'Woe is me,' mutters my wife, with hollow sympathy. But, in pregnancies less miraculous than Mrs Manoah's, mothers glimpse God's grace, fecundity, loving labour, in deeply incarnate ways, ways that we men can barely touch.

How do we all live faithfully, 'on the edges' of God's incarnate activity? With Manoah, might it include learning to trust the testimony of those on the inside, sitting lightly to our need to do/see/hear/feel it for ourselves? Learning that we aren't in control of the moments of encounter when they offer themselves? And learning to enjoy those moments, fully present, for as long as they last, rather than worrying about the next thing, however great or small? And if we begin to attend in those moments of grace, then perhaps we might slowly become of some use, when we're really needed.

When have you found yourself in on the heart of what God is doing? How has that felt? When have you found yourself closer to the edges of God's incarnate activity? How has that felt? What moments of grace have you been given at the edges? How have they changed you?

Abba, Amma, when I find myself on the edges of your incarnate activity, bless me with trust, patience, attentiveness, readiness.

'What have I done?!'

1 Samuel 2:12-17

The theologian Stanley Hauerwas tells of the vow his mother made, that she would dedicate her child to God if she conceived – as in the story of the birth of Samuel (just after today's passage). In this sense, Hauerwas describes himself as 'Hannah's child' (*Hannah's Child: A Theological Memoir*, SCM, 2010), but he asks himself, how much of his destiny was determined by his mum's vow, and did she really need to tell him about it?

Eli faces the opposite question: how much must he bear responsibility for his sons turning out to be a bunch of contemptuous scoundrels, and could he have done anything about it? I can imagine the old man tearing his hair out in despair, weighed down with the burden of parental – and priestly – guilt.

Philip Larkin suggests in his poem 'This be the verse', that parents 'f*** up' their children, with a tragic inevitability. As a priest and a father, I sometimes worry that 'God' and 'daddy's job' risk getting muddled as Rafi grows up, in ways that might make him resent both. Thankfully, we baptised him when he was still tiny – not to determine his destiny, but to throw open his care and nurture to a much wider and more diverse community than simply his two parents. And to throw ourselves in trust on the promise that, however much he and we mess up his life between us, the possibility of God doing an unlikely, unexpected, new thing, is just around the corner.

Amma, Abba, bless me with a community beyond my familiar walls, ease the burdens of guilt I carry alone, and surprise me with the new things you are doing that I can barely imagine.

'Listen, children...'

Proverbs 4:1-4

Is this God talking? Standing in that place and making those words one's own feels an audacious thing to do, but that hasn't stopped generations of fathers – Jewish and otherwise – daring to do so. I'm not sure I could.

'Listen carefully, my child' begins the Rule of St Benedict (www.osb.org), whose monks and nuns make three vows – 'obedience', 'stability' and 'conversion', vows that may perhaps contain within them the seeds of a life-giving wisdom, for parents, for children, and for communities that include both and others too.

In a world of hyper-mobility, where one computer company asks us 'Where do you want to go today?', 'stability' invites us to stay where we are, to stick with the people we're with, and to learn wisdom the hard way, through the knocks and struggles and difficult next-door neighbours.

In a world where the loudest voices wield the power, 'obedience' invites us to listen carefully, patiently, to the 'still, small voices', the youngest, the oldest, and the least articulate, in our midst – genuinely expecting insight and challenge to emerge from among 'the greatest in the kingdom of heaven' (Matthew 18:4).

And in a world where 'growing up' is for children only, 'conversion' announces a lifelong journey of growing up and learning from our mistakes, where we so-called 'independent' adults need to, as Jesus suggested, follow, rather than lead, little children into God's kingdom (Mark 10:15).

Commit to listening to a little child talking about what's most important to them (at least once, ideally more often). Expect to learn something that will change your outlook and/or your priorities.

Abba, Amma, bless me with patience to seek you in this place where I find myself; attentiveness to listen, especially to the unlikely voices; and an openness to grow and learn and change, today, and my whole life long.

Fathers

Perplexities of fatherhood

Notes based on the Jerusalem Bible by

Everlyn Chadi Kombe

Everlyn is a theological teacher at the Kenya Baptist Theological College in Kenya. She recently completed an MA in Applied Theological Studies at the Queen's Foundation, Birmingham.

2 Samuel 18:19-33

Hard lessons

Fatherhood in biblical times was a demanding role, no less than in our own time. I am writing from a Kenyan context of both Christian faith and indigenous tribal religions and shall draw on both to illuminate some of the challenges facing African society in its practice of fatherhood.

It was reported to Charo, the chief of the village in the Mijikenda community, that people were being disturbed by witchcraft, so a witch-hunter was brought in. Witchcraft has often led to family breakdowns and is also one of the sources of poverty in the Mijikenda community. To Charo's shock, the witch was Charo's own daughter. This incident is not unlike what David faced when his own son became a traitor. Although Yahweh protected David and gave his army victory, what kind of victory is it that involved the death of his own son? Society expected him to rejoice and express gratitude to Yahweh, and to reward the troops for the victory. On the contrary, David was torn between his feelings as a father and his duties as a king.

Sometimes fathers try to protect their children who are involved in serious crimes, failing to see that their action may cause great harm. David and Charo both discovered hard lessons through such difficulties, learning to trust in God despite the bad things that happened to their children.

Lord, help us to discern your will in both the bad and good things that happen to our children and to respond wisely.

Listening for true guidance

Matthew 1:18-25

Ben approached the church father, Mashanda, for a loan to take his sick father Joshua to the hospital for an operation (healthcare is very costly in my country). Joshua was diagnosed with cancer and had to undergo an operation within ten days. Alas, Ben did not have the 200,000 Kenyan shillings needed for the deposit in this emergency. The church father talked to the elders about the issue, but Ben's request was turned down because the church's limited funds were intended for the construction of the church hall and could not be used for an individual's operation. After several desperate attempts to raise the deposit failed, Joshua died of untreated cancer. The construction of the church hall also stopped because of conflicts among the leaders.

Such struggles in deciding what to do and discerning God's will are not a new phenomenon. Joseph was a righteous man and obedient to the law. He obviously wanted an equally righteous partner, but Mary's pregnancy was problematic. His moral beliefs guided him to do the right thing, to divorce her without causing public disgrace. However, before acting, Joseph took time to listen to God's voice and to discern God's will. He chose to follow the will of God in faith instead of doing what custom and culture considered the right thing. Had the church father and the elders taken time to listen to God, perhaps Joshua's life would have been saved.

God, help all fathers to have the ability to discern your will and to act in ways that please you, even when this means going against convention and culture.

Everlyn Chadi Kombe

Doing the will of God

Matthew 21: 28-31

Namwamba had become Christian at an early age. At thirty years old he was already a priest. He sometimes boasted of his faith by accusing his brother Nguma of not being a Christian and warning that he would end up in hell. However, Namwamba's behaviour was not consistent with his profession of faith. He once raped a widow who had come to the church for alms. He was also caught forging an invoice to steal a large amount of money from the church accounts. These and other issues got him excommunicated. Meanwhile, Nguma, whom he had taunted, had become a Christian and began to show in his own life a profound commitment to live out his faith by doing God's will.

The parable of the two sons represents people like Nguma, who prove better than they promise, and Namwamba, who promise better than they prove in reality. The religious leaders during Jesus' time demonstrated outwardly how they were committed to the law but in practice they rejected the will of the heavenly father (Matthew 21:28-31). Their rejection does not reverse the father's will because the prostitutes and tax collectors who showed no concern for the law submitted at last to God's authority, proving better than they promised.

Following the father's will requires both words and deeds.

Heavenly Father, have mercy on us and help all people to show commitment to your word in theory and practice.

Everlyn Chadi Kombe

Hope for healing

Luke 8:40-56

Emmanuel's son was a drug dealer and a wanted criminal. Emmanuel was traumatised by his son's activities, so that he began having counselling sessions with the church's minister, Karanja. In one of the counselling sessions, Emmanuel described his son's condition as deathly.

'There is still hope, through faith and prayer, and with wise counsel, that your son could be restored back to normal societal life,' Karanja assured Emmanuel, but Emmanuel saw no hope. His son's lostness was as if he had already died to him. In contrast, Jairus was a father who saw hope and had courage. He was one of the official leaders of the synagogue and proud of his position, associated, as it was, with the synagogue leaders' antagonism to Jesus. However, Jairus believed that Jesus could restore his daughter to health. In faith, Jairus' daughter was brought back to life. Jesus can be trusted to restore life to those who are lost, whatever condition of lostness is at issue. Although no father can compel a child to receive the healing offer of Jesus, this offer is never withheld from any.

Lord, help all fathers who are facing difficulties because of their children. Give them hope and courage to trust in your loving care, and to continue seeking healing for their children, however hopeless this may seem.

Freedom and faithfulness

John 8:39-59

Benjamin, a Presbyterian Church minister in one of the churches in Mombassa, trained all three of his children from childhood to become preachers. However, each child preferred to follow a different career path. The elder son, Kioko, became an army officer, and everyone in the neighbourhood remarked that he was so different from his father. Even though all the children were devoted Christians, Benjamin suffered depression because of their refusal to follow his path for them.

In ancient Israel, the common tradition was that a son was apprenticed to his father. This was Benjamin's understanding: Kioko was Benjamin's son, and he therefore should emulate his father's work of preaching. Benjamin was devastated by what he regarded as his failure to convince his son to follow the same calling, so much so that he did not regard his children's strong faith as worthy of commendation.

The best gift that fathers can give to their children is to teach them faith in God. Children will choose their own careers, but this does not indicate a failure on the fathers' part.

Lord, grant fathers your wisdom to teach your ways to their children, so that they in turn may teach truth to the next generation.

Everlyn Chadi Kombe — Fathers

Suffering and perplexity

Mark 9:14-29

John's daughter was highly educated at the best universities abroad. As a father, John wanted the best for her and was willing to spend everything he had to fund his daughter's travels. Despite his best efforts to bring her up in faith, she became confused and ganged up with criminals in international crime. John was bewildered and distressed beyond measure, wondering how this had come to be.

Today's text tells of a father, frustrated by his son's condition, who looks to Jesus to heal him. The disciples' efforts to exorcise the demon were in vain, and they were perplexed. Jesus emphasised the importance of prayer. Prayer and faith make a powerful combination as a way of leaning on God, whatever the issues, and such practices enhance communication between believers and God.

John took faith for granted as a secure possession that could safeguard his daughter, but belief alone does not supply the believer with power. Rather, faith needs to be received as a gift from God yet at the same time is something that needs much labour and effort, through prayer, worship, trust in God, and many other elements. Even so, there is no guarantee that what we hope for our children will be granted; sometimes, our faith is deepened and challenged precisely by the suffering we experience through our families.

Lord, help all frustrated fathers to trust in you and to bring their perplexities into your presence.

Everlyn Chadi Kombe

The hospitality of the father

Luke 15:11-32

Sam was one of the elders of Wesley Methodist Church. He had been a faithful member of the church since childhood. He tried his level best to assist each new minister posted to the church and they mostly regarded him as very resourceful, being impressed that he could answer almost all their questions concerning the history of the church. Thus Sam earned the title 'father'.

However, Sam was traditional in his approach to faith and quite unwelcoming of new ideas, especially modern evangelical ways of worship. He adopted an anti-youth stance, declaring: 'our children are a lost generation, they do not abide by the traditions'. His attitude had an impact on church membership, such that concerned members remarked that the church was dying. Sam was summoned by the church leadership and, through counselling, became aware of his own resistance to new ways and the need to be accommodating.

Sam's attitude can be compared to that of the older brother in today's well-known story. He boasted of his faithfulness and was not willing to welcome the prodigal son back into the family, but the one who suffered the most from his harsh attitude was himself. He excluded himself from the hospitality of his father, as well as trying to exclude others.

Lord, give us strength to accept all people, even those we consider lost or misguided. Help us not to be a hindrance to others. Help everyone to experience your love through us.

Fathers

Care and counsel

Notes based on the New International Version by **Francis Sencherey**

Francis Sencherey is an Anglican priest. He is the chaplain and a teacher of Christian Religious Studies at St Monica's Senior High School in Ghana, West Africa. He is married with five children. He has enjoyed the benefit and wisdom of different 'fathers', including people who have had a fatherly influence in his life.

Hosea 11:1-4

Our father's care

In this week's readings, I shall relate the Akan ethnic group's concept of fatherhood, in which the uncle, stepfather, father-in-law, foster father, the guardian (male), the master in apprenticeship, the elderly man, 'the cockerel (akoko-nnini)' (the responsible single mother) and the biological father are each seen and recognised as father – with shared and corporate responsibility. This cultural experience of fatherhood, wider and more complex than in many Western societies, offers us a rich and wonderful model of God's paternal care.

The Akan forms the largest ethnic group in Ghana's population of about twenty-four million. Over ten linguistic groups make up the Akan people in Ghana. The Akan are located in the southern and middle parts of the country, stretching from the coast in the south to the Gonja state in the north, and from the Volta in the east to the Ivory Coast border in the west. They occupy about one half of the country's land surface and constitute about fifty per cent of the population. They possess more than five of the ten regions in Ghana.

As both women and men readers, I invite you each to learn this week from my experience of fatherhood, drawn from this context. You are encouraged to compare your own cultural and religious understandings of fatherhood with mine, to see where you are challenged as well as encouraged to imitate the perfect fatherhood of God, which goes beyond any and every cultural model.

Father God, teach us the true nature of your paternal love.

A father's counsel

Exodus 18:18-23

Traditionally, in Ghanaian society, the relationship of fathers-in-law with their sons-in-law has always been close, sometimes to the point of becoming custodians of family secrets, treasury and the future care of the family. They play a significant role in the transfer of family wisdom, similar to the way in which, in today's passage, Moses becomes a beneficiary of Jethro's (his father-in-law), wisdom.

The counsel of Jethro relates to the delegation of power, something that is encouraged to ensure the sound health and smooth running of society and to maintain purpóseful leadership. The leadership was Moses', yet his respect for his father-in-law opens an opportunity for counsel to direct that leadership. Moses stands tall as a prophet of God, yet the excellence of his father-in-law in politics becomes a guide for him. This enables Moses' political zeal to be governed by discretion.

Jethro, as both priest and leader, transferred his experiential knowledge to his son-in-law, who was willing to learn from him and apply his counsel to the situation. An Akan proverb says, 'When a child knows how to wash the hand, he/she eats with the elderly.' That is to say, when young people humble themselves, the elderly open up treasures of wisdom for their benefit. Like the pearl, fathers' counsel is not thrown before swine, but many children have benefited from the wise counsels of fathers.

Help us, heavenly Father, to learn from the example of scripture how to offer fatherly care and counsel to the next generation.

A father's discipline

Hebrews 12:7-12

'No discipline seems pleasant at the time, but … later on …, it produces a harvest of righteousness and peace for those who have been trained by it,' (verse 11). Right and loving discipline needs, of course, to be distinguished from the abuse of power by parents and others in positions of trust, something we are becoming much more aware of.

Being a true and a legitimate child is linked, in both biblical and some cultural contexts, to submission to discipline. The Akan says, 'The hen's feet step on the chick, yet it does not kill the chick.' The free-range hen fends for the chicks, and in doing so she sometimes inadvertently steps on her chicks milling about her. Her intention is not to kill but to provide food.

Jesus compares himself to a mother hen caring for her chicks (Matthew 23:37), although he is perhaps less careless of his young than many an earthly bird! Nevertheless, the Akan's homely saying may provide another way of thinking about how, as true children, we have to endure hardship as part of a discipline that brings us to the expected harvest.

As parents and people responsible for the care of others, we learn from God, our heavenly Father, the perfect way of discipline. Abuse never substitutes for love and parental irresponsibility does not produce the good harvest of discipline. It is only when discipline emerges out of genuine care and compassion that it will produce the fruits of right action and character.

Heavenly Father, help us to acknowledge and appreciate the hardship meant for our training, and to submit to your gentle discipline.

Francis Sencherey

God knows and remembers who we are

Psalm 103:13-14

Earthly fathers have compassion on their children and do good to them for different reasons – to compensate for their children's lack of knowledge, to care for them when they are sick or in trouble, to lift them up when fallen, to comfort them when they have been wronged, and for many other reasons. Although human fathers' compassion is not perfect or wholly consistent, it is generally offered with genuine love and true affection. It may not be wholly sufficient in the child's life, yet it is tender and a cause for good. It may be limited, yet it can still model for us something of the compassion of the Lord that is, nevertheless, a more perfect compassion – always reliable and sufficient, unlimited in its tenderness and available to all who will call upon it.

'The chick that is closer to the mother hen eats the thigh of the grasshopper,' is a proverb of the Akans. It suggests that closeness and dependence upon parental care ensures an adequate supply of one's needs. Knowing our own frailty and mortality, that 'we are dust' (verse 14), as the psalm puts it, we recognise our need to depend on the loving kindness of God. This does not mean failing to take appropriate and proper responsibility for our own livelihood and the wellbeing of those who are under our care, but it indicates the appropriate spiritual attitude of trust and intimacy that is demanded of all God's children.

God knows how we are formed, remembering that we are dust. God formed us from the dust and knows our nature. God, therefore, compassionately and tenderly considers our vulnerability, and the fragility of even our best efforts and accomplishments. God has compassion on our sorrows. The Lord cares, and knows that we are vulnerable.

Teach us to know who we are, that we may fear you and submit to your tender care.

Francis Sencherey

A father's charge

1 Kings 2:1-4

Here is a charge, and a set of instructions, given to a son and declared successor. He is charged to keep the will of the Lord his God. This is the way to succeed with honour and satisfaction. Although it may seem quite alien to a contemporary Western society, where much store is set by individual fulfilment and freedom of choice, in traditional settings it is axiomatic that children have a duty to fulfil their parents' hopes, even though increasingly this is being challenged.

Though the authority of a dying father may be great, it cannot be compared to that of the living God. God is faithful to his promises. Let us therefore keep the charge of the Lord our God carefully, as those who must give account. As we keep God's charge, God will surely honour the promise given to us.

The last word of a dying man is trustworthy; it is regarded as the very heartbeat of a dying soul and, therefore, has particular authority. Those to whom it is entrusted feel a great responsibility to honour the wishes of the dying person, and will not set aside their charge without very good reason.

On his deathbed, David charges and instructs his son Solomon to keep the statutes of God, so that he may succeed and prosper. Success, prosperity and perpetuity of the crown in the house of David were tied to Solomon's obedience to the Law of Moses. Therefore, Solomon was instructed to be strong and show himself as one capable of obeying God.

Pray that you may honour truthfully your earthly parents, in the way that is appropriate in your own cultural setting and that, by doing so, you may learn more deeply about the nature of the true worship and honour of God.

A communal relationship

Ephesians 6:1-4

Children are instructed to obey their parents, and the father is ordered not to exasperate the children but to bring them up in the training and instruction of the Lord. In teaching, the father is not to be abusive, but serve as a role model in conduct and speech to the child. He is to be an example of 'the fear of the Lord'. Once the child is taught the fear of the Lord, he or she will not depart from it.

An Akan proverb says, 'Okoto nnwo anomaa' – 'The crab does not give birth to a bird', in other words, the influence and character of the parent is seen in the life of the child. We see the parent mirrored not only in the physical appearance of the child, but very often, too, in the qualities and characteristics of the offspring. The meanness or volatile temperament of a parent is passed on to the child just as a happy, sunny disposition and a trusting nature may be handed on from parent to child. Although this is not a universal law (children can rework their psychological heritage and forge their own characters, to some degree), it is sufficiently true for the proverb to make sense.

The proverb can suggest at the same time the responsibility of the parent and the child in the formation of character. If the father is to instruct the child with tenderness and compassion, so the child has a responsibility to receive the instruction with humility and respect. Children are to obey their parents in all things that are lawful and good (but not in those that are not), for the Lord has commanded it. Parents are to seek to pass on to their children all that makes for sound health and prosperity, not only in their own families, but in the wider society too.

Teach us, good Lord, to honour both parent and child in all our conduct and relationships.

The Lord's counsel

Matthew 7:7-11

The imperfection of many earthly parents in relation to their children is shockingly evident in society today, perhaps more so than ever. We are increasingly aware of the different ways in which parents abuse their power, particularly through physical and sexual abuse, as well as in other more covert or unintentional ways. Even so, earthly parents, though they may be evil, are rarely wholly without love and affection for their offspring, giving willingly to their children what they ask for.

Jesus has spoken of prayer in the previous chapter as a duty commanded by God to be honoured, and which, if done aright, will be rewarded. Here he speaks of prayer as the appointed means of obtaining all that we need in our physical and spiritual lives. The asking, the knocking and the seeking are different metaphors for intercessory prayer, and in each case Jesus makes it very clear that God is fundamentally predisposed to grant the needs of his children, as earthly parents usually are.

God, our heavenly father, knows us intimately as his children and knows both what we are and what we need. The readiness of earthly parents to give good gifts to their children should encourage us to pray to God for what we need. If even imperfect parents can be trusted to give gifts to their children, how much more can the perfect heavenly parent be relied upon to meet every need of his offspring. And whatever love and tenderness earthly fathers manifest are themselves gifts from God, our heavenly father. However inadequate our own love as parents may be, or the love we have received from our parents is, there are few of us who cannot recognise something in this imperfect love of the enduring love of God.

Teach us, O God, to pray aright – to ask, to seek and to knock so that we may receive the abundance of your gifts for us.

Francis Sencherey

Order now for 2013!

It may seem early, but the copies of *Words for Today 2013* and *Light for our Path 2013* are now available to order.

Order now:

- with your local IBRA Rep*
- in all good bookshops
- direct from IBRA

online: http://shop.christianeducation.org.uk/

email: sales@christianeducation.org.uk

phone: 0121 472 4242

post: using the order form at the back of this book

If ordering direct, postage is free of charge.

*If you purchase 6 copies or more, and you live in the UK, you can sign up as an IBRA Rep and claim the 10% IBRA Rep discount on all IBRA products. You will also receive a free poster and samples to help you share IBRA more easily with family, friends and others in your church. Contact staff at IBRA to sign up now!

A whole year's Bible reading notes for only *17p* a week!

Consider a legacy

Help us to continue our work of providing Bible study notes for use by Christians in the UK and throughout the world. The need is as great as it was when IBRA was founded in 1882 by Charles Waters as part of the work of the Sunday School Union.

Please leave a legacy to the International Bible Reading Association.

An easy-to-use leaflet has been prepared to help you provide a legacy. Please write or telephone (details below) and we will send you this leaflet – and answer any questions you might have about a legacy or other donations. Please help us to strengthen this and the next generation of Christians.

Thank you very much.

International Bible Reading Association
1020 Bristol Road
Selly Oak
Birmingham
B29 6LB
UK

Tel. 0121 472 4242
Fax 0121 472 7575

IBRA
International Bible Reading Association

Readings in Mark (3)

Who is this?

Notes based on the New Revised Standard Version by

Barbara Calvert

Barbara Calvert is a Methodist minister in the Orpington and Chislehurst circuit. Previously she has been a Religious Education teacher, worked for Christian Aid, and been a university chaplain in Glasgow.

Mark 6:1-13

Discovering Jesus

I recall one particular year when I was a secondary school RE teacher, waking up on the first day of the Easter holidays. It had been an exhausting term, and I could really have enjoyed a lovely restful lie-in. But it was Good Friday, so there was our local ecumenical walk of witness to join. I remember lying in bed thinking, 'I am getting up early this morning, the first day of the holidays, simply because of a man who lived two thousand years ago.' That thought struck me afresh as extraordinary. But ever since Jesus began his Galilean ministry people have responded by participating, even in really extraordinary and courageous ways.

Each story this week invites us to enter into the deep faith question of who Jesus Christ is. We will not find answers by reading a book (or lying in bed!) but by participating in the communal life of the followers of Jesus. This is what the disciples discovered through being sent out as participants in the activities of the ministry of Jesus – proclaiming, healing and casting out demons. It was in doing this that they began to answer the question: who is this Jesus of Nazareth?

Jesus, help me to find you afresh this day.

Seek healing and leap for joy

Mark 2:1-12

How do you know when you are in love? This is a question I can remember troubling me when I was a teenager. What is it like to love someone? Will I know when I am in love? Love defies definition. Perhaps only when we experience love are we able to recognise it. Many lovers would describe the experience of feeling they can see into their lover's heart, of gazing at one another and seeing into their inner being, as if their heart and soul are intertwined. A popular symbol of love is two hearts overlapping and an arrow pierced through them both, bound together in a love that reaches to the heights and depths of human emotion.

Jesus is like a lover in this sense. Jesus can see into our hearts. Following a very successful preaching tour around Galilee, when Jesus healed many physical and mental illnesses, crowds have gathered outside his home in Capernaum. The friends who bring the paralysed man to Jesus are seeking physical healing for the man, so that he might be able to walk again. But Jesus looks into his heart and sees deep into his soul. Jesus offers healing of body, mind and soul.

Sin is much more than wrongdoing. It includes the confusion, doubts and shadows that dwell in our innermost being. Like a lover, Jesus sees into our hearts, looks into the depths of our souls, and cleanses us – bringing joy, meaning and fulfilment so that we can leap up and glorify God.

Jesus, help me to see you in your piercing love.

Come in, take a seat

Mark 2:15-17

As I write, my church is undergoing a major refurbishment. One of the things we are doing is taking out the pews and replacing them with upholstered, movable chairs. As the church is not a very old building, the pews are of no great merit. There were no special small, narrow and uncomfortable pews at the front for the maids from the Big House. And there were no labels indicating that this pew was for the local gentry family only. Nevertheless, people had their favourite place to sit, just as if it had their name engraved on it. So it's not surprising that some long-standing families have bought and taken back home the very pew their family occupied for so many years. In those days, people knew their place! Many of us will have had experiences of visiting churches and being asked to move because we have sat in someone's seat. Not very welcoming!

I wonder at the welcome Jesus received at Levi's house. Levi and his friends – fellow tax collectors and sinners, outcasts of all kinds – are partying together, rejoicing and enjoying themselves. And there, sat in the middle of them, was Jesus. But the religious, upright citizens are horrified. Jesus is friends with moral and religious outcasts, such company will contaminate him, and he is eating in their homes with scant regard for Jewish food laws. Jesus doesn't know his place. He is sat in the wrong seat.

And that's where we find him today. Alleluia!

Jesus, help me to see you in unexpected places.

Barbara Calvert

Living in God's Spirit

Mark 3:20-30

In January 2009 much of the world rejoiced as Barack Obama, on the steps of the White House, was sworn in as the first black President of the United States. Many Americans could not believe their eyes. Those interviewed, especially members of the black or Hispanic underclass, seemed to stand taller, to be able to look up and take pride in 'one of their own' becoming President. They couldn't be dismissed and trampled underfoot again.

But not everyone rejoiced. The traditional ruling elite, the right-wing conservatives, could not believe their eyes either. It was not long before malicious rumours were spread about Obama: he was not a true American citizen; he was a closet Muslim; he was pilloried for seeking to destroy wealthy people's access to health care; it was even whispered that he was a socialist! Obama had overthrown the traditional boundaries of the powerful elite, and its opposition became more threatening and more dangerous.

Jesus gave the underclass hope. His preaching tour around Galilee had been full of encounters with ordinary humble people on the edge – farmers and fishermen, women, outcasts, sinners, people who knew their powerlessness but saw in Jesus the hope of liberation. The religious rulers are outraged and scandalised by Jesus, who has overthrown the traditional boundaries and usurped their power. They recognise Jesus has supernatural power. The issue is what sort of supernatural power, where has it come from – the devil or the Spirit of God? To believe it was the Spirit of God would be to destroy for ever their right to govern for their own advantage, and to oppress the poor.

Jesus, help me to see you in every encounter.

Seek peace

Mark 4:35-41

The beauty of God our creator is revealed as we gaze at a cloudless blue sky, as we feel the gentle refreshing rain, the soft breeze and the warmth of the sun. But the power of God is revealed too in God's creation as thunder clashes, lightning strikes, hailstones pound, volcanoes burst forth and earthquakes rumble with awesome and terrible power.

The disciples have left the crowds behind. They are in a small boat far from shore, adrift from all the props of daily living. Bereft of all their securities, they are alone. And in that aloneness with all other distractions stripped away, they experience God. They experience God in the power of the storm, in the terrifying wind and the lashing waves that threaten to overwhelm them. But they also experience God in the sleeping Jesus. At a time of disaster the Psalmist too cried to God,

Rouse yourself! Why do you sleep, O Lord?
Awake, do not cast us off forever!
Why do you hide your face?
Why do you forget our affliction and oppression?
Psalm 44:23-24

God comes in Jesus as a storm, disturbing our complacency, challenging our inaction in the face of an unjust and suffering world. But in Jesus God also comes as prince of peace, offering us refuge and a safe harbour.

Jesus, help me to see you in both calm and storm.

Pause awhile

Mark 6:45-52

This passage, like many another in Mark's Gospel, begins with the word 'immediately'. Mark takes us through the events of Jesus' ministry at breath-taking speed. The events leading up to Jesus walking on the water take place immediately following the miraculous feeding. Jesus has fed the five thousand and then immediately sends the disciples away in the boat. The disciples disperse. Then Jesus sends the satisfied crowd away.

Now he is alone. The desire of Jesus to have some time alone provides us too with a pause. We are able to take breath, to reflect and, as if invisible bystanders, look on as Jesus goes alone up the mountain to pray. We have a pause in the relentless pace of Mark's narrative as Jesus isolates himself for a while to be alone with God.

After spending time in prayer, evening falls and we see Jesus coming down the mountain alone, and then his solitary figure standing on the seashore in the fading light. Jesus gazes out across the Galilean sea and sees the disciples in the boat struggling against an adverse wind.

In the struggles of the disciples with the oars, the tools of life, we can see our own struggles. Jesus comes towards us, walking on the water but he does not impose. He is there, at hand, inviting us to call out to him. Jesus feeds us, he soothes our fears, he calms the storms, he is with us but also he is set apart, walking on the sea of life, the holy one.

Jesus, help me to see you in the pauses of life.

Plunge in

Mark 11:27-33

Travelling around Europe as a student on Inter-rail, many years ago, I remember visiting Olympia in Greece and looking in awe on the remains of the original Olympic running track, dating back over two thousand years. Today, not far from my home in south-east London, I have watched with interest as the 2012 Olympic site has taken shape over the last few years. Our modern world requires huge sums of money to be spent and extraordinarily complex arrangements made. But the Olympic Games today are founded on the tradition of the Olympics of ancient Greece and then, as now, the success of the games depends on one thing, participation. Sportswomen and men have to prepare and train, come together and compete. And for the games to come alive, the stadium, race tracks, sports arenas and swimming pool need to be alive with the participation of the cheering crowds.

Throughout Mark's story of the Galilean ministry of Jesus, Jesus has challenged all those he encountered to participate: to walk on the water with him, to experience his healing, to share the feast together. In contrast, the religious leaders of the day keep their distance. They burden people with ever more complex religious rules and purity laws, and take refuge in the inner temple where, for many of the very people Jesus has reached out to, entry is forbidden.

Fearful of his power and his growing number of followers, the chief priests, the scribes and the elders seek the equivalent of a written statement from Jesus declaring the source of his authority. Jesus cannot give them any such thing. It would be meaningless. To recognise the source of his authority we are challenged to plunge into the pool and participate. The question then falls away.

Jesus, help me to see you in every challenge to follow you.

Readings in Mark (3)

He is...

Notes based on the New Revised Standard Version by

Helen-Ann Hartley

Helen-Ann Hartley is Director of Biblical Studies and Lecturer in New Testament at Ripon College, Cuddesdon, UK.

Mark 6:14-29

The word's out!

'King Herod heard of it, for Jesus' name had become known' (verse 14). So begins this dramatic account of the death of John the Baptist (or John the Dipper, as a friend of mine puts it, reflecting more accurately the literal actions of this wildly prophetic character). This complex account starts with Herod's curiosity and leads to a retrospective account of John's execution. Note, too, how Jesus' identity is refracted against the identity of others around him and before him. Throughout this week, our focus is on that identity and how it is revealed in a variety of contexts in Mark's Gospel.

This desire to delve deeper into the mystery of who Jesus is is often referred to as 'Christology' (picking up on one of the keys points of Jesus' identity, his 'Messiahship'). It is something that affects each one of us in our daily lives. As we shape ourselves as disciples against the pattern of Jesus, we need constantly to be thinking about how we can bear witness to Jesus in all that we do.

Reflect on how Jesus' life, death and resurrection influence your own life.

God our Creator, we thank you that you became one of us in your Son, Jesus Christ. May our lives be a blessing to others, and may we show forth the love of your abiding presence in all that we do this week.

'Who do people say that I am?'

Mark 8:27-33

This is perhaps one of the most well-known passages from the gospels, and the links from yesterday's reading are clear. Straightaway Jesus is identified with John the Baptist, and with Elijah, and with one of the prophets. There's clearly something about Jesus that resonates very powerfully with people's understanding of these other biblical characters. It is Peter, however, who proclaims the most fully formed understanding of who Jesus is, at least from the perspective of hindsight: the Messiah. But then Peter misunderstands the situation and is rebuked rather harshly by Jesus, who proceeds to foretell his own death.

Mark's purpose here is twofold: first, to clarify who Jesus is and, second, to link this to the pattern of discipleship that his followers are to embrace in their own lives. Both are important. Mark, presumably needing to explain to his audience how exactly the Messiah would be killed in the most shameful of ways, reinterprets this title to account for the reality of the cross. In so doing, Mark brings alive the reality of discipleship and confronts us with what that means for us today.

Following Jesus, indeed, proclaiming Jesus' identity, can be tough in today's world. But, as we think about who Jesus is to us, we might also think about how other people view Jesus (even as irrelevant), and how we might ourselves describe who Jesus is in ways that are helpful and meaningful.

Who do you say that Jesus is?

God our redeemer, we pray for courage in our lives as disciples to make known your presence in our communities. We remember those who struggle to proclaim their faith through oppression and danger, and we ask for your strength in their lives.

The sea, a crowd and a revelation!

Mark 3:7-12

Mark's Gospel is full of a sense of time and place. His narrative ebbs and flows like the tide and, so often, events focus around the Sea of Galilee. We can picture the scene of Jesus being pursued by a great crowd of people. There is clearly something about him that attracts people to him and, indeed Mark tells us that they came from all over. In this narrative, however, the revelation comes not from a person but from the unclean spirits that Jesus sought to banish from their human hosts. 'You are the Son of God' (verse 11) was their cry but, far from affirming their declaration, Jesus tells them to do the very opposite, to be silent.

Mark is keen to portray Jesus as powerful in word and deed but also to show that his identity takes him into the realm of opposition (so unclean spirits are a precursor to those who oppose Jesus by misunderstanding him). The declaration that Jesus is 'Son of God' harks back to the opening of the gospel and also links forward to the use of that title in Jesus' trial and crucifixion. Thus Mark is linking this narrative to the lives of his audience, who may well have experienced opposition. The sea itself is often a metaphor for chaos, and this is another significant feature of the story. In overcoming the sea, Jesus is witnessing to God's powerful acts in the world through him.

How do you experience opposition to your faith?

God of order, we pray for a bold declaration of your love in places of chaos in our own world.

Explaining Elijah

Mark 9:9-13

This narrative follows the story of the Transfiguration, which itself follows the Old Testament model of the descriptions of Moses on Mount Sinai in Exodus 24 and 34. The discussion between Jesus and his disciples in today's passage relates Jesus' identity to the cross and to Elijah and John the Baptist (once again, these two important characters play a role in our understanding of who Jesus is). Mark's point here is to link John rather than Jesus with Elijah. What emerges from this passage is a much deeper appreciation of Jesus' death and resurrection as vital events in the ushering in of God's kingdom.

Also mentioned in this passage is one of the other important titles attached to Jesus: 'Son of Man' (verse 12). This title, despite its mysterious qualities, perhaps tells us more about Jesus' identity than the title 'Son of God'. Even though 'Son of God' may sound to us a more honorific title, it was in fact commonplace for it to be used of human beings, whereas 'Son of Man', with its overtones of the divine figure in Daniel 7, is a far more evocative identity marker, indicating Jesus' divinity that itself is a vital part of his humanity. All this reminds us of the connection between Jesus' identity and the coming of the kingdom of God. Who we understand Jesus to be and how we articulate his presence in our world today is a continuing part of the bringing in of God's rule.

At this point in the week, who is Jesus for you?

God of the old and of the new, we thank you for the richness of your revelation to us and we pray that, through the work of your Son, Jesus Christ, and inspired by your Holy Spirit, we may continue that work of witness to which we are called daily.

The woman with the alabaster jar

Mark 14:1-9

I am always fascinated by the details Mark chooses to include in his narrative. Like the woman with the alabaster jar. Quite a lot of narrative space is given over to what she did for Jesus, and we are told that she was to be remembered for her actions. There are interesting parallels to this story in the Psalms, particularly the notion of the suffering just person who is surrounded by enemies and persecuted. Psalm 23:5 is particularly notable: 'You prepare a table before me in the presence of my enemies; you anoint my head with oil; my cup overflows.'

Here in Mark, Jesus is at table; his enemies watch; and his head is anointed (only Mark contains this significant detail). The anointing itself is certainly pointing us to a deeper understanding of Jesus' identity (anticipating his death). But more significant are the actions of the woman: she enters what would have been a male-only gathering; she touches Jesus, and her use of ointment seems extravagant. Jesus' point is that the poor can be served at every Passover, but that Jesus will depart from his disciples to face crucifixion. Thus, the woman allows us to see Jesus as the suffering Messiah. The question remains, however: how much do we remember what this woman did for Jesus, as Jesus commands us to do?

Take time today to reflect on the actions of the woman who anointed Jesus, and how your own actions help to bear witness to who Jesus is.

God, we give you thanks for the extravagant riches that you pour out upon us daily. Help us to remember the actions of this woman, and to appreciate the acts of kindness that we see in our midst.

Helen-Ann Hartley

How many for dinner?!

Revelation 21: 2, 9–11

I suspect that the demands of emergency catering for such a large crowd would defeat most of us and I have a good deal of sympathy for the somewhat exasperated words of Jesus' disciples. There is a wonderful painting of this scene by the artist Eularia Clarke, inspired by her visit to Canvey Island in the Thames Estuary. We see a great crowd of people feasting on fish and chips. Children are playing, some are so full they are taking a nap, and right up in the corner we see the hands of a preacher in a pulpit. What we take from this story is a sense of the reality of the incarnation, the meeting of a practical need (hunger), and the extravagance of God's mercy in providing the food.

Mark rather significantly places this narrative next to the banquet Herod held for his special guests, at which John the Baptist was killed. By contrast, Jesus' 'banquet' is open to everyone: the kingdom of God is not an exclusive domain only for the rich and powerful. Jesus' vision of power is quite different. There is one detail of this passage that is easy to overlook, however, and that occurs right at the beginning. The introduction highlights a contrast between Jesus' desire for solitude and his concern to meet the needs of the crowd. His observation that the crowd is a flock without a shepherd is yet another indication of who Jesus is in Mark's eyes.

Reflect today on the theme of hospitality, and the ways in which you receive and give it in your own life.

God of the banquet, we thank you that you are there to meet our needs. We pray for compassion throughout our world for those places and situations where the need is great; for the right and proper sharing of resources; and for wisdom to those in positions of power.

An ending, or is it just the beginning?

Mark 16:1-8

This is one of my favourite passages in Mark. It's easy to see why some found it to be such an unsatisfactory ending to the gospel that alternative endings were suggested. Mark, however, ends his gospel in this way quite deliberately, abruptly even, much like his bold declamatory start (Mark 1:1-3).

I once heard a novelist asked why some of his books end by leaving us with more questions than answers. One of his books ends with two characters having a conversation off the page, so we never really know what happens next. His answer was quite simple: 'Life is not neat.' The women leave the tomb afraid, saying nothing, or so we are led to believe. A more accurate translation of the word 'fear' ('afraid' in NRSV) is 'awe' (verse 8), a reaction that so many characters have in the Bible to the presence of God.

Surely the women must have said something to someone (the other gospels certainly think so)? Mark's point, however, is more for us, the readers of his gospel. We are invited to read his narrative again, but this time in the light of the resurrection, which has been poured out upon us. The result of this is that, as disciples, we are then charged to go forth and proclaim who Jesus is. Thus Mark suggests that the real ending of the gospel might not be its literal end, but rather that the ending lies in our own lives – lives that are lived out in his resurrection light.

God who revealed yourself in the life and work of your Son, Jesus Christ, we give you thanks that you journey with us in our lives as disciples. We pray for ourselves, for our hopes and fears, and ask you to bless us this day, and always.

Not to the swift

Running with an attitude

Notes based on the New Revised Standard Version, by
Gary Colville

Gary Colville is vicar of St Peter's with St Margaret's, Rochester. In 2009 his sabbatical took him 'around the world in eight Olympic sites' to study the churches' involvement in the Olympic Games. Gary is a member of the Rochester Diocese Olympic Focus Group. For information on how the church is involved in the London Olympics go to www.morethangold.org.uk.

Hebrews 12:1, 12–13

Let the games begin

At the end of this week the 2012 Olympics and Paralympics will begin in London. It will be a pentecostal experience of over fifty days, featuring forty-six sports.

Most of us will have at least a grudging admiration for athletes and some of us find them awe inspiring. There may be some who are critical of the costs involved in putting on the Olympics and many of us will wonder about the legacy of it all. We should pray that, in time, the aspirations of encouraging younger people to aim high and to contribute great things to society will find fruition. Moreover, an area of great deprivation has been transformed to offer better opportunities for employment, housing and perhaps a more level playing field: 'a straight path' for the disadvantaged, the disabled and the impoverished.

I hope and pray that God will give us all the right attitude towards this great sporting event and that, as we run the race of faith together, we will be looking to Jesus, the pioneer and perfecter of our faith. He is the one who runs, walks, stands or lies beside us all the way.

Lord, you seized me and I could not resist you. I ran for a long time, but you followed me. I took by-paths but you knew them. You overtook me. I struggled, you won. Here I am, Lord, out of breath, no fight left in me, and I've said 'yes' almost unwillingly…

Michel Quoist, *Prayers of Life*, Gill & Son, 1963, p.110

Keep your eyes on the prize

Hebrews 12:2-4

Holding something as we pray or meditate can provide a helpful focus and perhaps even motivation in our discipleship. I find it helpful holding on to a cross; this has often led me to insight and a refreshed commitment to follow Christ's way. It was at the foot of a cross on a Good Friday that I was convinced and convicted of my sin and forgiveness by God through Jesus Christ. Through the power of the Holy Spirit I was empowered to offer myself for service in Christ's church as a priest. Before that I'd been a police officer and a professional firefighter and a bit of a sportsperson too! In all these arenas I needed to have the right focus and motivation; people's lives depended on it.

Athletes competing in the Olympics similarly need the right focus and motivation. I remember Colin Jackson, a world record holder, telling me that it was absolutely necessary to have the right focus going into a race. Colin was honest enough to recognise that it was when this was lacking that he didn't perform at his best.

Today's reading exhorts those running the race of faith to keep our focus on the prize and to find our motivation as we 'look to Jesus' so that we do not grow weary or lose heart.

What is it that keeps you focused and motivated and what is it that distracts?

Pray or meditate, perhaps with a small cross in hand, that God will help you keep your eye on the prize, and that you will be willing to give yourself for others as Christ gave himself for you at Golgotha.

Values for the race

1 Timothy 6:1-6

One of the funniest emails I've ever had (and I've had a lot) arrived with the title: 'Why can't I own Canadians?' You won't be surprised that it came from a citizen of the USA! The humorous content had a serious intent; the writer was seeking to challenge those of us who justify dogmatic theological views by appealing to scripture, especially those who take a few sentences from the Bible to justify so-called Christian values regarding human sexuality. We were urged to consider carefully how the Bible has been used throughout history to justify slavery (hence 'why can't I own Canadians?'), the subjugation of women, support for the death penalty and the exploitation of creation. There are many worldly values that need to be challenged in the name of faith.

As far as the Olympics are concerned, an important value has been added to the excitement of a major global sporting event, and that is that the games should provide a lasting legacy to the nation in which they take place. Working through 'More than Gold', the churches have recognised the importance of this aim, and this year will be focusing on a prayerful protest to end slavery, especially the exploitation of the sex trade. This is a global concern and, in my humble opinion, is as urgent as global warming. Until we see an end to such evil in our midst, I hope and pray that this will remain a core value underpinning the race of faith.

Your will be done, Lord, we pray. We know it's not your will that so many are exploited and cruelly treated in the sex trade. Let your people go free, we plead. Help us to use our freedom to set free all who are enslaved by the evils of our time.

Strength for the weak

Isaiah 40:20-31

When reflecting on the state of any individual, group, business or church, organisational theory offers a tool through SWOT analysis, which focuses on key strengths, weaknesses, opportunities and threats. In my case, there are always more strengths than weaknesses, many more opportunities than threats; my glass is always half full. I resonate with a rabbinic saying quoted by Lionel Blue: 'Your successes make you clever, your problems [or weakness] make you wise' (in *The Godseeker's Guide*, Continuum, 2010).

The Paralympic games begin on 29 August and those who, in the past, may have been considered weak will thrill us with their strength, ability and grit. Many Brits have been inspired by Dame Tanni Grey-Thompson and others of her ilk.

In today's reading, we find the prophet urging all God's children to give everything in running the race of faith, no matter their physical or mental condition, leaving nothing in the tank, the locker or hidden under a bushel. Even if you are faint, weary or feeling powerless, trust that the God who chooses the weak to shame the strong will give you the strength you need – or is using your weakness for a reason. As we wait for the Lord to unfold God's will, may we find our strength renewed and invigorated.

When have you experienced God's strength in weakness? How will you encourage others to know such strength – especially those who feel weak and powerless?

Lord, you choose the weak to shame the strong and the foolish to shame the wise. Help us to learn more about you from those the world considers weak but whom you have made strong in the Spirit.

The spirit of self-discipline

2 Timothy 1:1-7

If you put a picture of me aged twenty against a picture of me on the eve of my fifty-third birthday, you would probably conclude that I have little authority to speak about self-discipline. I haven't just let *myself* go, but the other person who now inhabits this body with me also seems to have got away!

I was in Canberra, Australia, at the Institute for Sport at the invitation of the chaplain. I was grateful for their warm hospitality and I learnt much about how Christians need to be alongside sportspeople. At this Institute, and others like it throughout Australia, this 'sportaholic' nation prepares and trains its future sporting heroes. Young men and women, the best Australia has to offer, put themselves through the self-discipline that this strict regime requires for success. It was estimated that, for every gold medal that Australia wins, around $11 million is invested. No surprise then that mediocrity is not acceptable and failure results in being sent home.

As far as we are able in running our race of faith we must also submit ourselves to the rigours of being self-disciplined in prayer, study of God's word, worship, seeking healing and showing love to all. Yet we should also take heart, as we remind ourselves that it is God who gives us the spirit of self-discipline (verse 7), not we ourselves who manufacture it.

What and who helps you to remain self-disciplined?

Help us, Lord, to run our race of faith with determination and self-discipline. May the example of the saints, those holy spiritual athletes, inspire us to live for you. Instil in us a deep desire to pray, and send your Holy Spirit to train us in the way of your commandments.

Gary Colville

Not to the swift

Ecclesiastes 9: 11-18

Today the London Olympics begin and it'll certainly make for a memorable birthday! I'll be celebrating by watching the opening ceremony – although most probably at a community festival here in Rochester rather than as one of the fortunate 100,000 who will be in the Olympic Stadium. Not everyone will have been swift enough to get their ticket, but everyone who can get near to a TV screen or a radio will be able to participate. Many millions around the world will be watching or listening to find out if their favourite athletes bring home that elusive gold medal. Some may be looking out for calamity to strike the favourites and no doubt a few surprises will unfold in London.

No one knows what the results will be and that's what's intriguing and compelling, drawing us into the spectacle and keeping many of us up to all hours. There will be some athletes who will claim it was their destiny to win, but what about those for whom calamity awaits? Surely wisdom teaches us that success is unpredictable and is quickly forgotten. Do you remember who won the bronze medal in the 1956 Melbourne Olympics? Not many will remember it was John Landy, a highly successful Australian athlete. John is immortalised in a bronze statue outside the Melbourne Cricket Ground, where he is shown helping to his feet Ron Clark, who had fallen during the Australian National trial race. Despite the importance of the race, John knew in an instant that real success comes 'not to the swift' but to the wise.

Lord, we pray for all the Olympic athletes, that they will be wise in the ways they seek success in the games. Help us all to apply our hearts to wisdom.

Gary Colville

An athlete's prayer

Psalm 19

As we pray that the world may become a more peaceful place, I urge you to pray for peace and security for all at the Olympic Games. With thousands of athletes around, things can and do go wrong. I remember David Tyndale, the Archbishop's Officer and Chaplain to Sydney 2000, telling me about a Nigerian athlete who had tragically died during training and how the chaplaincy team had cared for all involved, including the man's fiancée, who was an athlete herself. Prayer was a vital component of that pastoral care.

So let us pray for those competing in the games, as well as for the thousands of faithful Christians who will be chaplains and volunteers, offering the hospitality of their homes to athletes and their families and running hundreds of community festivals up and down the UK. As well as the many medals being won, we pray that lives may be won over to Jesus, our Lord and Saviour. This psalm reminds us that there is something that is more precious and enduring than gold, even Olympic gold, and that is the fear and love of God.

Lord, we pray for the wellbeing and safety of all the athletes and all people involved in the Olympics. We remember all Christians involved in ministry and mission at the games, that they will be effective in all they do. Help us each to run the race of a faithful life with compassion and commitment, so that we will reach our finishing line to find you waiting for us, our Lord, our Rock and our Redeemer.

Gary Colville

Not to the swift

Sunday 29 July

Live the ongoing race

Notes based on the New Revised Standard Version, by

Janet Corlett

Janet Corlett is a Methodist minister serving at Bermondsey Central Hall and the South London Mission (London, UK). She has previously served in the Republic of Honduras. Prior to ordination she competed at club, county and national levels in a variety of disciplines including yacht racing and surf life-guarding, as well as track and field athletics. She was women's captain of Oxford University Athletics Club in 1983–4 and in 1999 won medals at both the British and World Veteran Athletics Championships.

2 Timothy 2:1-5

Be strong in grace!

Each sport in the Olympic Games has its own rules and regulations but all have a common prohibition against 'outside assistance'. The marathon runner near collapse cannot be helped over the finish-line. A coach cannot enter the competition area and give advice to the javelin thrower who keeps recording no-throws. Performance-enhancing drugs are banned.

Now in this reading Timothy is being told to be like an athlete: well trained and disciplined, competing according to the rules as he follows Christ. I wonder what rules spring to your mind as you read this? Paradoxically I think Timothy (and the reader) is being urged to break the 'no outside assistance' rule. Jesus commanded us to 'love the Lord your God with all your heart, and with all your soul, and with all your mind' and 'love your neighbour as yourself' (Matthew 22:37, 39) but knew this was impossible for us without divine intervention. Timothy is told to 'be strong in the grace that is in Christ Jesus' (verse 1) and this should be the goal of our spiritual exercises too.

Gracious God, pour out your love into my heart today. Give me the grace to hear your voice and the humility to obey.

What is your goal?

Philippians 3:7, 10-12

It takes a certain degree of sacrifice to reach the elite level in any sport. All the athletes you see competing at the Olympics will have their own particular story of giving up many things in order not to give up on their goal. The key to their success is a persistent, single-minded, even ruthless focus on improving their performance. Every aspect of their life comes under scrutiny: diet, sleep patterns, relationships, psychology, rest times and leisure activities. Whatever does not help their performance is discarded without regret when set alongside their hunger for their goal.

When Paul was confronted by Jesus on the road to Damascus, he didn't so much change his goal (being right with God) but rather he ditched his zeal for 'the law' as unhelpful – straining instead to know Christ and the power of his resurrection. Paul is happy to give up anything that gets in the way of being found in Christ. He knows that this will mean giving up any attachment to wealth, success, honour and even personal safety in order to be ready to be like Christ (Philippians 2:5-11).

In long-distance running the finishing line never moves, but in the spiritual race a word of grace intervenes once again. We are left with the wonderful image of Paul straining forward with all his might to grasp hold of Christ only to find that Christ has already caught hold of him.

What do I need to do in order to grow strong in grace? Is it possible that not only the bad, but also some of the good things in my life might be getting in the way of something that is better in Christ?

Janet Corlett

Paul's top coaching tips

Acts 20:17-21

Paul would have made an excellent sports coach. As we will see over the next few days, he is good at giving advice and encouragement, warning of pitfalls and knowing exactly what sort of training will build us up and make us strong. Best of all, he is like a coach who can speak directly from his own experience as an athlete.

When I was learning to throw the hammer, David my coach was great at using the technical language of physics and mechanics to explain precisely what I was doing wrong. However, it was often his son Tim who could actually demonstrate to me how the physics worked in practice and at high speed. Then it was down to me to imitate him and very gradually find the repeated actions becoming second nature.

Paul knows he is coming to the end of his career on the track of ministry and he is coaching those who are to continue in the race, testifying to the good news of God's grace. Paul didn't have to leave them a long technical training manual to teach them how to share the good news. They had seen him in person being both helpful and humble, testifying and in tears. All Paul had to say was 'you've seen me doing it – now practise doing it yourselves until it becomes second nature'.

Gracious God, grant me the grace to be humble enough to learn from others. May I so learn the way of Christ that if others imitate me I may never be ashamed.

Body-building with grace

Acts 20:31-35

When reading the Bible, one always has to ask what a 'therefore' (verse 31) is there for. Here Paul is coaching the elders of the church in Ephesus, warning them of savage wolves to come; 'therefore' they need to be alert. Paul is particularly concerned about those within the church who will proclaim a distorted message; 'therefore' they should not only watch over the flock but also watch over themselves (verse 28) and follow his example.

In the Olympic Games in ancient Greece, the strongest and most versatile athletes competed in the Pentathlon: jumping, running, discus, javelin and wrestling. These days the events have multiplied, with ten for men and seven for women. It makes me wonder what the ten disciplines would be if we had a Christian Decathlon? Paul puts generosity at the top of his decathlon list and hints at how the love of money and covetousness in church leaders can weaken and injure the body of Christ. He coaches them and us to build up the body with the word of grace (verse 32). Grace reminds us continuously of our own complete dependence on the generosity of God in Christ, and encourages us to keep asking for more grace-muscles so that we may be strong in the decathlon of love, joy, peace, patience, kindness, generosity, faithfulness, gentleness, self-control and grace!

When I am generous, am I able to give without fanfare and without expecting any recognition?

Generous God, give me grace to keep praying for and longing for all spiritual gifts rather than the riches of this world. May I use all the gifts you have given me to build up the body of Christ.

Victory over evil

Timothy 4:1-8

When my sister was little and saw, for the first time, men playing football, she said to our mum 'Why don't they give everyone a ball?' Olympic sports are all inherently competitive: only one person or one team wins the gold, leaving all the other competitors without that thrill of victory. When using games as a metaphor for the Christian life we have to be careful not to stretch the point too far. In this reading the focus is not so much on being competitive as being persistent and having the stamina to keep going. Then the righteous judge will award a crown to all who cross the finishing line, to those who never give up longing to see Jesus.

I am naturally a very competitive person and I have had to learn not to try to compete with other Christians. I can, however, fight the good fight for victory over everything that would knock me out or get me disqualified from the race. As a preacher and a pastor I am also called to help others to stay on track. This means not only giving positive encouragement, but also being persistent in warning those who are going astray – even if this makes me unpopular. Maybe this is why Paul suggested, in yesterday's reading, that leaders should not rely on gifts or payment from those to whom they preach lest they are tempted to scratch the itching ears.

Am I carrying out my ministry fully (verse 5)? Do I long for the Lord's appearing? Ask God to increase that longing.

Aspiring to win

1 Corinthians 9: 24-27

As in yesterday's reading, the emphasis here is not on competition but on the goal, the athletes' complete and utter focus on the prize. What is the prize that we should be straining to win?

Near where I live there is a place of worship called 'Winners' Chapel' and I imagine my fellow bus passengers asking themselves 'can I worship there if I'm a loser?' or 'what will I win if I go there?' Paul has just been talking about winning or gaining people (verses 19-22) but in verse 24 he changes the meaning to attaining or catching hold of 'the prize', echoing his words in Philippians 3: 12-13 where the goal is Christ himself and a full sharing in Christ's righteousness, sufferings and resurrection.

Athletes know that to be winners they have to be disciplined in all areas of their lives. There is no point putting their body through rigorous training and controlling their diet carefully if they then have a hidden and destructive habit. Sometimes as Christians we can seem satisfied with a low level of attainment and complacent in excusing our lack of discipline. I wonder if we will be inspired this week by the hard but healthy discipline of Olympic athletes to put a bit more focus and rigour into our spiritual training? Thus we may aspire to a fuller knowledge of Christ and greater glory for God.

Do I have anyone to act as coach in my spiritual training?
What progress in spiritual growth can others discern in me?
How do I distinguish between a healthy and a harmful discipline?

Janet Corlett

Stamina for the ongoing race

Acts 20:36-37

At first sight these verses may seem a strange way to end our Bible readings with an Olympic flavour – but look again and there are some important words to ponder over: knelt, prayed, weeping, embraced, kissed. They are all active words and they are actions that we may very well see from athletes as they cross the finish line, score a goal, receive their medal or participate in the closing ceremonies. I wonder which word here catches most in your imagination as you think of 'living the ongoing race'?

For me the most resonant word here is 'prayed'. This word draws together many of the strands we have explored during the week, linking the discipline and focus of athletes in training to the discipline and focus of those who follow Christ. Prayer is our most important training ground. We pray for 'outside assistance' and we long 'to be strong in the grace that is in Christ Jesus' (2 Timothy 2:1).

In prayer we focus on God and strain forward to know Christ better. In prayer we listen attentively to the coaching of the Holy Spirit. In prayer we fight competitively against the forces of evil and tap into God's resources to help us move from prayer to radical action. We willingly give regular time and energy to prayer when we are interested in winning glory for God rather than glory for ourselves.

Gracious God, thank you that we are fearfully and wonderfully made. We marvel at the sacrifice and commitment of all the Olympic competitors. Give us grace as you help us bring focus and discipline into our Christian growth, training and service. May we grow strong in grace and be effective ambassadors for your kingdom.

Missing the mark

Prophets, kings and judges

Notes based on the New Revised Standard Version by

Ben Knighton

Ben Knighton is PhD Stage Leader in the Oxford Centre for Mission Studies. Unexpectedly called of God to East Africa, he worked for the local church among the Karamojong and then the Agĩkũyũ. In 2011 he will be writing on Gĩkũyũ religious history as a Leverhulme Research Fellow. For the past three years he has co-taught, with Professor Terence Ranger, a course called 'Gods, Kings, and Prophets' on the MSc in African Studies at the University of Oxford.

Romans 3:21-26

All have sinned

As a chief of sinners, I am specially qualified to open this series on 'Missing the mark'. 'Sin' is one of the few words from Old English that is more theological than the biblical languages. While *chata* and *amartano* are used respectively for an arrow and a spear missing the mark, 'sin' is simply an offence against God. I would suggest that British resistance to the term, therefore, has nothing to do with an ecclesiastically imposed word, but with the pride that refuses to admit sin.

Paul's fellow Jews referred to 'gentile sinners', while Israel was holy and set apart. Paul insists that righteousness belongs to God alone, who justifies by grace as a gift. The sins of saints in the passages of the Hebrew scriptures for this week underline the need for grace, be the person ever so high: prophet, king or judge. Delilah and Solomon sin in their alliance with other nations against Israel. But Israel, Moses and Jeroboam sin as Israelites against God. Jonah, in being loyal to Israel, sins against God's mission.

Where do you recognise the taints of sin in your own life and that of your society?

Lord, let me never forget that I stand by grace alone!

Israel turns aside to other gods

Exodus 32:1-6, 18-24

Israel was called and rescued out of Egypt to worship the God of their ancestors on Mount Sinai. Here, while Moses is up the mountain receiving a national covenant from the one who had revealed himself there as 'I will continue to be who I am being', the people grow impatient and say they can make their own gods. Aaron obliges, but the god he moulds is not the God of Abraham, but a god of Israel's Semitic relatives in the eastern delta of the Nile, and of the peoples they are due to overrun, the Canaanites and Syrians. Like other bull-cults in this interdependent area, Baal and Hadad offered strength and fertility through their symbols. The Hebrew word translated 'calf' (verse 4), extends to a three-year-old bull who has long been able to sire progeny; so 'bullock' would have been a better translation but for its association with castration. Thus the Israelites choose to abandon Abraham's mission (Genesis 12:3) to the Afro-Asian borderlands by making a god in the image of a dumb ox. However much they worship, it is merely an image and no god.

The story illustrates Paul's point from yesterday perfectly. Right at the very moment of God's special revelation, Israel, including its priesthood, sinned en masse, breaking at once the first three of the Ten Commandments. Being called from among God's people is no proof of sinless perfection. All have fallen short.

What does our culture put in place of the living God?

O Lord, let our eyes stay on you, so that we do not exchange dust for glory!

Moses was the greatest

Numbers 20:1-13

A response to Israel's apostasy might be to claim that it nevertheless showed that Moses remained righteous. In this story Moses appears to be again taking up his great roles of intercessor and leader. The people moan bitterly in the dry wilderness, and yearn to revert to their previous normality. For the Israelites now, the grain and fruit of Egypt appear sufficient compensation for slavery. Their only consistency is in moaning, a theme present since Numbers 15.

In Exodus 17:1-7 Moses was the agent of a solution, striking the rock to produce abundant water. All he had to do was ask of God, and follow God's commands. The phrase 'And Moses did so' marked the end of the problem. The people's quarrel with their leaders was over.

In Moses, as J A Thompson has said, were concentrated all the great offices of Israel: prophet, ruler, judge and priest. If some who held these offices were great, Moses was the greatest. But here in Numbers, even Moses lapses. He does not intercede for Israel, but addresses them rudely, 'Listen, you rebels' (verse 10). Then instead of commanding the rock as Yahweh had commanded (Numbers 20:8), he strikes the rock twice with his staff. Moses was taking God for granted and not diligently following his words, so his lack of trust and holiness bar him from the promised land (Numbers 20:12).

Help me to remember scripture, whenever I am tempted to presume too much!

How can you say, 'I love you'?

Judges 16:4-22

Samson judged Israel for twenty years; he receives more attention in the book of Judges than any other. His glory lay in his physical strength in an era of hand-to-hand battle; his weakness lay in his dependence on women. From a Philistine wife to a Gaza prostitute, he then falls in love with Delilah. There is no word that he married Delilah or that she or the prostitute were Philistines; it is more likely that they were Hebrews or Canaanites living under the overlordship of the encroaching Philistines. It turns out that the prostitute is the most discreet of the three, for both wife and lover prove treacherous. Delilah is given an enormous inducement, for there were five lords of the Philistines (Judges 3:3), which meant 5,500 pieces of silver, just for the secret of his strength.

The bitterest taste is left by Delilah's techniques. She manipulates his declaration of love to goad him into the unwise actions that put him in imminent danger of his enemies capturing him. When he is not so foolish to give away the secret, she accuses him of mocking her, but she has offered no love to be mocked. The process is completed by persistent nagging and pestering. Such selfish methods should be dismissed, for they are manipulations, not expressions of love.

Would you resist great wealth in order to remain true to your love?

O God, help me love you first, who can love most!

Ben Knighton

Too wise to be trusted?

1 Kings 11:1-13

Solomon was the greatest king of Israel, for the extent of his borders, his power and wealth was not achieved by other compatriot kings. However, Kings and Chronicles differ markedly in their evaluation of Solomon. The priestly account, valuing temple worship, makes no criticism at all (2 Chronicles 1 – 9), but emphasises the Mosaic orthodoxy of his worship (2 Chronicles 8:12-15). The Deuteronomist in today's passage builds on the ban of intermarriage with the peoples of the promised land (Deuteronomy 7) to extend it to the diplomatic marriages practised by all dynasts everywhere. When all Israel had clamoured, 'we are determined to have a king over us, so that we also may be like other nations', Yahweh told Samuel, 'Listen to their voice' (I Samuel 19 – 22). So Solomon has only been building the divinely ordained institution of monarchy, about which the Deuteronomist has always had misgivings. Schooled with prophets in the northern kingdom, whose kings showed their tendency to apostasy, the writer is likening infidelity to Yahweh with the misdirected love of women (contemporary readers may find this problematic!). So the great king symbolises the spiritual adultery against which the prophets warn, and his kingdom will be split.

O Lord, be I ever so poor, it is possible to be faithful to you. If I think I stand in this world, then open my eyes, so that I do not fall!

Many gods, many kings

1 Kings 14:1-18

The 'heavy tidings' (verse 6) that the prophet Ahijah has in store for Jeroboam's queen is simply that he has made other gods for himself by casting images. Just so that Jeroboam does not have to relate to King Rehoboam and worship at the temple in Jerusalem, he makes two golden bullocks, and tells the northern kingdom, 'Here are your gods, O Israel, who brought you up out of the land of Egypt' (1 Kings 12:27 to the end). This is the same wording that is inserted into Monday's reading from Exodus. It is the scriptural antithesis of worshipping the one, true, living God, but very convenient in making Dan and Bethel feel good about themselves.

There is an ultimate unity underlying all things, which monarchs and leaders should be careful to promote. Jeroboam, in the dividing not only of the kingdom but of the worship of Yahweh, has fractured that unity. The future will continue to be fragmented and plural, for there will be many kings of Israel. Jeroboam's dynasty lasted only two years after his death. Of all the sins of the leaders in the Hebrew scriptures, none is assured of such a bleak end as Jeroboam's line. Its end is already present here, starting with the royal son, for it will be the prey of dogs or vultures.

Where do you perceive a unity in all things? What kinds of plurality witness to the unity of God, and which are the manifestation of sin?

You who are three-in-one, teach me to believe in you as the source of all unity and truth.

The people repent, the prophet does not

Jonah 3:1-5, 10 – 4:11

Jonah enjoys preaching judgement to the capital of Assyria, for this will be Israel's biggest coup. Such a humbling of a great power centre in the fertile crescent, existing since 4,500 BCE, would have attributed more power to the prophet than all the chariots of Solomon. Yet God's mission is not calamity, although the freedom he has given creation has produced abundant possibility of disasters. It is salvation.

God sees that the Ninevites have turned from their evil ways – in New Testament terms, 'repented of their sins'. The prophecies of the Hebrew scriptures in general implied that the response of repentance would avert the judgement foretold. Jonah says that he fled because he knew God was ready to relent from punishing. However, the story gives no record of that, but rather tells of Jonah's fear of crying out against the wicked city. Jonah also demonstrates that he has a problem with anger management and, through the weak spot of his temper, Yahweh shows him that he cares more for his own passing convenience while he ghoulishly awaits the overthrow of the city, than for the lives of 120,000 people. Livestock also weigh heavily in God's scales.

Are you aware of occasions in your own life when deceptions to cover up your own dishonourable motives made you angry with others? What can you learn from Jonah?

O Lord, teach me to stop digging my way into sin and turn round.

Missing the mark

Sunday 12 August

Disciples and congregations

Notes based on the New International Version by
Eun Sim Joung

Eun Sim Joung holds a PhD from Birmingham University, UK, published as *Religious Attachment* (Cambridge Scholars, 2008). She has been a visiting lecturer teaching women's studies and leadership at a number of universities, and helped her husband's church ministry in Korea. Besides looking after her two children in England, she is translating and writing articles on the pastoral care and education of Korean Christians, especially women.

Matthew 26:47-56

Sin, then and now

The Greek word Paul often uses for sin means 'missing the mark', defacing God's image in us. This week we will be exploring aspects of failure in the life of disciples and church congregations, both in the first and the twenty-first centuries.

In today's passage, religious leaders were waiting for the Messiah but missed the mark by being jealous of his fame and threatened by it. Judas followed Jesus to fulfil his own zealous hopes but missed the mark by failing to model his zeal on that of Jesus. The crowd once followed Jesus and cried 'Hosanna in the highest' (Matthew 21:9), but missed the mark by being foolish and turning into a mob. Peter stood up for Jesus but missed the mark by not seeing God's bigger picture. Other disciples were told that their master would be crucified but missed the mark by being unwilling to take up a cross of their own. All deserted Jesus and fled.

Studying and meditating on this week's Bible passages, we may be led to recognise our own ways of 'missing the mark'. This need not be a disempowering experience as we realise that we are justified and sanctified, not by our own deeds, but by God's free and generous grace.

Following at a distance

Luke 22:54-62

Peter was the dearest follower who declared, 'Even if all fall away, I will not,' and insisted, 'Even if I have to die with you, I will never disown you' (Mark 14:29, 31). What went wrong then? He followed at a distance and sat down with the people who seized Jesus. Eventually he disowned his master three times, as Jesus predicted.

Most of the time keeping a distance is a safe option, particularly when we are in a dangerous or complicated situation. Keeping a distance gives us room to mislead ourselves somehow, and thereby to miss the mark. We do not correct wrong because we do not think it appears necessary or important. We do not come forward with the truth because we think that the truth would make things worse or more complicated.

We live in a very confusing society in which the truth makes us weak and miserable. There are also times when our hearts and minds are divided. We immediately recognise what has gone wrong but whisper to ourselves, 'It will be all right after a while'. All these examples result from an attitude of cutting ourselves off from the situation, the problem, or other people, in order to avoid taking full responsibility. By following at a distance, we lose the will to act decisively and we become preoccupied with our own safety rather than the truth.

There is good news, however, in our story. The important thing is that Peter wept bitterly after he remembered the word Jesus had said to him.

Lord, forgive all our attempts to distance ourselves. Forgive the times when we have sat down with dishonesty and untruth, consciously or unconsciously. Give us the courage to follow you closely and not disown you. Show us how to act to correct our wrongdoing.

Eun Sim Joung

Failing to level up

John 21:15-19

Imagine how awkward the situation is, as Peter meets Jesus again. He certainly remembered and doubtless tortured himself with the memory of his denial, whilst he engages in this very personal conversation with Jesus.

The implications of the Greek text are not apparent in English for, in Greek, Jesus uses different words for 'love' in his three questions. The first two times he asks Peter if he loves him, Jesus, with *agape* love, that is God's selfless love, yet the third time he asks only if Peter loves him with *phileo* love, or brotherly love – a lower standard. Jesus is asking Peter if he can bring his love up to Jesus' standard of *agape* or unselfish love. Peter replies, 'Lord, you know that I love you' (verses 15-17), but with *phileo* not *agape* love each time in his reply. We know that he hadn't been able to keep his earlier boast of *phileo* love when he declared that he would never disown Jesus. He could not bring his love up to Jesus' agape-standard.

As disciples of Jesus and congregations of the church, we are the same. We declare 'we will' today, but tomorrow we fail to keep the promise to love God and others. Today's passage, however, reminds us that our hope is in Jesus, who lowers expectations to meet us where we are, but who never gives up on his hope for us. Jesus left his own heavenly realm, came in human form, died for us and waits for us to meet him where he is, in the realm of all-generous, all-forgiving love. When we respond to his love, we are raised to the level of our full potential.

Lord, forgive us our lack of confidence and competence, our low standards and endless failures in loving. Thank you that you never give up hope for us.

 Eun Sim Joung

Honesty that matters

Acts 5:1-11

In recent years, Korean society has been overtaken by countless examples of celebrities and public figures being found out for their duplicity; even church ministers have been found to be dishonest about their qualifications, education, money and sexual crimes. Jesus was particularly strict on religious leaders and the rich who had power, position and money but were unrepentant hypocrites. Christian belief is fundamentally concerned with honesty to the self, to others and before God.

Ananias and Sapphira were wealthy, land-owning members of the early church community who were keen to contribute to the common good. However, by withholding some of the proceeds, they deceived themselves, the apostles and the Holy Spirit. What motivated their dishonesty? It is not entirely clear, but it seems they wanted to gain glory and praise in the eyes of others for a generosity that was not really theirs. They were calculating in their efforts to gain both human and divine glory – the very opposite of a simple and honest generosity. There was no compulsion for them to sell their property in the first place, and neither did they have to give the money to the apostles. Perhaps if they had been really honest with themselves, they would not have sold their property in the first place, recognising that they were not ready to make the kind of wholehearted gesture for which the gospel asks.

Peter recognises that dishonesty with the self and with others is a spiritual matter, and cuts to the heart of our standing before God. It is a sin, as Peter asserted, a lack of truthfulness before God.

Lord, give us the courage to be true to ourselves and to others, to confess our weaknesses and faults when needed and to be transparent before you. Lead us not into the temptation of seeking glory from others. Let us be humble before you and give all the glory to you.

Lack of willingness to yield

Acts 13:13; 15:36-40

Paul and Barnabas had a strong disagreement about whether to take Mark on their mission journey, and eventually they separated because of this. Both were engaged in God's mission but in their different characters they approached things differently. Paul, being a self-disciplined person, could not accept the weakness in Mark, while Barnabas, as an encourager, was ready to give Mark another chance. Neither of them was willing to yield.

In Christian history, people have been killed by other Christians because of differing theological convictions: lay people were beheaded by clergy because they translated the Bible into their own language to read for themselves; people were burnt to death because they sang gospel songs rather than traditional hymns in the church, and so on. Each of these factions was involved in God's work but had different ideas and approaches. This led them, in extreme situations, to kill or to be killed themselves.

Such situations still happen today, though in different forms. In Korea, many churches suffer acute pain and division in the event of appointing a new church minister. Such a significant event in the life of a church is one of the works of God and can be an exciting event. At the same time, it can cause many troubles in the church. Some churches are divided into warring factions and even take legal action against each other.

Look around your fellowship, and ask yourself whether there are any unresolved issues between you. How do you hold the contradictions between different members of the body of Christ in a way that contributes to spiritual maturity rather than wounds and divisions?

Pray for yourself and others within your church who are divided on aspects of your approach to faith, for grace to hold the contradictions together and to find ways of sharing together in God's work.

Eun Sim Joung

Inconsistent practices

Galatians 2:11-21

Peter's inconsistent and immature acts caused trouble on not a few occasions in his life, albeit he was one of the great apostles. Can inconsistent acts be a form of 'missing the mark'? From this incident in the life of the earliest Christian community, it seems so.

Peter, we know from Acts, had been instructed by the Holy Spirit, in a vision, that nothing was unclean if God had made it clean (Acts 10), and that, therefore, gentiles could be baptised as Christians without being required to be circumcised or keep the entire Mosaic law. Having been practising this new understanding, and enjoying full table fellowship with gentile Christians in Antioch, he became afraid of other Jewish Christians who might condemn him for this. So he acted inconsistently by drawing back and separating himself from the gentile believers. This act had a ripple effect, leading other Jews astray to join him, including significant leaders like Barnabas. Peter's inconsistent practice was not only his own personal problem, but was a gaping wound in the body of Christ, causing segregation between Jewish and gentile Christians.

Paul challenged Peter's inconsistent act, revealing it to be a cause of division and sin, one sinful act that was having dangerous repercussions in the life of the whole Christian community. Paul saw the implications of Peter's confused act clearly, and confronted Peter in front of them all so that the hypocrisy could be rooted out from the community.

Lord, forgive our inconsistent and ignorant acts that can lead others astray. Let us be conservative only in keeping the truth of the gospel, but radical to overlook all inessential and unnecessary rules. Let us have courage to live in the freedom of the gospel.

Eun Sim Joung

Bewitched?

Galatians 3:1-5

Why does Paul use the word 'bewitched' in upbraiding the Galatians? While I was reading the passage and wondering, I read a somewhat similar news article from a Korean newspaper. A radio presenter was condemned for his addiction to gambling. He had a good reputation but his gambling addiction destroyed his life. He was given a second chance to recover his honour, but he could not stop gambling. He disappointed his family and his audience yet again. He lost his job and his reputation. It seemed he was bewitched.

We usually think of addiction in relation to categories such as drink, drugs or gambling. Symptoms of addiction are common across all kinds of addiction, such as intolerance, withdrawal, self-deception, loss of willpower and distortion of attention. Although we rarely consider addiction in the realm of religious faith, some Christians display similar symptoms, suggesting that there may be a form of religious addiction at work.

Although the Galatians had become Christians, it seems they were still addicted to a slavish observation of the Law and an obsession with maintaining their own righteousness in the eyes of the Law. Their baptism in Christ, far from manifesting in a new freedom and spiritual maturity, was being undermined by their contradictory behaviour. Paul once again emphasises that they are justified not by observing the law, but by faith in Jesus and the sanctification of the Holy Spirit.

Spend some time honestly and prayerfully reflecting on your own life and where you see any addictive tendencies, either in your faith life (in terms of obsessive patterns of religious activity, perhaps) or more widely. Many people are addicted to shopping, or TV, or their mobile phones, for example. Ask the Holy Spirit to reveal to you the root of your addiction and pray for courage and grace to become free of all that would bind you.

Eun Sim Joung

Genesis 37–50

'Listen to this dream that I dreamed'

Notes based on the New Revised Standard Version and the Hebrew text by

Robert Parkinson

Robert Parkinson is a Baptist minister. Ordained in 1982, he has served congregations in the United States of America and the UK. Married, with three grown-up children, he is minister of Didsbury Baptist Church, Manchester.

Genesis 37:1-11

Joseph dreams

Joseph starts out gifted and becomes good. His dreams of greatness will be fulfilled but in ways he cannot imagine. Joseph's story is our story too. Not that most of us can claim the same giftedness as Joseph, nor even that we face the same trials and opportunities. Still, we are on a journey of becoming. We start out, to some degree or another, with abilities of our own. How we use and develop them can make all the difference, but talents alone are not enough. Gifted people are not always good people; so the Joseph story urges us to journey with God, through life's difficulties, from mere giftedness to goodness.

Favouritism and boasting are implicitly criticised in today's reading. Even so, unless Joseph is gifted, favoured, spoilt and boastful, there is no story. God, it will transpire, is at work in, through and despite human gifts and weaknesses. In this we can all take comfort and courage.

Please help us, O God, to use whatever gifts we possess with humility. Open our eyes to your hidden presence and guide our steps that we might grow in grace through times of trial.

Joseph at the hands of his brothers

Genesis 37:12-24

I am intrigued by the episode of Joseph's encounter with the stranger in this passage. It is not really essential to the story and if left out it would not be greatly missed. So why include it?

Perhaps the incident serves to heighten the sense of suspense, as it delays the action while emphasising Joseph's vulnerability. The reader already knows that Joseph's brothers are so jealous of him they cannot speak peaceably (shalom) to him, and that he is, therefore, a poor candidate for seeing if all is well (shalom) with them. We fear that Joseph's eagerness to visit his brothers is perilously misplaced, for we know what Jacob and Joseph do not, and we anticipate the unfolding drama in nervous apprehension.

Joseph the gifted child is now the lost child. Naïve and vulnerable, he is found wandering in the fields. Joseph is easy prey to strangers but the stranger helps him. Of course, in so doing he unwittingly delivers him into the hands of his brothers. Still, the point is made: not strangers but brothers are the cause of Joseph's downfall. Vying for their father's favour, consumed by jealousy and contemptuous of 'this dreamer' (literally, 'this lord of dreams' verse 19), they conspire to kill him.

In a world inordinately suspicious of strangers, we might recall that in the biblical story it is often strangers or outsiders who most readily demonstrate God's way.

Recall an incident where a stranger was kind to you. Are there strangers in your path toward whom you might act more kindly?

Journeying God, we do not want to be naïve about the dangers that sometimes lie close at hand, but neither do we want to live in suspicion of others. Help us to be open to others, to be hospitable and welcoming to strangers. Keep us from prejudice and help us so to live that others, whether near or far, will have no need to be suspicious of us.

Joseph and Potiphar's wife

Genesis 39:1-10

The Joseph story, like much of the patriarchal narrative, is vulnerable to feminist critique. Nowhere is this more apparent than in the incident of Joseph's encounter with Potiphar's wife. Here we are presented with a woman who, though powerful, is the unnamed personal property of Potiphar. However, perhaps the most objectionable aspect is its motif of 'woman as seductress', a theme that perpetuates the pernicious gender stereotype by which women, blamed for the sexual sins of men, suffer devastating consequences throughout the world.

The episode is ameliorated somewhat by Joseph's complete innocence. The story does not attempt to absolve male sexual aggression on account of women's wiles, for Joseph does no wrong. I am not sure whether it helps to know that Potiphar might be thought of as a eunuch (the Hebrew word for eunuch is translated 'officer' in verse 1). Any suggestion that this makes the advances of Potiphar's wife more excusable may itself betray a male perspective.

Despite its difficulties, the passage has plenty to say to today's reader. Both men and women can suffer sexual harassment, just as both men and women experience sexual temptation. This episode in Joseph's life alerts us to the deep consternation caused by sexual harassment, particularly in the workplace. It urges us to take such matters seriously. It also encourages the reader to stand firm against temptation even when it would be much easier to give in.

God of grace and justice,
we seek your help:
protect all who are harassed,
confront those who harass,
strengthen all who are tempted,
and help us to do what is right
even when it would be easier to do what is wrong.

Joseph prospers in adversity

Genesis 39:11-23

We tend to think prosperity means faring well, getting what we want and having plenty. What is remarkable about this passage is the way in which, with God's help, Joseph prospers in the midst of adversity. This, of course, is a feature of the whole story. When first he arrives in Egypt, we are told, 'The Lord was with Joseph, and he became a successful man' (verse 2) but now he is in prison and surely no good can come of it. Yet the narrator interjects again, 'the Lord was with Joseph and showed him steadfast love … and whatever he did, the Lord made it prosper' (verse 23). Even when all seems lost, God is still at work for the consolation of God's people.

We take courage from this story when facing adversity ourselves but we cannot allow it to dilute our compassion for others. If God cared for Joseph, those who claim to follow God must care about those who are unjustly treated today. For in our world too many people – women and men – are subjected to sexual harassment, or are falsely accused, or are imprisoned without cause. It is only right that we attempt to do something about it. While ensuring that we do not mistreat people ourselves, we can support organisations such as Amnesty International. We can call attention to the plight of the unjustly imprisoned as we also remember them in our prayers.

Visit the website of Christian Aid or Amnesty International and get involved in campaigning for peace and justice.

In adversity, help us to trust you;
in prosperity, help us to follow you;
in all circumstances, help us to accept your definition of
prosperity and success.

Robert Parkinson

Dreamer turns interpreter

Genesis 40:1-15

Joseph, it seems, has become something of an expert in the field of dreams. His own dreams needed no interpretation, their meaning was obvious to all. The enigmatic dreams of bakers and cupbearers, however, required further scrutiny. Enter Joseph who has graduated from dreamer to interpreter of dreams. If his journey has begun to shape his personality, he has lost none of his cockiness. 'Do not interpretations belong to God? Please tell them to me' (verse 8)!

If we are looking for evidence of change in Joseph's character, we might find it in the fact that now he listens to the dreams of others and seems genuinely concerned to hear and to help. He still uses the opportunity to put a word in for himself. 'Remember me when it is well with you,' he tells the cupbearer, 'and so get me out of this place' (verse 14). None of this is criticised in any way.

We are back to the tangled web. Life is complex and mixed. We experience good and bad. Sometimes we can effect an improvement to our circum-stances and sometimes we cannot. We act and are acted upon. Human beings are at work and, somehow, so is God. If there is anything new in this scene, it is Joseph's confidence in God. Perhaps he is discovering that reverence for God (with whom he now seems to be in close communication) is the beginning of wisdom.

Living God,
forgive us when we live as if you were not there.
Help us to experience the confidence that comes from
knowing that you are God.

Joseph is forgotten

Genesis 40:16-23

This incident establishes Joseph as dream interpreter par excellence. It thus sets the scene for his eventual discovery, release and elevation. In the meantime, Joseph will have to wait. He is, it seems, forgotten. This, I think, is the point of this episode.

Like Joseph, the people of God felt forgotten and abandoned, when in and around the year 586 BCE they were exiled in Babylon. All kinds of reasons could be adduced for their desperate situation. It was caused, at one and the same time, by their allies, their kin, themselves and their God. Certainly the prophets would say that the people had contributed to their own downfall, but also that God was involved too. Though silent and hidden, the Lord was at work chastising, purging and preparing God's people for their eventual restoration.

There would undoubtedly be problems if we adopted this approach to all the world's troubles. Bad things happen to good people, and desperate situations sometimes go unresolved. Still, the Joseph story does not intend to answer all the questions. It has, however, provided encouragement and consolation to the people of God, from the time of the exile to the present day. When family and friends have deserted you, when you find yourself living in a strange land with foreign values, when you are forgotten by all and God is silent, God has nevertheless not forgotten and will yet have the final word.

God, give us the courage and tenacity to keep on hoping, believing and serving even when we feel lost or forgotten.

Pharaoh dreams and Joseph is remembered

Genesis 41:1-13

In my life I have made a number of decisions that I regret. Yet, as a result of those decisions other things have happened that I would not want to undo. Who, then, can say whether my doing differently would have helped or hindered the general direction of my life? Does not the story of Joseph make a similar point? The forgetfulness of the cupbearer kept Joseph in the place he needed to be when Pharaoh finally dreamed his dreams. He could have been released earlier, but how then would he have come to the attention of Pharaoh? How then could his skills have become known to one so powerful as to provide a life-changing opportunity for Joseph?

Life is not always so ambiguous. Many will have had experiences about which they feel either profoundly happy or completely regretful. Nevertheless, in the ordinary course of everyday living there are countless occurrences about which it is difficult to judge. Was it good that Joseph languished in prison for two more years? Was it good that his brothers had conspired against him, and his father's heart had been broken? None of this was good. But none of it would defeat Joseph or the purposes of God. Remembered at last, Joseph was on the verge of a new existence, an opening that would throw new light on all that had preceded it.

God of wisdom and understanding,
help us never to forget that in you we are never forgotten.

Genesis 37–50

'One in whom is the spirit of God'

Genesis 41:14-16, 25-32

Defending our faith

Dreams have earlier been used in the book of Genesis to communicate God's will to humanity in a manner best described as unambiguous. But of the dreams in Pharaoh's court this is not the case. The oblique symbols of cows and ears of corn need to be interpreted by a gifted expert. Enter Joseph! Pharaoh was considered to be 'god-in-the-flesh'. So what does the prisoner of Pharaoh do? Joseph acknowledges the presence of God in his gift of dream interpretation. He declares that 'God has revealed to Pharaoh what he is about to do' (verse 25). Clearly and unambiguously Joseph states the superiority of the God of his forebears over any god Pharaoh may have thought himself to be.

Consider the time in which Joseph's story unfolded, when people languished in prison for a lot less! To this day, all over the world, Christians are imprisoned for defending the faith of our forebears, and for their worship of the one true God. This text teaches me to stand firm and share solidarity with my brothers and sisters in faith who suffer for the sake of the gospel, and to appreciate the privilege I enjoy in knowing the salvation gifted to me, and to us all, by our God.

Consider becoming part of a letter-writing campaign that supports Christians imprisoned for their faith.

God of our forebears, keep me faithful to the sacred teaching I have received. Day by day may I grow in courage to uphold my faith.

Notes based on the New Revised Standard Version by

Debra Snoddy

Having completed undergraduate studies in Theology and Classics at St Patrick's College, Maynooth, and postgraduate studies in Louvain, Belgium, Debra worked as a diocesan pastoral worker for the Roman Catholic Diocese of Armagh. She is now a lecturer in Biblical Studies at All Hallows College, a college of Dublin City University.

The temptation of Joseph

Genesis 41:33-45

This is a truly remarkable text! Joseph dares to tell Pharaoh that his God, the God of his fathers, has revealed the truth of Pharaoh's dreams. He then proceeds to tell Pharaoh what needs to be done to save Egypt from the coming famine, and Pharaoh accepts the wisdom of Joseph's words. This element of the story is perhaps not that surprising; the Egyptians were open to the possibility of the existence of other gods, and Pharaoh is relieved to receive knowledge and guidance, wherever its origin. What is surprising in the text is the elevation of Joseph to the lofty status of second-in-command to the king. He has moved from prison to palace, all in a day.

The prisoner's fidelity to the truth is rewarded, but it comes with a price tag attached. In an attempt to neutralise his identity and the source of his power, Pharaoh gives him an Egyptian title, an Egyptian name and an Egyptian wife, with direct links to the Egyptian cult. No doubt, Pharaoh thought to make a good Egyptian of Joseph, hoping he would fall in with the Egyptian ways of doing things. By elevating him, he placed the potent temptations of power, possessions and prestige in Joseph's path.

Would Joseph comply? When we are tempted in similar ways, do we? Spend some time reflecting on the temptations that confront you. It may be helpful to make a list. Ask for God's help in overcoming them.

Loving God, guide me along the right path, preserve me from the temptations of this world, keep me true to your name, and give me wisdom to resist the seductions of power and compromise.

Due diligence

Genesis 41:46-57

Joseph proves himself to be a reliable emissary of the Pharaoh, diligently overseeing the task set for him. To all appearances he is a trusty employee of Pharaoh. But has he forgotten the God of his forebears? Has he succumbed to the temptations of power, possessions and prestige? The answer to both questions is a resounding 'no'! Though he is in Pharaoh's employ, Joseph knows himself to be first and foremost the servant of God, owing God the primary allegiance. By giving his sons Hebrew names, rather than Egyptian ones, Joseph shows all Egypt where his loyalty really lies.

This part of Joseph's story can be a source of comfort to us. We all must earn our bread, sometimes working in environments where we struggle to keep our allegiance to God at the same time as remaining loyal to our employer. Like Joseph, we need to do our work as diligent employees whilst remembering that we owe our primary loyalty to God. There may be times when we cannot please God and our employer, and when we are compelled to make difficult choices, whilst at other times service of God may more readily be fulfilled through commitment to our work and the institutions of which we are part.

Do you experience tension between your faith and your daily work? If so, where and how? Where do you find support to enable you to bear these tensions and remain faithful to the gospel?

Faithful God, help me as I earn my daily bread to remain faithful to my calling as a Christian. I am grateful for all the good things you have given me. Help me not to take your blessings for granted.

The stern face of the governor

Genesis 42:1-17

Why is Joseph so harsh with his brothers? After twenty-two years of exile from those who loved him, was it payback time? Perhaps Joseph is relishing and enjoying his power, flexing his muscles and toying with the temptation to retaliate and wound those who have been the cause of his suffering. Will Joseph use his power for good or ill?

W C Kaiser reflects further on this passage, suggesting that Joseph's motives may have been partly to obtain information about his father's family without revealing who he was, and partly to bring his brothers to a proper realisation of the dreadful wrong in which they had been involved (Walter C Kaiser, Peter H Davids, Frederick Fyvie Bruce & Manfred T Brauch, *Hard Sayings of the Bible*, Downers Grove, IL: Intervarsity, 1996, p.133).

Faced with a choice of how to use his considerable power, Joseph chooses compassion, yet this is not a weak compassion that leaves untruth or injustice unchallenged. True compassion calls people to account for their actions and to come to take responsibility for their deeds.

In times of doubt, how can we be enabled, like Joseph, to choose reflection over resentment? Do you have experience of such choices in your own life?

Lord God, in times when resentment may threaten to overtake me, strengthen me as you strengthened your servant Joseph. Empower me to be the best possible version of myself and not a pale shadow of resentment or revenge. May I always be your servant, one who is both wise and compassionate.

The weight of guilt

Genesis 42:18-28

Have you ever been wronged by someone, and then found yourself in a position that gave you the capacity to take revenge on the person who had wronged you?

The three days have given Joseph a breathing space and his brothers ample opportunity to reflect on their misdeeds. Imagine their shock and horror when the Pharaoh's emissary visits and says, 'I fear God' (verse 18) – a clear reference to their own God, whose worship and honour their deeds have betrayed. The impact on the brothers is profound. They finally admit their wrongdoing against their brother and so come a step closer to being made right with their God again.

It is the nature of true compassion to lead the way back to God. But Joseph's brothers have not made it all the way back to God just yet. Finding the money replaced in their sacks on the journey home, they lose heart and tremble in deep fear. They have finally learned to fear a just retribution for what they had done in the past.

In my life there are people who have wronged me. How can I show true compassion, in word and deed, rather than seek vengeance?

Forgiving God, come and make your home in my heart. Fill me with the compassion only you can give, so that I may do what is right rather than what will make me feel good.

Debra Snoddy

Questions of trust and faith

Genesis 42:29-38

On their return, the brothers go to Jacob and report all that has occurred in Egypt. But he too is perplexed by the return of the money and fearful of the demand that the brothers go back to Egypt with Benjamin. He blames the brothers for his not inconsiderable troubles, and clearly does not trust them. How bad it is in a family where there is not trust! But there is more. Not only does he not trust his own kith and kin, but Jacob does not trust God any longer, as his reply to Reuben's reckless statement shows (verse 38). How desolate the person who loses trust in God! Jacob would rather condemn his people to starvation than trust that God is working in his life and the lives of his people. Faith without trust is no faith at all.

In my times of trial, am I like Jacob? Do I say I have faith but then fail to trust that God really is at work in my time of tribulation? How can I be a positive support to others in their times of trouble?

God of hope, grant me the gift of true faith in you.

Taking responsibility

Genesis 43:1-10

Jacob has rarely taken responsibility for his actions and once again in chapter 43 he blames his sons for his troubles, seeming to have no concern for Simeon's situation as the imprisoned hostage in a foreign land. However, Judah – the one who originally suggested that Joseph be sold into slavery – says that he will bear sole responsibility for the safe return of his youngest brother, Benjamin.

Is Judah trying to make restitution? No, since he believes that Joseph is 'no more'. Rather, he is demonstrating that he is willing to shoulder all the responsibility and endure consequences of his past sin. He has made the journey of true repentance and metanoia back to God. In accepting that there will be consequences, he demonstrates that he has really changed, in the depths of his being, in his heart and soul.

And what of us? Who are we in this story? A Jacob? Or a Judah?

Eternal God, keep me faithful to your teaching and never let me be parted from you. May I always and everywhere know that there is no sin beyond the reach of your mercy and healing. Give me the gift of knowing your love.

Genesis 37–50

'It was not you who sent me here, but God'

Notes based on the *JPS Hebrew-English Tanakh*, Philadelphia: Jewish Publication Society, 1999, by

Irit Shillor

Rabbi Irit Shillor serves the Harlow Jewish community as well as the Jewish Community in Hameln, Germany. Born in Jerusalem she moved to the UK in 1982, where she taught Mathematics for many years. She was ordained in 2002.

Genesis 43:11-15

Father and son

The story of Joseph's reacquaintance with his brothers is a troubled one. Joseph, in a position of power, can take his revenge on his brothers for what they did to him, when they threw him into a pit and then sold him to the Egyptians. Joseph, it is true, plays with them for a while, as the suspense builds up. But what will the final outcome be? What kind of a person is Joseph? This selection of readings presents a man in conflict, a man who is trying to do what is right. How would we have behaved in his place?

We also encounter Jacob, the father who mourns the death of his beloved son, son of his beloved Rachel, and must now face the possibility that his youngest child, also a son of Rachel, might disappear for ever, too. Jacob is a passive player in this enfolding drama. He seems to take very little responsibility. Originally he sent Joseph to seek his brothers, though he knew of the enmity between them. Could the outcome have been prevented? Now Jacob sends Benjamin to Egypt, at Joseph's command, unable or unwilling to change what he regards as fate.

God, give us grace to accept with serenity the things that cannot be changed, courage to change the things which should be changed, and the wisdom to distinguish the one from the other.

Reinhold Niebuhr

Deception?

Genesis 43:6-30

What sort of game is Joseph playing? He is clearly at this point still intent on deceiving his brothers and, as far as we know, they still have no idea who he really is. But is Joseph also engaging in self-deception? Does he really not care about his brothers, especially Benjamin? Or are his tears a sign that he is aware of his feelings, even at this relatively early stage?

What sort of person is Joseph? Clearly a master strategist, he is able to rule Egypt with a firm yet just hand. He has brought about the increase of Pharaoh's wealth as well as that of Egypt as a whole. So, he is no longer the selfish, rather spoilt brat we encounter earlier, his father's darling.

His experiences had, no doubt, a part in shaping Joseph. He is cold, calculating, businesslike. His interrogation of the brothers is quite ruthless. And yet, there are his tears. We glimpse another side of Joseph, which we encounter again in the following sections.

You give but little when you give of your possessions.
It is when you give of yourself that you truly give.

Kahlil Gibran, *The Prophet*, William Heinemann 1926, p.24

Questions

Genesis 43:31-34; 44:1-17

I imagine the scene – a sumptuous meal, over which Joseph presides. The brothers, a hungry lot (after all, they came to Egypt to procure food) eat ravenously, perhaps not daring to lift their eyes to the face of their benefactor. But is it possible to concentrate on food to such an extent that the outside world is blotted out? They also drink together, and surely raise a glass. How is it that none of them recognises in Joseph something of themselves, of their father, or of their youngest brother, Benjamin, who is, after all, Joseph's nearest kin? And if they do, do they turn away in confusion, thinking they must be imagining things?

It is a difficult situation, especially with Benjamin being clearly favoured. Breaking bread together should make them all friends, but the next morning the deception recommences, as Joseph makes sure that a 'stolen' cup is put in Benjamin's bags. When it is found he chides them saying: 'Do you not know that a man like me practises divination' (Genesis 44:15)?

The twelve brothers were equal the night before, and now Joseph is once again unquestionably in charge. This seems like a cat and mouse game. Is Joseph trying to make sure that no matter what the future brings, his brothers will know who is the boss?

God, direct me in your way, lead me in the path of integrity, for people lie in wait for me. Do not put me in the power of my foes; the false witnesses, who pant for violence, are rising up against me.

Psalm 27:11-12

Judah's plea

Genesis 44:18-34

Judah, who is not the eldest of the brothers, takes a leadership role and pleads for his brother Benjamin and for his father. Judah acted as the leader also when the decision was taken not to kill the young Joseph, but to sell him to the Egyptians. The eldest, Reuben, is not much of a figure, as indeed is the case in many of the Genesis stories. The second-born seem usually to have more in them than the firstborn. Is this Genesis reflecting real life in which the firstborn may not live up to parental expectations?

Judah relates the history of his family, telling about the death of one of his brothers and the heartache it would cause his father to lose the youngest, too. It is a poignant recital. Judah must have found it quite difficult to say (in verse 27): 'Your servant my father said to us, "As you know, my wife bore me two sons,"' thus acknowledging that his father regarded only Rachel as his true wife. How sad he must feel while making the admission. And Joseph, does he feel shocked to hear it said so openly? Does he hear the hurt and the sadness in Judah's dignified recital of the events? After all, that was always how he saw it (see Genesis 37:9).

Rabban Shimon ben Gamliel says, 'The world is preserved by three things: by truth, by justice and by peace'

Pray for an increase of each.

Sayings of the Fathers, 1:18

After deception

Genesis 45:1-20

'Joseph could no longer control himself ... [T]here was no one else about when Joseph made himself known to his brothers' (45:1). But 'his sobs were so loud that the Egyptians could hear' (45:2). What made Joseph make himself known to his brothers at this point? He must have been very moved by Judah's telling, but what was it that moved him to such an extent?

Let us not forget that Joseph cried earlier, so his emotional state was quite vulnerable. But the story he was hearing was not new – after all, it was his own story. But there is one major difference between his memories and Judah's recital. Joseph was hearing, for the first time, the role his father played in the story. For the first time Joseph hears about his father's sorrow, indeed devastation, at what he believed was the death of his beloved son.

Surely Joseph could have imagined that sort of reaction from the father who loved him so dearly? Why, then, was he so shocked? The text gives us a clue: 'Joseph said to his brothers, "I am Joseph. Is my father still well?'" (45:3) Had Joseph not thought about his father all these years? I imagine he knew that his father would be mourning him. Why didn't he try to send a sign of life to his father, or to find out whether he was still alive? Why not take up contact with his family? Admittedly, he must have been very angry at the way he was treated, and for a long time was not at liberty to communicate with the outside world. But now, as a man in power, all was possible.

Was it guilt, as much as sensibility, that made him cry so bitterly?

Loving God ... teach me to be like You ... kind, loving and generous ... Please help me develop true sensitivity and genuine compassion.

Rabbi Nachman of Breslav, *Likutei Moharan* 1:105

Jacob's reaction

Genesis 45:21-28

Jacob, uncharacteristically, moves into action. The news that his son Joseph is still alive does not give him a heart attack, as I would have expected at his age. Rather, it gives him a new lease of life. The man who was so old and weary that he couldn't join his sons on their journey to Egypt is now bouncy and full of beans and asks to go immediately to Egypt to see his long lost Joseph.

Now this, it seems to me, is further punishment of the brothers. For Joseph, Jacob is prepared to forget illness and discomfort. Joseph proves, yet again, to be the favourite. But this time he is no longer the unbearable, spoilt child – he is a generous and powerful man. This time the brothers cannot justify any action against Joseph. He was more than generous towards them. Having said that, he did deceive them for a while, but they are powerless to act against him in any way. The tables are turned, the powerful become powerless and vice versa. Where does that leave Jacob? He belongs to neither group but pulls the strings in the background. But he, too, has a string pulling him. Joseph is for him the memory of Rachel. So instead of expecting Joseph to fulfil his filial duty and come to see him, it is Jacob who travels to be near Joseph.

He [Hillel] used to say, 'If I am not for myself, who is for me? But if I am only for myself, what am I? And if not now, when?'

Sayings of the Fathers, 1:14

All's well that ends well

Genesis 46:1-7

But does it? Jacob receives God's blessing when setting off to Egypt and the promise that 'Joseph's hand will close your eyes' (46:4). God also reiterates the promise to make Jacob into a great nation. It is true, of course, that Joseph was with Jacob when he died and that the Israelites became a very large tribe in Egypt. But if all had been well, they would have merged into the Egyptian population and lived there happily ever after.

Perhaps it is just as well that it did not end well. The Egyptians got fed up feeding the Israelites, put them to work and oppressed them to such an extent that they made a bid for freedom and created what was to become the Jewish nation. Had it all ended well we would never have had Moses, the Ten Commandments or the Jews.

Jacob, Joseph and the other brothers found a life of comfort in Egypt. They thrived there and were well regarded by the Egyptians. But it is true that it is not comfort and wealth that fuel the creative process, but rather the difficulties we encounter and the hurdles we overcome.

Grant us peace, goodness and blessing; life, grace and kindness; justice and mercy. Source of our life, bless us all together with the light of Your presence, for in the light of Your presence You give us, our Living God, law and life, love and kindness, justice and mercy, blessing and peace.

Forms of Prayer, The Movement for Reform Judaism, 2008, p.287

Genesis 37–50

Sunday 9 September

'God intended it for good'

Notes based on the Revised Standard Version by

Mike Holroyd

Mike lives and works in south-west England but has close links with Scotland through his membership of the Iona Community and part-time doctoral study at the University of Aberdeen.

Genesis 46:28-31

Joseph is reunited with his father

This week the Joseph story concludes with wonderful images of true forgiveness and reconciliation. As we engage with the story, we visit the full array of human emotions and are offered the opportunity to reflect on our own lives and the life of the world.

Today's short extract from the Joseph narrative demonstrates the power of story, and is full of emotion. The father makes the journey to another land. He is so delighted to find his precious son is still alive that he is contented for his life to end. I wonder if Jesus had this incident in mind when he told the parable of the prodigal son? The New Testament seems to show no explicit awareness of the Joseph narrative, but it is inconceivable that Jesus would not have known the whole saga.

While Jacob is overwhelmed to be reunited with Joseph, Joseph is equally delighted to see his family. We do not know exactly what is going through Joseph's mind, but it appears that his initial response is one of joy and relief. This part of the story raises profound questions about forgiveness and reconciliation, and reminds us how rare these attributes are in the modern world.

Joseph is now the one with power, but after weeping with delight, his priority is to let his boss know of the need to celebrate.

O God of new beginnings, help us to live with a heart of forgiveness and a life that shows it.

Joseph's family settle in Egypt

Genesis 47:1-12

It's not what you know but who you know! This seems to be true for Joseph's family. Embarrassment is brushed aside as representatives from the family present themselves to Pharaoh. There's a deal to be done here, and they are just hoping that Joseph does not bring up the past. Pharaoh is sympathetic and grants them residency.

Surely this is one of the greatest examples in the Hebrew scriptures of God's wide and generous vision of the role of every human being? Pharaoh is hardly one of the 'God squad', and yet his apparent hospitality towards Joseph's family is crucial in the development of the family of God's people.

Many times in life we are forced to see things from a different perspective than our habitual one. Perhaps we are put in a situation where we have to accept help from someone with whom we have little in common. Extreme need often takes us out of our predefined social networks and compels us to learn from others, seeing the Christ in strangers.

What prevents you from seeking what you really need? Is there a sense in which you feel that you should be able to cope with every situation, always in control? Perhaps you need to learn from Jacob and his willingness to seek new solutions to his problems.

Spend some time this week looking at your life and where you could do with some assistance from others. Swallow your pride, and make that journey to ask for help. Learn to rejoice in your interdependence. Pray for the grace to make this journey.

Joseph and the famine

Genesis 47:13-31

This is hardly an egalitarian solution to an economic and humanitarian disaster, and is certainly not to be used as a blueprint for anyone needing professional advice on macro-economics! However, although there is a huge power differential, Joseph is concerned with ensuring that even the poorest have adequate supplies. Making sure that all the people of the land had enough to eat must have been no small task, but the story takes us back quickly to the personal narrative – Joseph must face his father's imminent death, and Israel has some demands to make.

Sometimes our professional or domestic responsibilities have a kind of momentum of their own that enables us to find appropriate solutions to the problems we face. But as well as our professional or domestic narratives, we find that our personal needs demand attention. Joseph has fallen on his feet in terms of career, but he also recognises the importance of his family relationships and the need to fulfil family obligations.

A sense of vocation is important and, whatever our work happens to be, it is crucial in helping us to develop feelings of worth and identity. However, we need to ensure a balance between work, faith, relationships and our own needs. If our work or vocation takes over completely, we may soon find that there is a dissonance between our outward purpose and our attitude towards the things for which God has given us responsibility.

Thank God for your calling, and pray that you may be faithful to that calling in every area of your life.

Joseph brings his sons to Jacob

Genesis 48:1-12

How much do we really value older people in our societies? Even though he is unwell, and at the end of his earthly life, Jacob is still in control, engaging with his prophetic memory and asserting his right to adopt Joseph's sons. If we are to understand anything from this cultural act, it is that Jacob has a particular care and concern for Joseph and his sons – and he knows what he is doing.

I have worked with older people for over ten years. It is a delight to hear time and time again the wealth of wisdom and experience that older people bring. We have a tendency to think that just because someone is frail or unwell, they somehow have less to offer. The ageing process is not an easy one of course, but this intimate interaction between Jacob, Joseph and his sons reminds us of the wisdom of life that may come through longevity. As we shall see tomorrow, this wisdom should not always go unquestioned. The true wisdom that comes with age is strong enough to be challenged and questioned; it is secure enough to engage in dialogue and never assumes ultimate authority.

As you reflect on Jacob's life, reflect also on the older people whom you have known. Thank God for their lives and pray that God will increase your capacity for grace and wisdom as you get older. If you are of senior years, thank God for your wisdom and experience and find someone to share it with today.

Mike Holroyd

Jacob's blessings

Genesis 48:13-21

As a person with a visual impairment, I love this part of the story. Jacob displays a subversive streak by wanting to bless the younger son as the firstborn. So Joseph assumes that his father's failing sight must have caused him to make a mistake. Jacob must have got it wrong! How could he possibly go against the established norms and bless the younger son with his right hand? Joseph tries to remedy the situation by taking his father's right hand away from Ephraim's head. But Jacob will have none of it; he knows what he wants and he is going to do it his way.

People with impairments are often expected to be conventional, to live life in safety without any risk-taking. Any departure from the norm is often perceived to be a result of disability or illness. But actually, Jacob's visual impairment is irrelevant in this story. He does not need to be able to see the boys fully to know which one should receive the prior blessing. Perhaps Joseph is trying to surmise what it would be like if he could not see well, and interprets his father's action in the light of his own limited understanding. Therein lies his mistake. Everyone is unique, and individuals learn how to live with their impairments in their own way – we should never impose our own projections on someone else.

Thank God for the diversity of human experience and the different ways in which we use our physical bodies to bless others. Pray for courage to live dangerously for God and for others, whatever your own physical or other limitations.

Mike Holroyd

Jacob's death

Genesis 49:29-33; 50:1-14

I am always amazed at how some people like to make quite detailed plans for their own funeral arrangements. It is, of course, helpful to know what a person's wishes are in such circumstances. Jacob is quite clear about where he is to be buried – with his ancestors, and next to his first wife, Leah.

Many cultures find death difficult to talk about. Much of the Western world has professionalised the whole process of death. In fact, we have transformed it into a sanitised process rather than seeing it as an integral part of life's journey. Ancient cultures seem to represent an understanding of death as a part of life much better than many of us do today. This part of the Joseph story compels us to face up to our own mortality, but not in a morbid way. Jacob identifies his roots as he describes where he is to be buried, but Jacob is also looking forwards as well as backwards. He knows that he has played his part in a much bigger plan that continues in the hands of the creator, beyond his own life's end.

And so have each of us. God's generous spirit is not concerned with what we have achieved, how righteous we have been in life, or what material heritage we leave behind. Rather, God delights in us because of who we are – whether young or old, full of health or less healthy.

Allow the divine purposes of God to work through you today. Do not resist the Spirit as she enables you to journey through life and what we perceive as death. You are every bit as great as Jacob, because in God's realm all are great, all are lovely and all are cherished as God's own. Spend time meditating on this thought and pray to accept it for yourself.

Joseph reassures his brothers

Genesis 50:15-26

The brothers knew they were safe while Jacob was around. They had sold Joseph into slavery all those years ago, and now that Jacob was finally off the scene, surely their brother's retaliation would follow swiftly? So they have to come up with a plan pretty quickly. Jacob can no longer offer his physical protection, but neither can he vouch for the accuracy or otherwise of their story.

Joseph does not need their made-up story, because he is already living in a liberated state of forgiveness – something his brothers have still to learn. In a world where the books have to be balanced and the scales kept level, we too often struggle to absorb the reality and full implications of forgiveness.

Joseph does not try to explain or excuse the actions of his brothers; he knows that they intended wrong. Their deeds cannot be explained away or justified. But he knows too that God uses even the wrongs in life to bring about a better future that will extend far beyond the life of Joseph and his brothers.

When will we learn the truth that shouts from the pages of scripture and from the cross of Christ, that forgiveness is unconditional and non-contractual? Jesus did not say to God on the cross, 'If they say sorry, and mean it, then please forgive them'; he said, 'Forgive them; for they know not what they do' (Luke 23:34). This is unconditional, just as Joseph's forgiveness is unconditional.

I firmly believe that unforgiveness is the most significant cause of physical, psychological and spiritual ill-health today. The story of Joseph shows us that there is another way, that relationships can be restored and that the future of both the forgiver and forgiven can be far better than we can ever hope or imagine.

Forgive us our sins, as we forgive those who sin against us.

Jewish festivals

The biblical pattern

Notes based on the Hebrew Bible by
Rachel Montagu

Rachel Montagu teaches Judaism and biblical Hebrew. She believes teaching people to understand the Bible in Hebrew, without translators' interpretations, is empowering. She lives in London and has been involved in interfaith dialogue for many years.

Leviticus 23:1-3

The Sabbath: the day of delight

The Sabbath, the most important Jewish festival, is described so briefly here that we have to look elsewhere to understand what makes it a day of delight (Isaiah 58:13). In Exodus 20, the Ten Commandments say, 'Remember the Sabbath': follow God's example of six days of creation, then one day of rest and of time for the soul (Exodus 31:17).

Judaism teaches that the Sabbath is a day of warmth, light and joy, study, prayer, special foods and family closeness. Abraham Joshua Heschel said that Judaism has no tradition of creating splendid sacred spaces and cathedrals but instead sanctifies time, shaping a day of spiritual delight (*The Sabbath*, New York: Farrar, Strauss & Giroux, 1984). Tova Mordechai, who was brought up a Pentecostalist but later reclaimed her mother's Jewish origins, was thrilled by the palpable rest and peace she felt during the first Sabbath she spent with a Jewish family (*To Play With Fire: One Woman's Remarkable Odyssey*, Urim, 2005).

Lighting candles to welcome the Sabbath and blessing my children is a high point of my week.

Gather family and/or friends to share a meal. Before the meal follow the Jewish Sabbath custom of blessing the food and also every person present, either with the biblical blessing (Numbers 6:22-27) or your own words.

The Jews had light and joy, gladness and delight – let it be so for us too.

Esther 8:16

Passover: reliving the Exodus

Leviticus 23:4-8

This brief description of the major festivals celebrated in the biblical period can feel far removed from Jewish life today, partly because of Leviticus' focus on sacrifices, which have not been part of Jewish life and liturgy since the Jerusalem temple was destroyed in 70CE.

Passover, Pentecost and Succot were pilgrim festivals where everyone who could went to the Jerusalem temple to celebrate together. These verses give the timings of the festivals and mention the key words: Passover and unleavened bread. The Exodus story (Exodus 1–12) tells how God passed over the Israelite houses whose doors were marked with lamb's blood during the tenth plague, and that the children of Israel ate unleavened bread because their hasty departure meant there was no time for slowly fermenting and baking sourdough bread. In temple times, every family offered a Passover lamb to remember the pre-Exodus feast. The Mishnah, the first rabbinic code written down around 200CE, describes how, after the lambs had been killed on the afternoon of the fourteenth, everyone waited, chanting psalms of praise, for their turn to have the blood of their sacrifice thrown on the altar. Following the pattern of the week of creation when 'it was evening, and it was morning', the Jewish day of the month changes once it becomes dark, not at midnight. After sacrificing the lamb on the afternoon of the fourteenth, they took it home to roast and eat it to re-experience their ancestors' Exodus a few hours later on the evening beginning the fifteenth.

Today and tomorrow are Rosh Hashanah: wish any Jewish friends and colleagues a happy New Year.

Blessed are you, Eternal our God, who redeems and rescues.

First-fruits: the first of your crop

Leviticus 23:9-14

During the biblical era, the three pilgrim festivals celebrated and thanked God for the harvest won from the land through God's benevolence. During the middle ages, the Jews were no longer mostly farmers or, if they did farm, they no longer farmed the land of Israel with its special agricultural commandments. Nor did they have a temple to which to bring harvest offerings. Then theological interpretations – that Passover commemorated redemption, Pentecost revelation, and Succot God's protective care – became more significant than the barley, wheat and fruit harvests.

The custom of reaping a sheaf immediately after Passover became a demarcation line in the rabbinic period, between the Sadducees, who read the Bible literally, and the early rabbis who interpreted it more freely. 'Sabbath' here seems literally to mean the first Sabbath after Passover, but since Passover can fall on different days of the week, that would make Pentecost a movable feast. Therefore the rabbis interpreted it to mean 'count from the day of rest, the first day of the Passover festival'; on festivals some work forbidden on the Sabbath was done, but it was still a rest day. This meant Shavuot always fell on the same date, fifty days after Passover.

Here we read about offering the first sheaf of the harvest to God. Firstborn animals were also sacrificed. There was also a complex system of tithes, which were brought to the temple to support the priests and Levites (who had no agricultural land) and the poor.

Blessed are you, Eternal our God, who provides for all my needs.

Feast of Weeks (Shavuot) or Pentecost: a kingdom of priests

Leviticus 23:15-22

This festival takes place seven weeks (*Shavuot* in Hebrew) after Passover, on the fiftieth (*Pentekonta* in Greek) day. The festival commemorates God giving the Ten Commandments (Exodus 19 – 20) on Mount Sinai, which completed the covenant begun at the Exodus. Some books on Judaism consider Sinai the formative experience of the Jews, others the Exodus, but they are linked by the reaping of special harvest sheaves in the biblical and temple periods and by the counting of seven weeks, still done today. Another link is the declaration made by those who brought their first fruits to the temple (Deuteronomy 26:1-10), which is included in the contemporary Passover seder.

In biblical times, bringing first-fruits was vital to the festival. Like leaving the corners of the field for the poor and other vulnerable people to harvest, like the gleanings left for the poor, this was a significant part of the biblical commandments for social welfare.

The early rabbis taught that the Ten Commandments were given in the wilderness so they could not be regarded as any nation's possession but were open to all. An interpretative legend, more self-mocking about being 'chosen', was based on the phrase 'under the mountain' (Exodus 19:17): God tried giving the Ten Commandments to nations who refused them. A murderous nation refused when they heard 'Don't murder', a licentious nation when they heard 'Don't commit adultery'. Finally God lost patience and told the children of Israel: 'Accept this teaching or I drop Mount Sinai on you'!

Join or start a book group that meets to read religious books so you can add discussions with others to the pleasure derived from the books themselves.

Blessed are you, Eternal our God, who gives us your teaching.

Remembrance of trumpets

Leviticus 23:23-25

The Jewish festivals, like Jewish thought in general, balance universalism and specific Jewish identity. Exodus 12:2 says that Nissan, the month of Passover, commemorating the creation of the Jewish people when God redeemed them from slavery, is considered the first of months. Passover, therefore, is considered first in the cycle of pilgrim festivals. But, from a contrasting universalist perspective, the festival described in Leviticus as 'the day of remembrance of trumpet calls' was in early rabbinic writing described as the anniversary of creation and, therefore, became the New Year. This is the day when the year changes, even if it is in the seventh month (compare our different fiscal, school and calendar years). On Rosh Hashanah 2012, the Jewish year changes from 5772 to 5773; this number is derived from adding up the years described in the Bible.

The 'trumpet calls' mentioned here were developed by the rabbis into a wake-up call in preparation for the Day of Atonement; the shofar (usually a ram's horn; the long kudu can be used but not cow-horns because the sin of the Golden Calf renders them inappropriate for summoning to repentance) is blown a hundred times. Since the Bible describes how ram's horn trumpet-blasts destroyed the solid walls of Jericho, hopefully they are powerful enough to kick-start the Jewish community into remembering all they have done wrong, and need to put right, before Yom Kippur.

The Rosh Hashanah Additional Service has three themes: remembrance, shofar-blowing and God's kingship, since on this festival we acknowledge God's rule and judgement over us.

Blessed are you, Eternal our God, who helps us remember what we have done.

Day of Atonement: all is forgiven

Leviticus 23:26-32

In biblical and temple times forgiveness for sin was achieved by the sacrifices offered by the High Priest. Once the Romans had destroyed the temple, Jews repented and returned to a state of 'at-one-ment' with God by prayer, willingness to apologise for, and put right, sins committed against one's fellow human beings, and by doing good deeds, including giving to charity. The early rabbis decided that the 'afflicting the soul' mentioned here meant refraining from that which the body enjoys rather than actually physically damaging oneself. So on Yom Kippur Jews don't eat or drink (this applies only to those aged over thirteen, and healthy enough not to be harmed by fasting), have sex, wash for pleasure, as distinct from basic hygiene, anoint themselves or wear leather shoes.

The Sabbath and Yom Kippur are both described in the Bible as a 'Sabbath of Sabbaths' and so they share the distinction of being Judaism's most important day. The splendour of the High Priest and the temple service is described in Ecclesiasticus 50. The author emphasises the priest's impressive appearance, the choral singing that was part of the temple service, the way the people valued the priest's blessing and the drama of the moment when all prostrated themselves, while the High Priest, this one time in the year only, entered the Holy of Holies and uttered God's name. The departure of one of the two goat-offerings to the wilderness with the sins of Israel symbolically confessed on its head ensured that the people knew their sins were gone.

Blessed are you, Eternal our God, who delights in forgiveness.

Feast of Tabernacles: celebrate, celebrate, celebrate

Leviticus 23:33-44

Tabernacles (*Succot* in Hebrew) is the only festival on which Jews are commanded to celebrate; these verses say 'celebrate' four times. Like wheat at Shavuot and barley at Passover, Succot is a harvest festival, celebrating gathering autumn fruits. And, like them, it commemorates an aspect of the journey from Egyptian slavery to the promised land: living under God's protection for the forty wilderness years described in Deuteronomy 8:2-4.

In temple times, those who had travelled to Jerusalem for the solemn splendour of the Day of Atonement stayed to celebrate Tabernacles, the party time. During the festival, there was a water libation of which it was said, 'the one who hasn't seen it, has never seen true joy'; solemn rabbis would dance and sing. It is hard for us to understand animal sacrifices now, but if they measure a day's importance, Tabernacles was very important indeed; a grand total of seventy animals was sacrificed during this week (Numbers 29:12-34). It has been suggested that the seventy sacrifices are part of the universalistic approach of the seventh month festivals – one for each of the seventy nations who traditionally made up the ancient world. During the festival, Jews ate and slept in succot or temporary shelters ('tabernacles' doesn't quite convey the meaning) as a reminder of the frail dwellings they lived under both when harvesting and for the forty years in the wilderness. The same word is used in the Jewish evening service when we ask for the shelter of God's peace until morning.

Blessed are you, Eternal our God, who spreads a shelter (succah) of peace over us and over all the world.

Jewish festivals

Jewish festivals today

Notes based on the Hebrew Bible by

Rachel Montagu

For Rachel's biography see p. 264.

Genesis 21:1-14

Rosh Hashanah: A new beginning

Rosh Hashanah and Yom Kippur are called the 'days of awe' because of their solemn message that at this time Jews stand before God's judgement. But Rosh Hashanah is also a cheerful New Year celebration, a time for sending greeting cards and eating apple and honey, hoping the coming year will be sweet. Jews from Eastern countries eat a series of foods before the evening meal; a short blessing is said for each, invoking a good year via puns about the food – for instance the Hebrew for carrot is the same as for 'decree' so the invocation for carrots is 'may God grant us a good decree'.

In synagogue all the cloths and scroll covers are white, a visual reminder that we hope our sins will be forgiven. The shofar is blown a hundred times, ending with the longest blast the shofar-blower can manage. My father was the shofar blower at my childhood synagogue; I used to worry for his health as his face turned puce while he held the notes as long as possible. The 'Unetana Tokef' prayer declares that today God decides our fate for the coming year.

The story of the 'binding of Isaac' is one of the most frightening and challenging in the Bible; its theme of obedience to God and willing self-sacrifice is appropriate for the day. According to Jewish interpretative tradition, Isaac is thirty-seven years old; old enough to understand and consent to martyrdom.

Blessed are you, Eternal our God, who blessed the years.

Yom Kippur (Day of Atonement): Prayer, repentance and loving actions

Jonah 1

The ten days of repentance between the New Year and the Day of Atonement are used to do everything we can to put right any wrongs done to other people; we cannot take the easy step of confessing to God without first apologising to those we have hurt. Because prayer, repentance, and kind deeds can ameliorate a harsh fate decided at Rosh Hashanah, on these days those rarely seen at synagogue services attend.

During the quick, easily-digested meal eaten before the fast, parents can bless their children. I apologise to my sons every year for being too impatient a mother, but at least they know I want to do better.

Yom Kippur services start with a brief prayer of forgiveness for all who have wronged us during the past year and a prayer welcoming those who have left the synagogue and return only on this day; then all the scrolls are taken out of the ark and the haunting 'Kol Nidre' is sung.

Because there is no time needed for preparing and eating meals, the services on Yom Kippur continue unbroken from morning until dark. As well as saying the many prayers of repentance, singing the many beautiful special tunes and hymns, Yom Kippur is a wonderful opportunity to think about our lives and decide whether we want to make changes. If we worry whether God will forgive us, the Book of Jonah, which is read during the afternoon, reminds us that God wants to forgive if we only show the same willingness to repent as the people of Nineveh.

Reflect on whether there are changes you need to make in your life, including human relationships where forgiveness is needed.

Eternal, Eternal, God of mercy and graciousness, slow to anger and full of loving-kindness and truth, forgiving sin, transgression and wrongdoing, who considers your servants to deserve forgiveness.

Exodus 34:6-7

Rachel Montagu

Succot (Tabernacles): 'Answer us, save us'

Ecclesiastes 12

Ecclesiastes' world-weariness seems at odds with the joyous mood of Succot. Some of his message, like 'much study exhausts' (verse 12) will be hard for enthusiastic readers of this book to understand! Ecclesiastes is a man struggling with the Hebrew language to find words to express his search for the meaning of life.

During Succot Jews eat in temporary shelters, roofed in natural material. In kindly climates they may sleep in them too. Some synagogues use this as a basis for youth projects working with the homeless. The Torah commands Jews to wave the four species: citron, palm, myrtle and willow. This is done while singing psalms of praise in the morning service and during processions round the synagogue chanting 'hoshanot', special prayers with the refrain 'Save us'.

Seven weeks after Passover, Jews have Shavuot to celebrate God giving the Torah or teaching. Succot re-enacts this; the seven days of the festival are followed by a day celebrating God's teaching; the extra festival day after Succot (Leviticus 23:36) is now called Simchat Torah, Rejoicing of the Torah, and marks the beginning and end of the annual cycle of reading the Pentateuch (Torah in Hebrew). The last verses of Deuteronomy are read, followed immediately by the first verses of Genesis. Before the reading, the scrolls are processed round the synagogue and in many communities the congregation sings and dances with them and all participate in the readings. The diarist Samuel Pepys visited London's first synagogue on Simchat Torah and thought all the happy dancing looked very chaotic.

Eternal our God, all is vanity – except the pure soul which will in the future account for itself before the throne of your glory.

Pesach (Passover): Tell your children!

Exodus 15:1-18

It says four times in the Torah 'tell your children about leaving Egypt'. The Passover seder is an exercise in home education: extended families gather round the dining table to read the Haggadah, which means 'telling the story'. Everything possible is done to excite children's curiosity about the seder and they ask the questions that launch it. The first seder I conducted felt more a sign of becoming an adult than even the first time I voted. Many families try to add extra readings and wide-ranging discussions of freedom and responsibility so that the seder lasts long into the night. Some end by reading the Song of Songs, read on Passover because of its message of God's love.

During the seder, Jews eat the unleavened bread and bitter herbs mentioned in the Bible, vegetables dipped in salt water, bitter like the tears the slaves shed, and charoseth, a paste of apples, nuts and raisins, to remind us of the mortar Pharaoh's slaves used. Four cups of wine or grape juice are drunk as a reminder of God's four promises of redemption in Exodus 6:6-7. Moses' name is never mentioned in the Haggadah; all the emphasis is on God as rescuer, not on Moses the intermediary.

Passover cooking can be a challenge because during Passover Jews avoid all products containing anything fermented, leaven or ordinary flour. Many synagogues now have a community seder on the second night so the congregation can celebrate together. The eighth day of the festival commemorates God's next act of salvation, the crossing of the Red Sea.

Who is like you, Eternal our God, among the gods, who is like you, splendid in holiness?

Exodus 15:11

Shavuot (Pentecost):'We will do and we will understand'

Exodus
19:9 – 20:2

The Ten Commandments are read during the festival morning service. There are many ways to analyse the Ten Commandments. One way is to interpret the first five, from 'I am your God', the introductory commandment that justifies the rest, to 'Honour parents', as commandments between God and humanity, and the rest as commandments between human beings. Then 'I am your God' parallels 'Don't murder'; murder destroys a person made in God's image. Adultery and idol worship both betray a covenantal relationship.

The children of Israel promised, 'We will do and we will hear.' This might seem the wrong way round; commentators suggest that 'hear' means understand, and only by doing commandments can we understand them.

While most festivals are celebrated in a way that involves children, an increasingly popular way to observe Shavuot is staying up to study through the night, ending with a dawn service. The traditional subject matter was to summarise all Jewish teaching by reading the first and last paragraphs of each book of the Bible and section of the Talmud. Today popular study texts include Ruth, which is read on Shavuot: Jews are either descended from those who stood at Sinai or from converts, and Ruth is an exemplary convert.

Dairy foods are eaten – just as milk is ideal nourishment for a growing body, God's teachings are ideal food for the soul. Traditionally, British Jews ate cheesecake; today children are often given ice cream after morning services.

Yom Kippur services are very beautiful because of the special prayers and music. But spending a whole day in synagogue while fasting can be exhausting; be sympathetic to any Jewish friends and colleagues who seem tired today.

Blessed are you, Eternal our God, who has given us words of teaching to study.

Rachel Montagu

Chanukah (Dedication): by God's spirit

Zechariah 4

Chanukah commemorates the rededication of the temple after Antiochus desecrated it by sacrificing pigs. His taxes and religious persecution triggered a rebellion led by Mattathias, a priest, and his five sons. Inspired by God, their knowledge of the country helped them win against a larger, better-equipped army of mercenaries. Because they succeeded in hammering the opposition, they were called Maccabees – hammers, in Hebrew. Their story is found in the apocryphal books of Maccabees.

Chanukah is celebrated by lighting a special nine-branched candlestick for eight days; one light is lit by the serving light on the first day, two on the second; by the eighth day all the lights are lit. This commemorates a Talmudic legend: when the Maccabbees came to rededicate the temple there was only enough oil to keep alight the great temple lamp for one day, but miraculously it lasted the eight days needed for more to be prepared. Some Jews light candles but others prefer oil-lamps because lamps were used in the temple. It is customary to place Chanukah lamps where they can be seen by passers-by to publicise God's miracle.

Today Chanukah has become more important; it gives diaspora Jews a festival to celebrate in December. For Israeli Jews who have fought so many wars against larger, well-equipped armies, the message of the Chanukah prayer reflects their experience: the weak defeated the strong, the few defeated the many.

Blessed are you, Eternal our God, who has performed many miracles for all who serve you.

Purim (Feast of Lots): Lots to celebrate

Esther 9:1-19

Jewish history has been flippantly summarised: 'They attacked us, God saved us, Let's eat!' Purim is the biblical festival that best fits this template – Haman decided all Jews must die because Mordechai the Jew refused to kowtow to him. 'Purim' means 'lots': Haman cast lots to decide the date for massacring the Jews. Esther's intervention with King Ahasuerus could not nullify Haman's decree, due to the foolishly rigid rules of the Persian Empire, but at least it ensured the Jews could defend themselves. The death toll in this chapter may sound horrendous to a modern ear but their refusal to attack those who did not attack them, or to take spoil, was great chivalry in its day.

Purim is celebrated by fasting beforehand to commemorate Esther's fast, reading the book of Esther in synagogue, giving to the poor, sending food to friends, and eating a special meal. Later in Jewish tradition it became the carnival day for fancy dress; Jewish schools put on mocking plays and parodies and Jewish newspapers carry incredible stories.

The Book of Esther offers profound challenges about diaspora living and collective punishment. Is anti-Semitism the inevitable response to difference? Haman tells the king that the Jews are a people with different laws, whom the king should not let remain at peace. Esther's place in the Bible has been challenged because it never mentions God's name, although later commentators decided 'deliverance from another place' (4:14) meant God, and deemed beautiful, literate and brave Queen Esther a prophetess. Esther and Vashti have both been admired as heroines of resistance.

Blessed are you, Eternal our God, who rescues the vulnerable.

Rachel Montagu

Jewish festivals

The festivals in the ministry of Jesus

Notes based on the Revised Standard Version by
Ann Conway-Jones

Ann Conway-Jones is an Anglican, and chair of Birmingham Council of Christians and Jews. She is fascinated by the fact that Jews and Christians share scriptural texts, yet often interpret them very differently.

Matthew 12:1-4

Sabbath debates

As a Jew, Jesus participated in weekly Sabbath observance, and the yearly round of festivals. The same was true of the first disciples – we read of them going up to the temple to pray (Acts 3:1). Gradually, however, Christians devised their own celebrations, such as meeting to share the Lord's supper (1 Corinthians 11:20). And they discovered new meanings in the Jewish festivals. The process started in the early church, as we shall be discovering this week; but it took time. Some Christians in the fourth century attended synagogues on Sabbaths and festivals. We know this because John Chrysostom (who became bishop of Constantinople) got very cross about it! It seems that the laity was more relaxed about interfaith exchange than the clergy.

Today we read of Jesus in a dispute about how to observe the Sabbath: exactly which activities are allowed, and which are prohibited, by the fourth commandment? Vigorous debate about the interpretation of God's law was, and is, an important part of Judaism. In entering into such a discussion, Jesus was not criticising Judaism, but being quintessentially Jewish.

God of discussion and debate, teach us to listen, and to appreciate the value of other people's ways of thinking.

Sabbath rest

Hebrews 4:1-11

As a joyful day of rest and recreation, the Sabbath is a foretaste of heavenly rest. Here in Hebrews we find anxiety over who will enter this promised future rest. The author quotes from Psalm 95, which meditates on the stormy relationship between God and Israel in the wilderness, as narrated in Numbers. God often expresses anger at the people's lack of faith, and sometimes threatens to disinherit them, but always relents. The relationship never comes to an end. Psalm 95 and Hebrews 4, however, reflect the anger rather than the subsequent forgiveness. Hebrews talks of 'us' and 'them': 'they' have been cut off because of their disobedience, 'we' are now the people of God. It has been suggested that the letter was written to Christians of Jewish origin mourning the destruction of the Jerusalem temple, in order to reassure them that by persevering with Christ they could still enter God's promised rest. But one group is reassured at the expense of another.

Is the Sabbath rest of God really something to fight over? Is it appropriate to gloat over other people's mistakes? Does not our relationship with God have ups and downs? The tone here reminds me of sibling rivalry – competition for a parent's love. What is God's response? Understanding and forgiveness of the anxieties involved perhaps, along with encouragement to take a break. Can we lay aside our differences, and enjoy a Sabbath rest together?

God of rest, grant us moments of stillness in our busyness, when we may see life in perspective.

Christ, the Passover lamb

1 Corinthians 5: 6-8

Whether or not the Last Supper was a Passover meal is debatable. But Jesus was certainly crucified at Passover time. In John's Gospel he is described as 'the Lamb of God' (John 1:35), and he dies as the Passover lambs are being sacrificed, ready for the evening celebration. Revelation uses imagery of 'the Lamb who was slain' (Revelation 5:12). And here Paul calls Jesus 'our paschal lamb' (verse 7b). The blood of the first Passover lambs averted death from Israelite houses (Exodus 12:21-27). This imagery, therefore, proclaims Jesus as overcoming death. Paul also finds new symbolism in the unleavened bread of Passover, and the preliminary spring clean. But this symbolism applies not to Jesus but to us. We are to clean out the 'old leaven' in our lives, ready to celebrate with 'unleavened bread', representing the integrity of our Christian lives.

This is a good example of the Christian reinterpretation of Jewish festivals. Religious traditions stay alive by being reinterpreted. Jews and Christians have both discovered new symbolism in Passover. The first Christians linked it with the death of Christ. The rabbis coped with the destruction of the temple and the experience of exile by developing a new Passover liturgy for the home, with ritual questions and symbolic foods. So long as we are honest about what we have done, and don't expect our symbolism to speak to Jews, there needn't be a problem. Each tradition has its own integrity.

God of freedom, avert from our lives malice and evil, that we may live in sincerity and truth.

Festivals in perspective

Colossians 2: 16 – 3:4

Paul warns the Colossians not to let anyone pass judgement on them. It is not clear exactly who he is writing against. His opponents seem to value the observance of festivals, and dietary restrictions. But there is also mention of angels. It has been suggested that the ascetic practices referred to were preparations for the receipt of mystical visions. Paul also urges his readers to 'seek the things that are above' (3:1), but his emphasis is on Christ, rather than angels. In Christ dwells 'the whole fullness of deity' (2:9). And all who are baptised are knit together into the body of Christ. There are to be no claims of spiritual superiority.

Getting the balance right between 'the things that are above' and 'things that are on earth' (3:2) is not always easy, particularly when it comes to celebrating festivals. These usually involve necessary 'earthly' tasks: cleaning, preparing food, sorting out accommodation for guests, buying presents. But things can get out of hand, especially if people get competitive. The purpose of the festival becomes lost. Competitiveness, however, can also enter into the spiritual side of festivals, as this letter testifies. Who can celebrate in the most humble fashion?! Paul continues the letter by emphasising human relationships: 'forbearing one another', 'forgiving each other' (3:13). What matters is not our individual achievement, but our contribution to the harmony of the whole body.

God of wisdom, teach us when to care for things on earth, and when to set our minds on things above.

Dedication festival

John 10:22-42

For those of us involved in Jewish–Christian relations, John's Gospel is a challenge. The gospel of love can seem to turn into the gospel of intolerance. Occasionally we get a glimpse of the historical Jesus: 'salvation is from the Jews' he says to the Samaritan woman (John 4:22). But no one reading today's passage for the first time would realise that Jesus was Jewish: 'Is it not written in *your* law?'(verse 34), he says to 'the Jews'. Scholars suggest that the gospel was laid down in layers, with the top layer reflecting a predominantly gentile church. It seems to be a frightened, defensive church, with an 'us and them' attitude, convinced that it alone has possession of the light, surrounded by an ocean of darkness. 'The Jews' becomes shorthand for the enemies of Jesus.

The feast of Dedication referred to (now called *Chanukah*) celebrated the victory of Judas Maccabeus over the Syrian armies, and the reconsecration of the temple (see 1 Maccabees 4:36-59). A persecuted minority held its own. The Christians who put together John's Gospel saw themselves as a persecuted minority. Is their beleaguered attitude appropriate for our situation today; or do we need to add a new layer to the gospel, one that recognises that all humanity are God's sheep?

God of love, help us to live with the fragility of our beliefs, and never to use them as a tool of condemnation.

Tabernacles

Matthew 17:1-13

On the top of a high mountain, Jesus appears to Peter, James and John as his heavenly self. His body and clothes are transfigured. His face shines as did the face of Moses after speaking to God (Exodus 34:29), and he wears the white garments of heaven (see Revelation 4:4). Moses and Elijah, key figures from scripture, act as witnesses. Peter asks Jesus whether he should make three booths, or tabernacles. In Greek, as in English, the word 'tabernacle' can refer either to the portable desert sanctuary, the precursor of the temple, in which the glory of God resided (Exodus 40:34-38), or to the booths that the Israelites were to build every year in remembrance of their desert wanderings (Leviticus 23:42-43).

Is Peter offering shelter, or is he wanting to mark this as a holy place? Since Jesus is appearing in heavenly glory, it would make sense for the reference to be to the sanctuary. Peter wants to provide a suitable residence for the divine. He does not realise that this glimpse of Jesus' glory is only temporary – no building is required. Following the resurrection, the church comes to understand itself as the body of Christ (1 Corinthians 12:27), the new temple (2 Corinthians 6:16). The glory of God is now to reside in the life of the Christian community.

God of glory, reveal yourself to us in the midst of our complicated, compromised lives.

Ann Conway-Jones

Pentecost

Acts 2:1-13

The Jewish festival of Shavuot commemorates the revelation of God at Mount Sinai, and the giving of the Torah. God came down upon the mountain, accompanied by fire, smoke and the sound of trumpets (Exodus 19:16-20), to seal the relationship with Israel, making it 'a kingdom of priests and a holy nation' (Exodus 19:6). The liberation from Egypt, commemorated at Passover, came to fruition. In Greek, Shavuot became known as Pentecost, from the Greek word for fifty, because the festival is approximately fifty days after Passover. This story in Acts marks the Christian reinterpretation of Pentecost. A new revelation took place, accompanied by wind and tongues of fire, which sealed the work of Christ, leading to the birth of the church.

The first letter of Peter picks up on the language of Exodus 19, and describes the church as 'a chosen race, a royal priesthood, a holy nation, God's own people' (1 Peter 2:9). Unfortunately, this kind of imagery led to the church seeing itself as the replacement of Israel, with disastrous consequences once it gained political power. Many denominations have now publicly repudiated suggestions that Judaism is obsolete, turning to Paul for support: 'The gifts and the call of God are irrevocable' (Romans 11:29). We need to find ways of making space for each other, so that both festivals of Pentecost can be celebrated.

God of wind and fire, send your Holy Spirit, to teach us new ways of speaking.

Readings in Mark (4)

Following Jesus 1

Mark 10:2-12

God made them male and female

What does it mean to be a Christian? For me the simplest definition of a Christian is a follower of Jesus. But what does it mean to follow Jesus? These next two weeks will be an exploration of that theme.

Today's passage takes us back to basics: 'From the beginning of creation, "God made them male and female"' (verse 6). Our beginning as Christians is that moment of inhalation when the Holy Spirit, God's breath of life, pours into our lungs and we become alive. The rest of our Christian life is about discovering the consequences of that moment. It is a first moment that repeats itself endlessly, breath by breath, not just at our physical birth or our rebirth in faith, but at every moment in which we return in conscious awareness to the source of our existence.

God makes us male and female: not just outwardly, but inwardly also. Each of us is a microcosm of humanity, striving for that unity and wholeness of which marriage is a symbol and sacrament. God calls us to grow up, to be united with the otherness we find in our beloved and in ourselves, to be one.

For our prayers over the coming fortnight, I have chosen well-known hymn texts (from *The English Hymnal*, 1906/1933). You could sing them as well as say them.

For your prayer today, simply breathe in and out and become aware of your breath as the life of the Spirit at work in you.

Notes based on the New Revised Standard Version by

Nicholas Alan Worssam, SSF

Brother Nicholas Alan is a member of the Anglican religious community, the Society of Saint Francis. He has been a friar since 1995, and has lived at Glasshampton Monastery in Worcestershire, England, since 2002.

Jesus called to him those whom he wanted

Mark 3:13-19

Jesus went up a mountain; often, following him feels like scrambling up the Himalayas behind a bounding Sherpa guide. Then he called and named his apostles, to be with him, to proclaim the message and to cast out demons. Like Adam at the dawn of creation, Jesus names us and makes us who we are. Our names invite us – Peter, be rock-solid; James, like thunder; Margaret, bright pearl of wisdom; Irene, peace.

Those three duties of the apostles are ours also, in our varied situations. First, to be with Jesus, to speak with him, eat with him and learn from him at work and play. Without this enjoyment of his presence, how can we share his life with others? Today we find him in the scriptures, and in our prayers, but also in those Christ-like people (of all faiths) who inspire us to take greater strides in the upward climb. Roped together there is less chance of falling, and even overhangs can be scaled. Then we are ready to speak and act out his message: that God is here among us; that this is the kingdom of God; and it is a place of healing and wholeness for body and mind.

Jesus calls us because he wants us. Do we share that validation with others, making them feel cared-for and esteemed?

Jesus calls us! – o'er the tumult
Of our life's wild restless sea
Day by day his sweet voice soundeth,
Saying, 'Christian, follow me':

Jesus calls us! – by thy mercies,
Saviour, may we hear thy call,
Give our hearts to thy obedience,
Serve and love thee best of all.

C F Alexander

Who are my mother and my brothers?

Mark 3:31-35

This time it is the family of Jesus who calls to him, but he does not answer. Or does he? They think he is out of his mind – 'Who does that son of mine think he is?' But Jesus is unperturbed. His answer to the call of his heavenly Father is unshakeable, and eventually brings even his brothers to be leaders of the church. His mother later follows his call to the end, standing faithfully at the foot of the cross, even when so many of those sat around him that day had subsequently fled in fear.

What is the calling of Jesus? To do the will of God, and so be his brother, sister and mother. Mary qualified on those grounds abundantly, showing us the way to say 'Yes' to God's Spirit. Jesus calls us all to be his family, to be related to him by blood and birth, to find in Mary our mother and know ourselves to be her son or daughter. We become in this way part of the family firm. Discipleship is not so much a lone enterprise as a corporate undertaking where risks and successes are jointly shared, and the losses are underwritten personally by the owner of the bank.

But to enter this family we cannot remain standing outside. Where do we find our relations in God? Jesus says: 'Right here!'

Who are your mother and sisters and brothers?

Let saints on earth in concert sing
With those whose work is done;
For all the servants of our King
In earth and heaven are one.

One family, we dwell in him,
One Church, above, beneath;
Though now divided by the stream,
The narrow stream of death.

C Wesley, and others

How many loaves do you have?

Mark 8:1-10

Jesus did not preach a gospel only of spiritual salvation. James, his brother, had understood his message well when he asked: 'If a brother or sister is hungry and you say "Go in peace and eat your fill," and yet you do not supply their bodily needs, what is the good of that?' (James 2:15-16, abridged). Jesus had compassion on the crowd and acted to satisfy their stomachs as well as their souls. But he does not act alone. First he asks the disciples: 'How many loaves do you have?' What do you have to contribute to this situation? How can you practically help your neighbour? Only when they have brought out all they have does he act to multiply their generosity a hundredfold.

Jesus takes what we have and what we are, and he gives thanks, breaks it and distributes it to all who have need. Do we want to be taken, offered up, broken and shared in this way? It is the basis of our eucharistic worship and the pattern of our Christian life, but perhaps most of us would rather look the other way or catch the first bus home. The reward for staying the course is infinite. Not just four thousand well-fed people eager to hear more teaching, but the seventy nations of the world gathered up into the kingdom, like the fragments filling the seven huge baskets at the end of the meal.

And so we come; O draw us to thy feet,
Most patient Saviour; who canst love us still;
And by this Food, so awful and so sweet,
Deliver us from every touch of ill:
In thine own service make us glad and free,
And grant us never more to part with thee.

W Bright

Do you not yet understand?

Mark 8:11-21

Which are more important, questions or answers? In this passage Jesus has ten questions to ask, but not many answers are forthcoming. He seems to be amazed at the lack of understanding and hardness of heart, both among the Pharisees and his own disciples. It's a theme that runs through Mark's Gospel and is echoed in John 14:9, where Jesus asks: 'Have I been with you all this time, Philip, and you still do not know me?'

The question is asked of us, the reader of the gospel, just as much as it is asked of those first disciples. Have we been with Jesus all this time, and still we do not know him, trust him, or follow his way to true life? The question is relentless. Like Paul on the Damascus road I find myself continually crying out: 'Who are you, Lord?' (Acts 9:5). Maybe the question is enough. It's not that Jesus wants us to solve the riddle of the number of loaves and baskets, it's that he is calling us to wrestle with the soul-encompassing question of who he is and what this kingdom is that he is revealing to us.

Wisdom says to her children: 'I love those who love me, and those who seek me diligently find me' (Proverbs 8:17). May we never tire in our seeking, until we become the question to which Christ is the answer.

Jesus, these eyes have never seen
That radiant form of thine;
The veil of sense hangs dark between
Thy blessèd face and mine.

Yet, though I have not seen, and still
Must rest in faith alone,
I love thee, dearest Lord, and will,
Unseen, but not unknown.

Ray Palmer

Those who lose their life will save it

Mark 8:34-38

Of all the sayings of Jesus, this has to be the most ruthless and the most kind. Ruthless, because it allows no room for escape; kind because it reveals the way to true life. But is there really anything to attain, or indeed anyone to attain it? How can a relinquished self be fulfilled? The sixteenth-century Spanish mystic John of the Cross says: 'To arrive at being all, desire to be nothing. To come to the knowledge of all, desire the knowledge of nothing' (*Ascent of Mount Carmel*, Book 1, Chapter 13, Numbers 10-12, ICS, 1979, translated by Kavanaugh).

What is this nothing? Is it not the simple relinquishment of all attachment to anything less than God? 'Because', as John continues, 'if you desire to have something in all, your treasure in God is not purely your all.' This is Lady Poverty, whose secrets Francis of Assisi knew well, as he called out to God over and over, '*Deus meum et omnia*': 'My God and my all'. This is the Wisdom of God, whom Paul revealed when he cried out: 'I have been crucified with Christ; and it is no longer I who live, but it is Christ who lives in me' (Galatians 2:19-20).

It is not a case of 'all or nothing'; rather it is all and nothing – going 'by a way in which you are not' (John of the Cross) to find God in all things.

Take up thy cross, the Saviour said,
If thou wouldst my disciple be;
Deny thyself, the world forsake,
And humbly follow after me.

To thee, great Lord, the One in Three,
All praise for evermore ascend;
O grant us in our Home to see
The heavenly life that knows no end.

C W Everest

Receive the kingdom of God as a little child

Mark 10:13-16

Children may have guardian angels in heaven (Matthew 18:10) but they are not always little angels themselves. Empathy and negotiation are learned skills, and sometimes there are many tears in the process. Why does Jesus ask us to be like children? Is it their innocence, their obedience, their simplicity that we need?

For some Christians the liturgical practice of speaking as children before a heavenly Father feels regressive for an adult believer. Children in those days were very often treated as servants, but didn't Jesus call us to be not servants but friends (John 15:15)? And children are so vulnerable to hurt in their relationships with adults, as the church has finally begun to admit. Can this still be a model for us when exploited innocence is the source of so much pain?

But children still have a voice with which to teach us holy things. Perhaps it is simply the willingness of children to be loved, to be blessed, to be held by those who truly care for them. Jesus plainly delighted in the company of children. May we also delight in Jesus, letting him bless us and love us into the kingdom of God.

How can we be more childlike with God?
How can we protect and cherish our children, and our inner child?

O holy Child of Bethlehem,
Descend to us, we pray;
Cast out our sin, and enter in,
Be born in us to-day.
We hear the Christmas angels
The great glad tidings tell:
O come to us, abide with us,
Our Lord Emmanuel.

Phillips Brooks

Readings in Mark (4)

Following Jesus 2

Notes based on the New Revised Standard Version by

Nicholas Alan Worssam, SSF

For Nicholas' biography, see p.285.

Mark 10:17-22

Why do you call me good?

The story about the rich young man is foundational in the history of Christian religious life. In the fourth century, Athanasius wrote the hugely popular *Life of Anthony*, about a man who heard this gospel text and, leaving home and family, became one of the first monks in the deserts of Egypt. Countless others over the centuries, including Francis of Assisi, have been similarly inspired to take the step that the rich man with Jesus could not take. But it is a call to all of us, regardless of our situation in life, to give up all that holds us back from God.

And Jesus helps us: he draws us out of ourselves. Mark says, 'Jesus, looking at him, loved him and said, "You lack one thing"' (verse 21). That word, 'loved' could equally be translated 'embraced' or 'caressed'. Jesus said only what the young man most needed to hear. But it was too much to bear. Maybe later he heard the invitation again and said 'Yes'. Whatever his response, ours is called for again and again as God invites us to enter the mystery of Jesus Christ, in whom 'every one of God's promises is a "Yes"' (2 Corinthians 1: 20).

In your prayer, allow yourself to be looked at and loved (embraced, caressed).

Then who can be saved?

Mark 10:23-27

The Hebrew scriptures are frequently ambivalent about material riches. Wisdom says: 'Riches and honour are with me, enduring wealth and prosperity' (Proverbs 8:18); and yet 'Better is a little with righteousness than large income with injustice' (16:8). Was the rich man in Mark's Gospel proud? Certainly he claimed to have kept the commandments since his youth. Was this his idol: not just greed (which Paul calls idolatry – Colossians 3:5), but his self-image as a blameless man?

The disciples are amazed that riches are such an impediment to entering the kingdom. Maybe they thought they were a reward for a righteous life. But Jesus knows the perils of material attachments, and the joy of being set free. So too Paul had 'learned to be content with whatever I have ... I can do all things through him who strengthens me' (Philippians 4:11, 13).

And are we not indicted also, who have more than we need in food, medicine, clothing and shelter? Abundance is not wrong – it is God's gift – but, unshared with those in need, it turns to poison in our stomachs and our hearts. To return to John of the Cross: 'To come to possess all, desire the possession of nothing' (*Ascent of Mount Carmel*, Book 1, Chapter 13, Number 11, ICS, 1979, translated by Kavanaugh). Who can desire this? But with God all things are possible.

What is holding you back from a closer walk with God?

O for a closer walk with God,
A calm and heavenly frame;
A light to shine upon the road
That leads me to the Lamb!

The dearest idol I have known,
Whate'er that idol be,
Help me to tear it from thy throne,
And worship only thee.

W Cowper

Look, we have left everything

Mark 10:28-31

At first Peter seems to have fallen into the same trap as the rich man: look at all the good things we have done! True, says Jesus, you will receive your reward, together with all the trouble that any reward will bring. But look beyond this narrow expectation of doing good for the sake of the benefits you will receive. Just do the right thing. All expectations will be overturned in the kingdom of God: the first will be last and the last first. Don't try to get to the head of the queue or you might just find the entrance moved to the other end.

So what should Peter have said? Perhaps that saying of Jesus in Luke's Gospel: 'We are worthless slaves; we have done only what we ought to have done!' (Luke 17:10). Yet who of us can say even that much? Better rather to let go of all self-judgement – 'Let the one who boasts, boast in the Lord' (1 Corinthians 1:31). Because of our poverty? Rather because of our riches in Christ. The more you leave behind, the more 'all things are yours ... and you belong to Christ, and Christ belongs to God' (1 Corinthians 3:21, 23). Then we can say with Paul that we are 'poor, yet making many rich; as having nothing, and yet possessing everything' (2 Corinthians 6:10).

How has God made you rich?

Dear Lord and Father of mankind
Forgive our foolish ways!
Re-clothe us in our rightful mind,
In purer lives thy service find,
In deeper reverence praise.

In simple trust like theirs who heard,
Beside the Syrian sea,
The gracious calling of the Lord,
Let us, like them, without a word
Rise up and follow thee.

J G Whittier

What is it you want?

Mark 10:31-40

Once more Jesus asks a question that pierces to the heart: 'What is it you want me to do for you?' (verse 36). It seems an innocuous question, but it is central to the Christian life. What we ask for and receive may be more than we bargained for. Never ask for two contradictory things (riches and peace of mind, say?) as you may get a taste of both and then have to choose in all earnestness which one to keep.

James and John ask for front-row seats, but can they pay the price of the ticket? In the end they do, but it costs them, and Jesus, every penny they have. What do you want Jesus to do in your life? It's a frightening question. Voice it too loudly, and it might just happen: tomorrow, or even today. Idle dreams may while away a prayer-time or a distant sermon, but what if Jesus took us at our word? Do we really want the things we say and sing in church on a Sunday morning?

Jesus has no illusions about the cost of his path. Nothing will be left to him at the end. But if he is to be submerged in death then he knows also that it is God who plunges him under. His own Father stands waiting, drenched in the same waters, looking for the gasping recognition that he is truly God's Son.

When I survey the wondrous Cross,
On which the Prince of glory died,
My richest gain I count but loss,
And pour contempt on all my pride.

Were the whole realm of nature mine,
That were a present far too small;
Love so amazing, so divine,
Demands my soul, my life, my all.

I Watts

Do not stop him

Mark 9:38-49

Are you with us or against us? It seems that the teaching of Jesus is at times designed to polarise, to force people into making a choice. You can't just sit on the fence. But this story gives a broader scope to the range of God's kingdom. 'Whoever is not against us is for us' (verse 40). Jesus gives people the benefit of the doubt. This saying is significantly more inclusive than the parallel saying as recorded by Matthew: 'Whoever is not with me is against me, and whoever does not gather with me scatters' (Matthew 12:30). Maybe Matthew's version reflects a more urgent situation than that of Mark, whether in the life of Jesus or in the life of the church. What is God saying to us today?

John struggled to include others in his vision of the kingdom. Jesus called him 'thunderhead' perhaps because of an explosive temper that would happily have razed a Samaritan village to the ground (Luke 9:54). Yet John's Gospel shows Jesus going out of his way to include a Samaritan woman into the circle of faith (John 4), and the first letter of John is full of exhortations to love one another (e.g. 1 John 4:7). Perhaps it was the mellowing of age that opened John's eyes to the all-embracing compassion of Jesus. Certainly all of us need to care for the 'little ones' among us, realising our own littleness and need of God's love.

There's a wideness in God's mercy,
Like the wideness of the sea;
There's a kindness in his justice,
Which is more than liberty.

But we make his love too narrow
By false limits of our own;
And we magnify his strictness
With a zeal he will not own.

F W Faber

The Son of Man came to serve

Mark 10:35-45

People sometimes ask me why I became a monk. There are many answers I could give. I could talk about the help of a commitment to regular prayer, or mention the support of community life. But perhaps the deepest reason is that I am here to save the world. Maybe that sounds a little megalomaniacal, but I believe it to be the vocation of us all.

Jesus says, 'The Son of Man came not to be served but to serve, and to give his life a ransom for many' (verse 45). This verse stands out as a pivotal text in Mark's Gospel, introducing the final cataclysmic week of Jesus' life. The title 'the Son of Man' is notoriously difficult to interpret, but a part of its meaning is simply 'a person like myself', or even 'the Human One'. It marks out Jesus as representative of the whole human race. And Jesus' whole life was an offering of himself – not just on the cross, but day by day as he taught and healed, and ate and drank with those he called friends. He lived as well as died for them, and he calls us to enter that gift. Yes, Jesus saves us, but he calls us also to share in his saving death and resurrection, and to offer up ourselves for the well-being of all.

What is your gift to the world?

O thou who camest from above,
The pure celestial fire to impart,
Kindle a flame of sacred love
On the mean altar of my heart.

Jesus, confirm my heart's desire
To work, and speak, and think for thee;
Still let me guard the holy fire,
And still stir up thy gift in me.

C Wesley

Do you see?

Mark 13:1-13

From my window I look out over the Severn valley. It's a beautiful view of woods and farmland. Often the sun will rise red over the hills, while clouds of mist still linger over the river. It is a scene that inhabitants of this hill must have gazed at for centuries, but it is a fragile landscape all the same. I read once in a book that if the Greenland ice-cap melts, sea levels will eventually rise 50 metres. Here we are 70 metres above sea level. That means the monastery will be on an island in a vastly expanded Severn estuary, in an archipelago once known as Great Britain.

The disciples of Jesus are amazed by the temple in Jerusalem, but Jesus is unimpressed. He clearly foresaw the fall of Jerusalem, and its destruction by the Roman army in 70 CE. Many of today's scientific prophets foresee a coming catastrophe in the world's climate while we carry on with business as usual. I write this in October 2010. Will anything much have changed by the time you are reading this in 2012? Storms and droughts, wars and rumours of wars are already a reality. How long will it be before we see the signs of the times and act?

There is always hope: 'the one who endures to the end will be saved' (verse 13). But what will be the cost and who will pay?

Jesu, Lover of my soul,
Let me to thy bosom fly,
While the nearer waters roll,
While the tempest still is high:
Hide me, O my Saviour, hide,
Till the storm of life is past;
Safe into the haven guide,
O receive my soul at last.

C Wesley

Eyes of God

Sunday 21 October

God sees us where we are

Notes based on Today's New International Version by

Judith Atkinson

Judith Atkinson hails from Cumbria, in the north of England, and is currently living in Sydney, Australia with her husband and son. She is an ordained priest in the Church of England, while for a 'day job' she works developing government policy and services in the areas of housing and homelessness, child protection and domestic violence. She is very interested in how people of faith can work to create communities that are good for all.

Job 34:12-15, 21

God sees us where we are

What does it mean for God to see us where we are? Verse 21 reminds us that God sees all our steps. If God were unjust, or untrustworthy, we would have reason to worry about such omniscience. But God is righteous and, more than that, our very existence is bound up in God.

This week we will be thinking about the wonder – and the consequences – of God being interested in our lives, including all their details. God sees where and how we live our lives and perceives our motivations, aspirations and intentions as well as our actions.

This is all part of God's astonishing invitation to us to be a covenant people, to 'walk in God's ways'. It isn't something abstract, or something private, which doesn't take account of the world in which we live. God knows and understands our world, as well as each person within the world – including the terrible and tragic parts of it.

Through responding to God, we are invited to be part of God's love and glory, wherever we are.

Teach us, dear God, to be part of your love and glory in the world.

God sees us in God's world

Genesis 1:26-31

As I write, Australia is currently debating what to do about one of its great river systems that needs more water. Scientists say that less water needs to be consumed, or unique wetlands will be lost for ever. At the same time, news stories tell of farmers and communities who fear losing their livelihoods and homes without water to grow crops. Our technology does not seem able to solve these huge problems or conflicts of interest, often presented as 'people versus creation'.

In the midst of such situations, it is important to remember that each one of us can make a difference. I remember catching a small segment of news about coffee growers and the pressures of falling prices. The reporter told (almost incidentally) of how fairtrade growers were still able to send their children to school and buy medical care – but others were not so lucky. It is truly humbling to me that something as modest as which coffee I buy can impact on a child's medical care in another country.

As we are reminded that God sees us where we are, there is an invitation to offer all parts of our lives to God – even the very small things – and allow God to help us to be part of the ongoing creation and redemption of this world.

Think and pray about something you can change that will make a difference in the lives of others, and something you can do to care for God's earth.

Judith Atkinson

Sharing God's grieving heart

Genesis 6:5-8

For my 'day job' I work in the area of child protection policy. It is not unusual for me to come across stories or statistics that evoke despair. It continues to shock me that human beings can be so cruel to the most vulnerable in our communities. The fact that God looks upon wickedness and 'his heart [is] deeply troubled' (verse 6) seems enormously important, and is a source of comfort to me. Why? Perhaps because it tells us that those who suffer are known to, and matter supremely to, God.

In Genesis, the story that Noah found favour with God proved to be a lifeline to the human race. We cannot assume that this would have been easy for Noah. Those who stand up for righteousness and justice often do so at huge personal cost. Advocating for the poor and suffering is often unpopular in a world that doesn't really want to hear. But even if not recognised in their lifetime, the examples of the righteous inspire us, and remind us that seeking righteousness will find favour with God.

Loving God, we grieve with you for the sin and destruction in your world. We pray for all who suffer at the hands of others. Thank you for the example of those faithful people who have shown us the righteous path. Give us courage to stand up for what is right. May our hearts find favour with you.

Seeing through God's eyes

Psalm 33:13-22

It sometimes seems that we need to seek God out, that we need to go to 'holy places' to find God. Whilst intentional journeying towards God – pilgrimage – can be important and even necessary at times in our lives, we are invited to recognise that God always sees us where we are.

Psalm 33 reveals to us how God's seeing of us, and our looking to God, are two sides of the same coin. It challenges the tendency to view the world as though God has nothing to do with it. We may trust in our own strength, but it is God who protects, who delivers, who helps. When we actively trust in God, our lives have focus. We know that we are not alone. Even though everything around us might be changing, and there might be things that scare us, we can hold fast to the promise that God's love is steadfast, and will give us hope.

Loving God,
help me always to hope in your steadfast love.
Teach my soul to wait on you
for you are my help and my shield.
I trust in you,
you fill my heart with gladness
as you watch over me.

God is in the detail

Psalm 139:1-18

One of my friends – someone whose life and faith were well lived – had this scripture read at her funeral. I had read or heard it many times, but it was in that moment, on that day, that this text was 'opened' to me. My friend knew that she was known by God, and she had acknowledged God's presence in every part of her life. I'm sure she would have been pleased that, as we remembered her, I saw and understood something new about God.

What an amazing thing it is to know that God cares about the events of our lives – that our lives start and end in God. Perhaps if we really pay attention to that, then we will be able to let God work in and through our activities and relationships. I recently had to ask people who had been homeless about the help they had received. In nearly every case the significant thing was not *what* service had been delivered, but *how*. It really helped if workers were kind. If they were judgemental, people usually had a negative experience. The service design or the funding was much less important than the nature of the human contact.

Take some time to think about how you show God to others. What do those who come into contact with you see of God? Think about the different people you have met, and the different situations you have been in recently.

Ask God to work in the details of your life and relationships.

Eyes of God — Judith Atkinson

Our covenant starts at home

Deuteronomy 26:15-19

The opening verse of today's reading reminds us that God looks at us and sees us where we are – really where we are. We are bound to the physical places that we find ourselves in, and it is from those real places that we respond to God and to those around us.

Moving country has shown me how much our identity is shaped by the place where we consider ourselves to be 'from'. But the history of the Jewish people also tells us that, while our physical home, or 'homeland' is important, even when separated from it we can still be grounded in our relationship with God. This covenant – this agreement – that God makes with his people, shapes the lives of those who walk in God's ways (see verse 17). Our covenant with God is the foundation of our identity, wherever we are.

But covenant also requires a response from us. Immediately before this passage, God's people are instructed to share their bounty with strangers and those in need. There are many people who find themselves in places where they did not expect – and sometimes never wanted – to be. How does our covenant with God require us to care for them?

Loving God, we pray for those who have lost their homes. We think of refugees and those who have been displaced by war, disaster and profit. May we remember our covenant with you, to walk in your ways and obey your commands, and to care for those in need, that you might make us a holy people.

Making covenant choices

Isaiah 38:1-8

This story reminds me of the psalmist's plea in Psalm 90 that God would teach us to count (or 'number') our days. When I imagine what Hezekiah might have been feeling at this point, I wonder if he was thinking about all the things he wished he had done: if he was regretting broken relationships, or despairing that he would not be around to protect those he loved. In imagining that, I am no doubt reading some of my own feelings and fears into the story! Although Hezekiah's situation is distant in terms of time and context, we can understand the grief he must have felt – his situation is so essentially human.

I seem to have seen quite a few Hollywood movies where the story involves the heroine or hero somehow nearly losing her/his life and, after receiving another chance, working out what is really important. Probably most of us don't have such dramatic reminders that we only have one life, or that we make choices all the time about how we live it. Yet if we are serious about being a covenant people, then our choices are important: they reflect who we are.

The encouragement of knowing that God sees us where we are reminds us that no choice or action is too small to reflect God's love and glory to the world. And that when we let God work through the small things, we can expect big changes within our own hearts.

Loving God,
I belong to you.
Let me be a channel of your love in this world.

Judith Atkinson

Eyes of God

God seeks us out

Notes based on the New Revised Standard Version by
Helen Stanton

An Anglican laywoman, Helen has worked for Christian Aid; in university chaplaincy; and in promoting social justice and responsibility. In recent years her work has focused on training people for ordained and lay ministries. Currently she is a Visiting Scholar and Associate Tutor at the Queen's Foundation in Birmingham, UK.

Psalm 32:8-11

God's gaze

Central to all our texts from the Bible this week is the idea that God seeks us; we do not need to seek God. This idea emerges very strongly in the experience of the mystics, among them Teresa of Avila, who taught her sisters to sit before a crucifix and just allow themselves to be loved. All we have to do is wait to be found.

When I was in my twenties I had a job that required me to abseil occasionally. I am terrified of heights, and found this aspect of my job very troublesome, but eventually I learned a technique for coping with it. As I let myself over the edge of the rock face, I asked a colleague to keep eye contact with me. Somehow gazing into the encouraging face of Joanna or John enabled me to overcome my fear and take the first steps of the descent. Today's excerpt from the Psalms reminds me that following in God's way may have its terrifying moments, but God keeps us safe in God's loving gaze. Likewise, we do not need to be cajoled, we have simply to look towards God and God's steadfast love will surround us.

In the cool air...

Genesis 3:8-13

Imagine walking in the garden at the time of the evening breeze, and being found there by God who is enjoying the dusk too. But the man and woman are hiding, they don't want to be seen, they don't want to be confronted with their vulnerability, with what they have done.

Many readings of what Christians have come to call 'the fall' have presented this moment, and its consequences, not as catastrophic, but as part of the process of maturation. If the garden stands for innocence, then being exiled from the garden comes to each of us, and though it may be searingly painful, it is necessary. Learning that we cannot always think well of ourselves may be the beginning of wisdom, the beginning of the recognition that we are in need of the grace of God.

In his poem, 'En Sourdine', Paul Verlaine writes of being with a lover under the black oak trees. In the quietude and intimacy of the poem, there is an intimation for me of God's presence in the garden. God does not compel humanity, but God's desire to be with us means that God is ever waiting for us. And more than that, God is so eager to meet us that he comes searching for us, like a shepherd searching for a lost sheep. Verlaine's poem is full of the despair of parting, but God's seeking for us, though it may mean we must confront who we really are, is not to banish us but to restore us to Godself, to enfold us in God's embrace, which is God's desire for us eternally.

Calmes dans le demi-jour
Que les branches hautes font,
Pénétrons bien notre amour
De ce silence profond.

Calm, in the dusk
– the shade of high branches,
let us fill our love full
of this deep silence.

Paul Verlaine, translation by Helen Stanton

Sight and insight

Genesis 15:1-6

If God keeps us in God's sights, today's text reminds us that God gives us sight too. Whether insight into matters of personal, local or global consequences, it requires us to share our insight with others, and act upon it ourselves. Many great Christians, and probably many who were not great, had very specific visions. Hildegard of Bingen, the twelfth-century Benedictine abbess, recorded her visions, dictating them to her secretary, who also depicted them visually. Her visions tell of the feminine in God, Wisdom, God's agent of creation.

Hildegard was struck by God's over-whelming love for the whole of creation, and the creation's love for God shown in its flourishing. Virtue was associated with what Hildegard called the greening of the earth, but the creation was tainted by the sin of humanity, and the Spirit's work was the restoration of the greenness of the world, the sign of God's presence and blessing.

Abram's vision in Genesis 15 is one of a multiplicity of descendants, no doubt a comfort to the great patriarch. I suspect that Hildegard, however, would have looked at the stars and seen God's life-giving Spirit resplendent and radiating God's love.

Try to find some time today to gaze at an aspect of God's creation, give thanks, and think about how you can help God to care for the earth.

For [Wisdom] is the splendour of the eternal
light,
And immaculate mirror of God's majesty,
And image of his goodness …

For she is more beautiful than the sun,
And above all the order of the stars;
Compared with the light, she is found before it…

Therefore she reaches from end to end mightily
And orders all things sweetly.

Wisdom of Solomon 7:26 – 8:1

Angels and strangers

Genesis 16:1-13

There seems to be a thread running through the Hebrew scriptures that reminds us that God speaks and acts through those who are not the chosen people, as well as those who are. Think of Ruth's covenant with Naomi (Ruth 1) and Cyrus as the Lord's shepherd and anointed one (Isaiah 44:28ff).

Today's text is another example of this, and it parallels what we read yesterday. Hagar, the slave whose name means 'stranger', runs away from the cruel treatment she is given by Sarai. The word of the Lord came to Abram, but an angel to Hagar. Was it really an angel or a literary device for an encounter with God, which no one, it was believed, could receive and survive? Hagar certainly believes she has met with God and she gives God a special name, El-roi, 'the one whom I have seen'. God's promise to her of innumerable descendants has been interpreted as the beginning of the Arab world, and even of Islam.

Hagar's story has been an inspiration to many of the black women of North America, as womanist theologian Delores S. Williams highlights in her study, *Sisters in the Wilderness* (Maryknoll: Orbis, 1993) how Hagar has 'spoken' to generation after generation of black women. As a family she and Ishmael validate the experience of many black American families in which a lone woman/mother struggles to hold the family together in spite of the poverty to which ruling class economics consign it (p.33).

Consider the 'strangers' in your community. How might they help you recognise the presence of God?

God, who seeks me out and knows me, open my eyes to see your face in unexpected places.

House of God, gate of heaven

Genesis 28:10-17

Since the second half of the twentieth century, people in the West have become rather dismissive of the beautiful buildings they associate with church. And it is true, church is a gathering of people, not a building, and sometimes people feel they spend all their time repairing buildings and not engaging in mission.

Today's text reminds us that there is a long tradition of marking out places of encounter with God. Great and beautiful buildings of another age can be awesome; they remind us of the beauty and transcendence of God; and they witness to the encounter with God that has happened there over the centuries. That can be so in a tiny plain chapel, or a great cathedral.

I remember when I saw for the first time the fan vaulting at Bath Abbey, in England. I said, 'It is like the polyphony of a great hymn.' It was and it is. I still have a strong sense that the building itself is worshipping God and, in admiring the building, being uplifted by it, I am joining in that worship too.

It is not only buildings, but other places identified by our ancestors in the faith, that give us a sense of God's presence. Artworks can do it too. And icons, the intensely focused images of Orthodoxy that promise the presence of God. Think about one such place for you, and give thanks. Think about the ways in which your own church building can be part of the church's ministry.

Creator God, whose creativity is seen in the work of all who make beauty, give us grace to approach the gate of heaven, wherever we may find it, with awe and love.

God of our ancestors

Exodus 3:1-12

God is not a God who stands aloof, nor even a God who watches from a safe distance, noting the suffering of the people. Here is a God who intervenes for our good. (There are certainly appropriate questions to be asked about the peoples of the land of milk and honey, and what the implications of this rescue are for them, but that is not the focus of this text.)

The God of the Exodus will lead the people away from oppression and into a place where they will be free and sustained. God convinces Moses to trust God, in part because of the burning bush, and in part because of God's history with the founding fathers (and mothers) of the community. Moses can rely on this God, because of God's track record.

I sometimes think that God's track record isn't that impressive: can we really rely on a God who did not prevent the Holocaust; who does not prevent thousands being massacred by their neighbours, or dying in flood and famine? When I ask these questions I find that I need to rely a good deal on the testimony of my ancestors in the faith. I recall Rabbi Hugo Gryn, who reported his experience of God weeping alongside him in Auschwitz; and the experience of the people of Chalatenango in El Salvador who knew God was with them when they returned to their own land after years in a refugee camp, harassed on their way by a violent and repressive army.

There are days when I see a burning bush, but many more days when the saints of the church – living and dead – remind me that God is with us, seeking us out to transform our lives and the world. Give thanks for your ancestors in the faith.

Not as mortals see

1 Samuel 16:1-12

Today's text is preface to one of the most important stories in the Hebrew scriptures: the anointing of David who, though profoundly flawed, becomes an idealised figure, presiding over the golden age of the history of his people. But today's text stops before David is found. Instead Samuel sets out and begins to see the sons of Jesse. Age and status are significant in this society, but not to God, and he has to explain to Samuel that, just because Eliab is impressive, that does not mean he is God's chosen one. God sees differently.

Repeatedly in the Bible, God chooses those who are the least significant in their family hierarchy. And in the gospels Jesus does the same: little children were not considered winsome; they were those of the lowest status. 'Unless you change and become like children'– like those of low status – says Jesus, 'you will never enter the kingdom of heaven' (Matthew 18:3).

One of the most important contributions that Latin America has made to theology is the doctrine of the preferential option for the poor. This doctrine asserts that God takes sides with those who are marginalised and oppressed – they are the most important in God's kingdom. Since as Christians we are called to follow the way of Jesus, we are asked to take sides with the oppressed too. God is not interested in success or status in the world; God is interested in poor people, and in the creation that is impoverished by the greed of human beings. And Jesus promises us it is amongst the poor that we will encounter him (Matthew 25:40f).

When he was asked what the rich needed to do to be saved, Salvadoran martyr Archbishop Oscar Romero replied, 'They must be converted to the poor' (broadcast on El Salvador Radio, 17 February 1980). What might this mean in your context, for you, for the churches, for society?

Eyes of God

The watchful God

Notes based on the New Revised Standard Version by

Francesca Rhys

Francesca Rhys was raised as the middle one of five in London, but has lived in China, the USA, Germany and the Democratic Republic of the Congo as a language-learner and teacher. She now lives with her partner in east Leeds, learning Yorkshire ways, and resourcing three churches as a Methodist minister. She told the youth club that three of the rocks on which she tries to build are: cycling, loyalty and dried fruit!

Psalm 53:1-3

God's searching

In the midst of our busyness, we think we have to seek God out, deliberately trying to make time to go to a quiet place or to church, before we can be in contact with God. This week's readings demonstrate that in fact the opposite is true, that it is God who seeks us out and watches over us. God always wants to be in contact with us to establish relationship. As did Jesus, God goes to endless lengths to reassure individuals of loving care and wise counsel.

We're in relationship with God, as illustrated by the congregation's lament in verse 1 of the Psalm, which is then answered by God. The prophetic liturgy sings of the need for wisdom and searching for God. God is looking for this too.

Can you see this dialogue mirrored in our life in the world? I've experienced a necessary partnership between the church youth club and the government's Youth Service. We people of faith who are seeking after God need the knowledge of specialists to help our evangelism be well-grounded. Our partners who are worldly-wise need our reminders of dependence on and relationship with God.

The God who never sleeps

Psalm 121

I don't like the thought of not being able to sleep, but I like the notion of a God who never sleeps! The ever-watchful God reminds me of living in New York City, 'the city that never sleeps'. On the corner of the street where my partner and I lived was a small grocer's shop, owned by a Korean Christian family and often staffed by Hispanic shop assistants. It was open twenty-four hours a day and it didn't close on a Sunday, so it was a reassuring sight at any time of day or night. Out front were gleaming fruits, vegetables and sprays of flowers. Stepping inside there was the usual stock of essential groceries, as well as big plastic bowls of water containing fresh bean curd (tofu), dark-green bunches of salad and bean sprouts.

What leadings does a shop like this give us to God? It always provides fresh goods, is colourful, open, warm, welcoming, and offers small enhancing things, accessible to all.

Do some shopping at a small business or grocer's shop or stall, rather than at a supermarket. Take time to enjoy the provision, freshness and diversity of the display.

Welcoming God, you who never need to sleep! Thank you that you watch over our comings and goings and keep us aware of your abundant grace in your everyday provision.

Good figs

Jeremiah 24:4-7

Here is a message of profound encouragement to people in a state of exile and deep suffering. Through the prophet, we hear of God's efforts to bolster the confidence and responsibility of those in exile in Babylon. God identifies these exiles as chosen ones, like perfectly ripe, beautiful and delicious figs. God's eyes are particularly and permanently focused on those who have suffered much: 'I will set my eyes upon them for good' (verse 6).

I conducted a funeral for the mother of eleven adult children born in the 1950s and 60s on a council estate in Leeds. By British standards there had been extreme poverty in the family, and severe physical abuse from their father. Two of the sisters, impressive survivors, told me their dreams and prayers that had been answered. One had dreamed of an encounter with her father where expressions of forgiveness were given and received between them. Along with their mother, both sisters had simultaneously had the same dream of assurance related to another sister who had died, that she was now perfectly happy. Prayers for reassurance were answered as requested, in the form of two butterflies, one appearing at night on the car windscreen in the supermarket car park.

Reflect on times of suffering or sense of exile during your life. Are you aware of God's affirmation and response to your needs and prayers?

Buy a ripe fig and admire it as a marvel of God's creation. Before enjoying it, imagine God looking at you with the same wonder with which you look at the fig.

And everyone beneath the vine and fig tree,
shall live in peace and have no fear.

Traditional song based on Zechariah 3:10

God sees people's distress

Lamentations 3:49-59

The period of exile for the Jewish people in Babylon from 587 BCE for about two generations was a devastating national tragedy. Alongside slavery in Egypt, it was the worst collective experience for the Jewish people in biblical history, leading to starvation, death, deportation and separation from loved ones. Traditional cause and effect theology, which apparently rewarded obedience, had to be revised completely. Eventually this led to less judgemental, more compassionate, understandings of God's feeling for people's sufferings.

Lamentations has a chaotic, incoherent feel to it, redolent of human reaction to severe loss. There's an unusual, helpful effect of English translation in this passage, since we hear of '[t]hose who were my enemies without cause' (verse 52) and then '[y]ou have taken up my cause, O Lord, you have redeemed my life' (verse 58).

What cause is particularly close to your heart or life over your lifetime? Trace developments in such a cause over your lifetime. Can you see how God has indeed 'seen the wrong done', and taken up the 'cause' (verse 59)? Over the past twenty years in the UK we have traversed revolutionary changes in attitudes and legislation towards lesbian, gay and bisexual people, although most churches, and indeed governments, continue to discriminate against sexual minorities throughout the world. 'You have seen the wrong done to me, O Lord, judge my cause' (verse 59).

Nobody knows the trouble I see,
nobody knows but Jesus;
Oh, nobody knows the trouble I see,
glory hallelujah!

African-American Spiritual

Liberal and radical?

Matthew 6:1-18

I feel fortunate to have been a member of a congregation that I would describe as both liberal and radical. This was a North American United Methodist Church that had an equal opportunities statement of welcome to everyone, and a congregation that housed the largest food aid programme in New York City. It had also offered shelter to a two-thousand-strong synagogue, when its ceiling collapsed, an arrangement that turned into a permanent sharing of worship space. On my Sundays off now, I like to get to a congregation in Leeds that has good partnership with local Muslims, financially supporting a number of asylum seekers and incorporating speaking in tongues, informality and participation.

Matthew is writing here about the greater righteousness of our intentions and of our heart. Right intention involves a kind of self-forgetfulness and humility, where things are done with only God as audience. As part of his Sermon on the Mount, Jesus emphasised the three practices of charitable giving, prayer and fasting, which have their roots in Jewish faith. These three are also central to the Five Pillars of Islam. There's a rigour and seriousness here: faith and its practices need to inform all aspects of our lives and lead us into radical discipleship and openness.

Find out if there are congregations in your area that could be described as both liberal and radical. Pay a visit to such a congregation, and consider what elements of its life and worship you could help introduce within your own church.

Searching God, you call us to be your disciples in every part of our lives. Help us be open to your leadings and committed to your kingdom. In Christ we pray.

Love virtue

1 Peter 3:8-16

This section of a pastoral letter to an early Christian congregation, probably in Rome after the Roman destruction of the temple in 70 CE, is about virtue and right behaviour in the face of abuse. The writer, probably a follower of Peter, reminds people that God is watching their actions and their attitudes that help foster group cohesion. The abuse being faced was not state persecution, but more along the lines of verbal or physical abuse from neighbours.

Virtue, and not seeking revenge or litigation, are countercultural values in our day. In what settings would you say you have been most aware of these values? In the past I've worked alongside the Chinese voluntary development and relief organisation, the Amity Foundation, whose name in Chinese ('Ai de') means literally 'Love virtue'. Amity provides an example of Christians and those of no faith working together in partnership to promote education, community development, medical and social service. The Amity Home of Blessings in Nanjing provides educational services for some mentally challenged young adults where one of the things they do together is make bread to sell at the Amity Bakery.

Look up the website of The Amity Foundation www.amityfoundation.org.

As we wait on you, O God, help us move with the Spirit,
and co-operate with generous hearts in our common life.
So may we proclaim in our life together the reign of God,
present among all people.

St Michael's Convent, *Nourish Body, Nurture Soul, Recipes for Life from a Convent Kitchen and Elsewhere*, self-published by the Community of the Sisters of the Church at Ham Common, Surrey, p.116

What will it be like?

Revelation 22:1-5

As the writer of Revelation, John sees his visions of the end times as the culmination of the prophetic vision of the Bible, so this passage conveys the people of God at last being fully bathed in the light of God's presence. What a culmination to this week's theme of the eyes of God being upon us!

Sometimes the imagery of Revelation can seem bizarre and remote, although this short passage is more accessible. You could try drawing a picture of the scene described here. It was brought vividly to life for me by the participation of two women, aged around 90, who were both lifelong Christians but who had contrasting experiences and personalities. When I presided at the monthly Communion service at their sheltered housing scheme, Tranquillity Court, they attended faithfully and took part. After reading this passage, I asked them and the others present, what they thought some of the twelve fruits on the Tree of Life would be. Edith said 'wisdom and Jesus'. Doreen said 'love'. For the next month's Communion I was away on holiday and, by the time I visited again, both Edith and Doreen had died. I imagined them now having made the transition to be in the light of God's presence constantly. They will have learned what the twelve fruits really are. I'm sure that, between them, they got it right.

O God, you who are beyond our imagining but embodied in love, Jesus, and wisdom, keep us in your gaze and in the light of all that helps us move in your direction. In the name of Jesus we pray.

Sunday 11 November

Eyes of God

Face to face with Jesus

Notes based on the New Revised Standard Version by

Paul Nicholson

Paul Nicholson SJ is a Roman Catholic priest belonging to the Society of Jesus (the Jesuits). He is currently Director of Novices in the Jesuit novitiate in Birmingham, England, responsible for the first two years of training for men from Britain, Ireland, Holland, Flanders, Latvia and South Africa. Since his ordination in 1988 Paul has worked chiefly in the fields of spirituality and/or social justice. Between 1999 and 2006 he was Director of the Loyola Hall Spirituality Centre outside Liverpool.

John 1:16-18

A Christ-like God

Around the time that I was preparing these notes, I read a selection of sermons by Michael Mayne, former Dean of Westminster and Head of Religious Programmes on BBC Radio, who died of cancer in 2006. An idea he comes back to again and again is that, in Jesus, God is revealed as Christ-like. Indeed for him, Jesus 'is the only accurate picture of God the world has ever seen' (Michael Mayne, *To Trust and To Love*, Darton, Longman & Todd, 2010, p.33).

The evangelist John, in today's reading, shares this powerful conviction, and our prayer this week will explore more of what it means to base our faith on such a belief. In Mayne's abbey church today they will be remembering those who have died in war. One of the aspects of God revealed by Jesus is his sharing in the world's suffering. God is neither aloof nor unmoved, but shows that same compassion that is to be seen in the Christ who wept over Jerusalem.

As you look at the world around you, where do you feel particularly moved to share this practical compassion of the Christ-like God?

Filling in the gaps

John 1:35-42

There's an enigma at the centre of today's reading. The two disciples, who have been followers of the Baptist, are invited by Jesus to go and see where he lives. They go, we might assume, with some enthusiasm, and spend several hours with him. But we are told absolutely nothing about where it was that they were taken to, or what they found there, or what was said. All we know is that, whatever it was, it was enough to convince Andrew that this man whom they had encountered was one anointed by God, and that he should bring his brother Simon (soon to be Peter) in on the action. The rest is, as they say, history.

The lack of detail has served as an invitation to some commentators, including Ignatius of Loyola, founder of the Jesuit order to which I belong, to supply what is missing from their own imaginations. What kind of place is Jesus likely to have been staying in? What might have been said, or done, there to move Andrew so deeply? Such an imaginative exercise, if nothing else, tells you more about your own idea of Jesus, and of the Christ-like God whom he represents. Of course, we have no further access to what might actually have happened on that day two thousand years ago. But God can today use your imagination to speak to your heart, as he spoke to Andrew's.

Lord, open the eyes of my imagination so that I may come to know you more fully, and then follow you more closely on the road to your kingdom.

How can these things be?

John 3:1-15

Nicodemus, we are told, 'came to Jesus by night' (verse 2), and it's natural to wonder why. Was he too busy, as a leader of the Jews, to appear during office hours? Was he anxious to maintain a reputation that could only be tarnished if it got out that he was associating with this upstart young rabbi? Whatever the reason, he starts from a position of puzzlement. Clearly God is at work in Jesus, as is evident from all that he does. But how? Jesus, using this puzzlement as a hook, draws Nicodemus in to a deeper appreciation of the surprising action of God's Spirit in the world.

If Jesus wants to draw you to a deeper knowledge of himself, and of the God whom he serves, what might act as the hook? What aspects of God's actions surprise or puzzle you? Maybe your answer is a traditional one. How can a good, all-powerful God allow so much suffering? Or your own 'hook' might be more individually-tailored. How can God expect you to live out what seem to be some aspects of his call to you? Such questions are not to be ignored or suppressed. They are truly opportunities. A prayerful reflection that tries to puzzle out such matters can be a powerful tool to deepen and extend your faith.

God of surprises, use the questions that I have to draw me to an ever-deeper knowledge and love of you.

Paul Nicholson

Are you looking at me?

Luke 19:1-10

Zacchaeus, I think we can assume, was quite anxious to see Jesus. Rich chief tax collectors today are unaccustomed to climbing trees, and it is unlikely to have been any different in Jesus' time. But these are the lengths to which he is prepared to go.

Jesus, it seems, was every bit as anxious to see Zacchaeus. Of all the people in the crowds who surround him, he singles out this man to dine with. And what is it that Jesus sees in him? Someone who was lost, admittedly, in need of the salvation that Jesus could bring. But maybe more importantly, someone who was open to receiving this salvation. Somehow the time was right, and so it was worth enduring the grumbling of the bystanders.

You may or may not feel yourself anxious to encounter Jesus today. But you can be sure that he is keen to meet you. After all, he has put this book into your hands, and helped you find the time to work with it. So what is it that Jesus sees as he looks at you now? What needs will he recognise in you that only he can meet?

Ignatius Loyola begins each of his Spiritual Exercises with an invitation to 'think how God our Lord is looking at me' (*Spiritual Exercises of St Ignatius: a translation and commentary*, George Ganss SJ (ed.) Institute of Jesuit Sources, St Louis, 1999, p.48. See also www.sacred-texts.com/chr/seil/seil15.htm). Maybe you could try that for yourself today.

Lord Jesus, what do you see when you look at me? Help me to experience myself as I appear to your loving gaze.

Jesus wept!

John 11:30-37

Today's reading is a snapshot, taken in the middle of a longer story, that of the death of Lazarus and of his raising to life by Jesus. Our glimpse is encapsulated in what is famously in the Authorised (King James) Version the shortest verse of the entire Bible, John 11:35: 'Jesus wept.'

What causes his grief? Briefly, it is the human condition. Sickness and suffering, death, loss and bereavement. Martha speaks for all of us when she suggests that Jesus could simply put a stop to all this. That he doesn't remains one of the main puzzles of the Christian faith. There must, we conclude, be a purpose to it all. But attempts to explain that purpose often fail to convince, especially when I am chiefly aware of my own suffering, or that of those whom I love.

In this reading, Jesus makes no attempt to give reasons for what has befallen Lazarus. The Jesus we are face to face with here simply weeps, as you or I would weep.

Think, for a moment, of some aspect of your own life, or of the world around you, that causes you pain. It might be anything from sickness in your own life to the environmental despoliation of the planet – you probably don't have to search too hard. Hold this before Jesus, who weeps in response to what he sees. Let your own prayer grow from that encounter.

Lord, I weep with you at the pain of the world. Let our shared grief draw us closer together, and help me to take your compassion out to all those I encounter today.

Seeing with the eyes of the blind man

John 9:24-39

For the second time this week (see Tuesday's passage) we meet Pharisees who are trying to make sense of what Jesus does. But if Nicodemus was prepared to give him a fair hearing, these men have already made up their minds. 'We know that this man is a sinner' (verse 24) and 'God does not listen to sinners' (verse 31). What more is there to be said? Yet it is noticeable that the man born blind, who, it might have been assumed, would be intimidated by these learned leaders, refuses to back down. He knows what Jesus has done for him, and has enough sense to recognise God at work in and through him. It is this recognition that leads him back to a further encounter with Jesus, who seeks him out and leads him to a more profound faith.

Religious faith seems to be perpetually tempted to judge whole categories of people as sinners, those through whom you can't expect God to work. Yet the message of Jesus is that God continues to work through the most unlikely people, himself included!

It's not always easy to recognise God in unfamiliar situations or unexpected people, as the Pharisees in this story demonstrate. It might be good today to make a conscious effort to view the world, and all those you meet, with the eyes of the man born blind.

It's easy, Lord, to recognise you in the nice, and the kind, and the sympathetic. Let me take time today to see you at work in the scared, and the hostile, and those who don't see the world as I do.

What are you thirsting for?

John 19:25b-30

I visited recently someone who has been very influential in my life, and is now dying. Although I wanted to go, I was nervous. What would I say? How was I going to react? In the event, the meeting was a good one. My friend helped put me at my ease, and made it possible for each of us to say what needed to be said. I may well not see him again in this life, but can face that now with a greater measure of peace. Who helped whom most in that encounter, you might well ask? My dying friend was in many ways the stronger one there.

Christ in this passage, undergoing an agonising torture and knowing that he is near death, continues to show compassion to those whom he loves. He makes provision for his mother in a society in which widows are a paradigm of those needing support. His closest disciple is given a role that will no doubt help him to deal with his own grief at Jesus' death. Jesus, to the end, was able to notice the needs of those who are close to him, and to give them gifts and graces tailored precisely to those needs.

What do you most need from God in your own life at the moment? What sense do you have of the ways in which God is working, even now, to meet those needs?

Lord, often you choose to meet me not in my strengths and achievements and successes; but in my weaknesses, my failures in the darkness of my life. Let me trust that you are there to be found, and so not run away from these challenging encounters.

1 & 2 Thessalonians

Sunday 18 November

Keep awake and sober

1 Thessalonians 1

Turned to God

The Manchester neighbourhood in which my family and I live is largely Muslim, and we love it. On the playground at school our daughter is learning to negotiate a diverse world at a young age, gaining skills for life. The Thessalonians knew far greater religious diversity. Thessalonica was home to several Hellenistic cults, including shrines to the Roman emperor. Most in the church appear to have been gentiles, not Jews. They had turned to God 'from idols, to serve a living and true God' (verse 9). Perhaps that's why Paul skips the words 'the law', 'justification', or 'the cross' in our letter. But the encouraging, just, community-building God who emerges has much to say to us this week as we 'keep awake and sober' for the coming of Jesus.

To say God is 'living and true' (verse 9) is not bland, but bold. Paul knew of other powerful, attractive belief systems, and the church knew persecution (verse 6). Paul is rarely safe. But perhaps his forthrightness is ultimately more respectful of other faiths than ignoring difference.

May a 'living and true' God guide us into genuine appreciation of world religions this week, as well as into a fresh, bold expression of our own faith in the present and coming Lord Jesus, wherever we live.

Notes based on the New Revised Standard Version by

Nathan Eddy

Nathan Eddy is Free Church Chaplain to the University of Manchester and Manchester Metropolitan University. He trained for ministry at Yale Divinity School and is ordained in the United Church of Christ, USA. Before ordination Nathan worked as a reporter for a daily newspaper in suburban Boston, Massachusetts. He has written on Paul for the preaching commentary *Feasting on the Word* (Westminster/ John Knox Press) and has written on young adult spirituality for other publications.

Mother of the church

1 Thessalonians 2:2-12

Paul is not noted for his celebration of women in the life of the church. So let's linger over his description of his own ministry during the unspecified period he spent living, working and sharing the gospel with the Thessalonians. 'We were gentle among you, like a nurse tenderly caring for her own children,' Paul writes in verse 7. He goes on to describe how he shared not just the gospel, but himself.

St Anselm of Canterbury in the eleventh century described Paul as a 'sweet nurse, sweet mother' and as 'the greatest mother' of the church. Paul was a person of his time, but perhaps his gender roles were not as rigid as they sometimes appear. Feminist Pauline scholar Sandra Polaski also points out how Paul's nurturing language here differs from other biblical talk of 'begetting' (*A Feminist Introduction to Paul*, St Louis: Chalice Press, 2005, pp.24–5). Paul's evangelistic ministry took place over time, over meals, in the midst of working days as he lived and breathed the city. He didn't zing off emails from Corinth or peddle a 'one size fits all' theology', although he was certainly authoritative. He supported himself so as to work with and alongside people, although the Philippians sent help (Philippians 4:16). In working with young adults I find this kind of ministry to be the only kind that is respected.

Can we share the gospel with our lives, over the long haul, appreciating the many varieties of care humans provide? This is our task.

God, you share your own self with the world in Jesus. Root us likewise in our cities, towns and villages that we might share the gospel out of our very selves. Help us discern the ministries of others without recourse to rigid roles. Make us a people of patient nurture and care of young people.

The coming of Jesus

1 Thessalonians 2:13-end

I subscribe to a British world news magazine. In a new issue I flip first to a map of the world with recent events: a multiple killing here, an election there, a coup attempt, a mine rescue. Our world churns with vitality and violence, week on week. What's it all about?

Paul writes of his pride in the Thessalonians at Christ's coming, which Paul imagines would come within their lifetime (1 Thessalonians 4:15). The idea of an end to history is strange to our minds, and not only because Paul was wrong about its timing. Perhaps with Richard Bauckham we should imagine history like a still-unfolding story (in *Hope against Hope: Christian Eschatology at the Turn of the Millennium*, Grand Rapids/Cambridge: Eerdmans, 1999, pp.49–50). We long for meaning in its drama. But meaning implies an ending, a time when all will be known and settled, when the churn of history – sometimes more just, sometimes less just – will make sense. Is history a tragedy, a noble but lost cause, or could it have a comic twist, with 'all revealed' in a surprise ending? Only if justice is ultimately made real, which Paul calls Christ's return. To believe in this unexpected event, a closure that arises from outside the processes of history, is called hope.

Paul's claim that the Jews killed Jesus (verse 15) conflicts with evidence given in the gospels. His words have had a tragic legacy since, a fact no interpretation today can avoid. These words too will have their final judgement.

Lord, we yearn for meaning. Give us a taste of your coming peace, here and now, that we might know that our labour and living, our serving and loving, our fighting for justice, are not in vain.

To see you face to face

1 Thessalonians 3

Paul yearns for the company of the Thessalonians. His words, as warm as a love letter, sing across millennia. Something uncanny is going on; many have noticed a 'slippage' between Paul's yearning to come to the distant Thessalonians (perhaps he writes from Corinth) and Jesus' coming.

When we imagine it at all, we have quite a jumble of images for Jesus' second coming – at best, cosmic and impersonal; at worst, utterly terrifying. Our verses today invite us to imagine a more down-to-earth (so to speak) second coming. Jesus is coming to us as one who knows us, and misses us as Paul missed the Thessalonians. Jesus is a friend who is far away; a lover who yearns to be near. The Thessalonians weren't better Christians than you and your church. Jesus longs for your company as much as he does for theirs.

The gospel is not private but it is always personal. In whatever way Jesus will come again, he will be as he was in life: someone who looks beneath the surface, who takes time to know and understand, who heals and seeks to include. Jesus prays day and night for us, that he might see us face to face. He takes seriously our struggles, the ways we are tempted. And through the Spirit he seeks to make us abound in love for one another, and so to glorify him and be blameless at his coming.

Read these verses slowly, imagining Jesus' prayer for your local congregation, in all its banalities, joys and struggles; your denomination; your local ecumenical group; and the one catholic church. What is the expression on Jesus' face? What temptations concern him? What are his feelings for you? Imagine the 'train' of saints that accompanies Jesus in verse 13. Beyond death, as in life, we are a part of a community. Whose faces do you see? What are they hoping for you?

A God of love in a world of violence

1 Thessalonians 4:1-12

I grew up in a small town in the dairy-farming countryside of Vermont, USA. That the Lord is an 'avenger' of injustice, as Paul writes in verse 6, is not something I ever heard in church. It makes me nervous. The theologian Miroslav Volf grew up in Croatia, saw his country ravaged by war, and taught in a Croatian theological college in the painful aftermath. In his view, if God were not angry, God would not be worthy of worship (*Exclusion and Embrace: A Theological Exploration of Identity, Otherness, and Reconciliation*, Nashville: Abingdon Press, 1996, p.304).

But does God need to 'avenge' injustice at the end of history? Must God be ultimately coercive? Many are uneasy at the prospect of divine violence. But imagining that the guilty will freely accept their share in the horrors of history seems naive. God is patient but God will not be complicit in suffering.

But won't faith in an 'avenger' encourage violence? Perhaps in giving ultimate justice to God we are instead freed to 'love one another' (verse 9) without fear. We do not love 'into the void'; there is solid ground beneath us and beyond us on which to build communities of self-giving love. The Thessalonians experienced persecution, but their love for one another was famous (verse 9).

How does your understanding of God reckon with a violent world? Jesus shows us both the reality of violence and its overcoming. God has final judgement, not human beings; thanks be to God.

Invite Jesus to read the news with you this week, especially the short stories of even small-scale violence. Imagine Jesus' sorrow. Feel his indignation kindle. Is it right that these things should happen? What can human society do about it? What kind of reconciliation is needed ultimately for a rule of justice and peace to be more than a fiction?

Real grief, real hope

1 Thessalonians 4:13-end

I serve as co-pastor to a diverse congregation gathered from the university community in Manchester. At a Bible study on this passage, we talked about patterns of grief in our cultures and across generations – from formal Victorian patterns of dress and propriety to mourners and incense at Buddhist funeral services in Singapore. Paul writes these words to the Thessalonians 'so that [they] may not grieve as others do who have no hope' (verse 13). We're not sure what was going on in the congregation. Perhaps someone died as a result of the persecution. Perhaps a natural death before the coming of Jesus, an event Paul said was imminent, was unsettling. At any rate, like humans in all times and places, they grieved.

Paul's description of Jesus' dramatic arrival is not a road map for the future. He discourages speculation about Jesus' coming, in the following verses. His intent is pastoral: he wants the Thessalonians to encourage one another, knowing that nothing can separate them from Jesus and one another. Allowing ourselves to be distracted by the physics or the musical instruments is hardly the point.

As grief visited the Thessalonians, grief will visit us, as well. Paul writes not that we should not grieve, only that we should not grieve as those who have no hope. In the midst of real grief is a real hope – hope in a presence, hope in a community that death cannot extinguish.

God, you make of us a people in this life and in life beyond this world. Help us stand in that strong love, shoulder to shoulder, in everything we do today.

Born among us

1 Thessalonians 5:1-11

Life in a multi-cultural society throws up surprises. Last year during the start of term we decided to erect a yurt in front of our busy campus chaplaincy to encourage people to slow down and rest, as at a music festival. On the first morning we attracted mostly Kazakh students surprised to find their national structure so far from home...

Paul tells the Thessalonians that they are destined for salvation, because Jesus died for them in order that they may live (verses 9-10). God chose the Thessalonians (1:4). Election or destiny, in other words, was no longer dependent on ethnicity. The Jews might have been called first, but the Thessalonians were sisters and brothers in the same family, a family of grace, not merit. God has chosen the world in Christ.

The working out of this rainbow-coloured destiny happens over time, like a pregnancy (verse 3), like Paul's own motherly care for the Thessalonians. What is being born among us is new and wonderful, though none of us knows exactly what it will look like. The resolution is coming from outside the world, not from within the processes of history. But it is coming to complete history and to complete our incomplete lives. The future is open to all, regardless of background. The future is coming to a world searching for meaning; to Kazakhs and to Mancunians; to all, equally. Good news, indeed.

God, give us patience in the open stories of our lives. Keep us from rushing to closure. Help us know the gospel is not only ours to share, but also ours to share in, with all people.

Nathan Eddy

1 & 2 Thessalonians

Never tire of doing right

Notes based on the *Poverty and Justice Bible* and the Contemporary English Version by **Mauricio Silva**

Mauricio Silva is a lay missionary from Chile. Over the past nine years, Mauricio and his family have worked in different inner city areas of Birmingham. His ministry has been related to providing support for asylum seekers and refugees, and promoting understanding and dialogue among people of different faiths and traditions. Mauricio is currently a member of the leadership team of Columban Lay Missionaries, an intercultural group seeking to live a simple lifestyle and journey with the poor and marginalised.

1 Thessalonians 5:12-end

Communities of resistance

The people of God in each generation strive to hear God's voice in their daily experiences. When Paul and his friends greet, instruct or pray for the community of Thessalonica they bear in mind the struggles facing that community.

Paul and his companions know well that the church in Thessalonica needed to be strengthened in unity in order to be better prepared to face persecution. Having this in mind, they persuade the community to cultivate the values of inclusiveness, respect for each other, esteem for their leaders and patience with those who are weak. Paul also knows that facing a hostile environment requires creativity. Christians today are likewise called to build communities of resistance that do not respond with hatred but with love to those who persecute them.

Our generation is confronted with a society that resists gospel values and spreads the belief that humans can live in a world without God's compassion and justice. We are all called to challenge trends and fashions that dehumanise communities, destroy identities and idolise human constructions. And this must be done in a spirit of communion and unity among Christians.

How do I contribute to building unity among Christians?

How do I personally testify to belonging to a 'community of resistance'?

Holy Spirit, infuse in our hearts the desire to build communities of resistance that faithfully testify to your message of peace and justice in unity and with love.

Resisting from our roots

2 Thessalonians 1: 1-4

In Chile we boast of our sense of solidarity. Chileans believe this is due to living in a dangerous land that is continually hit by natural disaster. One of our popular sayings is '*hoy por ti, mañana por mí*' ('I help you today – you'll help me tomorrow'). With this saying we acknowledge the mutual dependence among neighbours; solidarity is a defining quality of our identity.

I grew up under an oppressive regime that imposed on us the way we should behave, dress, think and speak. To dissent was considered tasteless and dangerous. At that time solidarity was suppressed and considered subversive. Instead of solidarity our people were offered 'suspicion'. We were trained to suspect our neighbours, our friends and even our closest relatives. The manifest result of spreading such a sense of mistrust was to build a society in which self-interest was the centre of everything.

The Chilean sense of solidarity has been a resisting force against oppression in the past. Nowadays, many indigenous groups and campesino communities are leading the way to help us rediscover this solidarity and resist selfishness and greed.

What place does my personal faith take in times of trouble?

How is my daily life an expression of the people of God's resistance to a civilisation of greed and selfishness?

Holy Spirit, in times of tribulation and fear, lead us to discover our identity as mutually dependent creatures.

Mauricio Silva

Mining for justice

2 Thessalonians 1: 5-12

Today's passage speaks of a triumph. 'God will give you relief from your troubles' (verse 7), is Paul's promise, and suffering will make the community fit for the kingdom. At times I struggle to see how this sense of suffering as a necessary element of faith can be reconciled with our efforts to build a kingdom of justice.

The events surrounding the successful rescue operation of the thirty-three miners trapped in the San José mine in Chile in 2010 can be seen in different lights. The international media portrayed it as an example of the triumph of hope over despair, of life over death.

Mining must be one of the most challenging jobs: it requires technical skill and high levels of physical strength in the individuals who are willing to work in hazardous conditions. These qualities were tested to the uttermost in the thirty-three trapped miners. We cannot imagine the sense of triumph and freedom that they must have felt once they reached safety. However, this triumphant grand finale must not detract from the cry for justice rising from thousands of other miners who continue to work in inhumane conditions every day.

Paul's reassurance of a final triumph comes also with a warning: we must not become part of structures that inflict pain and death.

Am I part of any structure that inflicts pain and suffering on others?

In what ways can I engage locally and globally in the struggle for justice today?

Spirit of truth, strengthen our endeavours with passion and love so that we may own the struggles of those who seek your justice and peace today.

A language of urgency

2 Thessalonians 2: 1-12

Every now and then we are warned about the threat levels from terrorism. As I write, the level is severe, which means that a terrorist attack is highly likely to happen. After the 9/11 and 7/7 terrorist attacks we have had to get accustomed to this sort of language, a security jargon used to keep us on alert mode.

Paul also used a language of urgency. He exhorts the church in Thessalonica to be attentive and alert, to become a discerning community that is not fooled by false claims or disturbed by false prophecies but remains faithful to the truth it has received. Reading the signs of the times in the light of the Lord's truth nurtures the community members' understanding of their faith, strengthens relationships and deepens their convictions.

Then and now, Christians live among many who claim to speak the language of truth. It is precisely in such a context that the community of believers needs to exercise its capacity for discernment. In a society dominated by a language of national security – which may promote individualism and suspicion – Christians must be that 'breath of Jesus' who disperses disunity and builds strong communal ties.

Do I offer an 'alternative language' to my immediate community, family, friends?

Do my priorities in life reflect the urgency of the kingdom of justice and peace?

Spirit of reconciliation, give us the gift of companionship and trust with each other, so we may help build strong and inclusive communities.

Today's voice of God

2 Thessalonians 2: 13-17

In communal cultures the voice of the elders, echoing the wisdom of the ancestors, helps the community to discern the meaning of present events, and becomes a source of authority (a divine-like authority) that guides the whole community to do and say what is right.

Paul trusts that the message he has conveyed to the community of Thessalonica will be treasured and faithfully followed by all its members. This is not a human message, Paul insists, it is God who has used Paul's preaching to transform individuals and communities.

The gift of faith we have received has been nurtured in the act of listening to others. For a Christian this implies not only listening to those who have preceded us in the journey of faith, but also to many in our own generation who join us in the struggle to find meaning and purpose in life.

Living in multi-cultural Britain, I realise that God must be using the voices of people from all walks of life when communicating with our world. I try to pay particular attention to the voices of those beyond my immediate Christian environment. After all, Saul of Tarsus was an unexpected instrument of God to many in the early church.

Which testimonies and voices have nurtured my journey of faith throughout the years?

What unexpected voices may tell us of God in our multi-cultural and globalised world?

Holy Spirit, we thank you for speaking to each generation. Open our senses so that today we may continue to listen to your voice teaching, comforting and healing.

A friendly God in a hostile world

2 Thessalonians 3: 1-5

As an immigrant, I have learned that prayer is an essential component of my relationship with those I have left behind. For Paul and his companions it must have been similar. Paul's prayer that God may guide the Thessalonians to be 'as loving as God and as patient as Christ' (verse 5, CEV) is an expression of his care for them, as well as summarising the core of the Christian message.

The love of God is reflected in the patience of Jesus, who, in fraternal solidarity, bears his sisters' and brothers' brokenness in order to be a sign of reconciliation. Christ's patience becomes God's love in action in the midst of a broken reality.

Working among refugees, I have become more and more aware of how much love and patience are needed within a context of despair and isolation. Living with others who do and say things differently may so easily trigger hostile attitudes, destroy communities and build barriers. People who flee from persecution and poverty bear the scars of a hostile world.

In this ministry I have also witnessed how Christian communities in this country have responded lovingly and patiently to the challenges of migration. The biblical tradition of welcoming the stranger has been exercised against an unfriendly political environment that generates a public feeling of distrust towards the newcomer. When Christians care and speak up for refugees, they participate in God's unconditional love and become, in Jesus, a symbol of reconciliation.

How do I exercise the biblical tradition of 'welcoming the stranger' in my life?

Spirit of life, mould us so we become as loving as God and as patient as Christ.

Mauricio Silva

The works of faith

2 Thessalonians 3: 6-16

Paul's words remind the community that working is a duty for the Christian. The Lord's coming cannot be an excuse for laziness; on the contrary, hard work is needed in order to build up the Christian community. The dichotomy between prayer and work finds no place in Paul's reflections.

William McNamara defines contemplation as a 'long loving look at the real' (at www.theyardleygroup.com/Burghardt_-_Contemplation_a_long_loving.pdf). The 'real' is God at work among us: the God behind the struggles for justice of those who work in inhumane conditions and among victims fleeing persecution and poverty. The 'real' is the God-with-us who walks along human paths.

Paul writes, 'never become tired of doing right' (verse 13, CEV). The challenge is to immerse ourselves in the struggle without tiring, to become part of our society with the intention to transform it. This tireless 'long look' must be sealed with love. The 'loving look' emerges from the certainty of being unconditionally loved by God. This certainty moves us to be present in the loveless places of today: places where people die of hunger, where workers are exploited, where women and children's dignity is undermined or where nature is desecrated. We take this 'long loving look' standing by the victims and the exploited earth, because we know that from that place redemption springs.

In what ways do I take the victim's side?

Holy Spirit of peace, bring our labours to fruition so that we may taste and see the kingdom of justice, peace and love we long for.

Wisdom

The identity and character of wisdom

Proverbs 3:13-18

Unwrapping wisdom

In New Zealand, the shops and advertisers have been selling Christmas since early November. The mail box at the gate is daily stuffed full of glossy advertising, telling us what the ideal gifts are for granny or grandpa, children, him and her. There are multitudes of suggestions for the person who has everything. Rarely are there suggestions for the person who has nothing. Supermarkets are overflowing with festive food, yet do not offer to match item for item in our trolleys with a contribution to the food bank. Travel brochures invite us to exotic places, promising that it will be the holiday of a lifetime. Wisdom and understanding are unlikely to be on many wish lists. Nor is a tree of life likely to feature highly.

Being connected to wisdom is not an insurance against sorrow and difficulty, any more than the gift of a best-selling novel or a holiday on a Pacific Island is a guarantee of lasting pleasure and relaxation.

To unwrap the gift of wisdom is to open ourselves to spaciousness and wholeness, in which pleasantness and peace will flourish. Through this week, we will be unwrapping the gifts of wisdom.

May I be open to spaciousness and peace.

Notes based on the New Revised Standard Version by

Lynne Frith

Lynne Frith is a presbyter in the Methodist Church in New Zealand, Te Haahi Weteriana o Aotearoa, and is currently appointed to a central city parish in Auckland.

Her creative expression includes stitching with threads and fabrics, writing poetry, tutoring in liturgy and homiletics, and being with family and friends.

Slip, slop, slap

Proverbs 8:12-21

To live with prudence is to use common sense, to have presence of mind, to be aware of consequences. At this time of year, in my country, when the sun is hot, the sea is sparkling and summer holidays draw near, there are constant reminders of how to guard against danger. The wise person will 'slip, slop, slap' – slip into a shirt, slop on some sunscreen, slap on a hat – to protect against the sun's fierce rays. Boaties are exhorted to pay attention to weather forecasts, to wear life-jackets at all times, to carry emergency beacons or flares. Swimmers do well to pay attention to ocean currents and the flow of rivers, always to swim in the company of others, and not to go beyond their depth. Ignoring such advice can have life-threatening consequences for self and others. Swimming with the current conserves energy. Staying off the oceans in bad weather saves lives. Remaining in the shade in the heat of the day is good for the body.

Just as the summer safety instructions are not difficult to follow, so it is with the ways of wisdom. Wisdom is kind to those who seek her out, who love her. Right living and just action bring the satisfaction of knowing that our living is not at the expense of any living thing.

How have you ignored safety instructions for a good life recently?

May I live wisely and well.

Small is good

Proverbs 30:24-28

Agur, son of Jakeh, laments his own stupidity, his lack of human understanding, his lack of wisdom. How often have you felt like Agur, full of critical self-examination perhaps, or so weary that all you can see is your unwise decisions, your impatience with the foolishness of others, your lack of experience?

When we are weary and stressed, whether because of overwork, or no work at all, illness or accident, the death of someone close or the ending of a relationship, it's not unusual to lose perspective on self and the world around us. Everyone else seems to cope well with adversity, while we are depressed and miserable. Everyone else is surrounded by caring friends and family, yet we are so alone.

It's all too easy to feel weak, powerless, out of control and at the beck and call of everyone around us. It is beyond our comprehension that in such a state wisdom might be found. Agur's oracle draws attention to the wisdom found even in the repetitive patterns and structures of existence, in the need for and provision of food, shelter, and community order. Just as the least and smallest of creatures may be seen to have incomprehensible wisdom, so, when we feel small, powerless and disordered, we too may find stores of wisdom to strengthen us.

May I find hidden stores of wisdom.

Survival in tough times

Ecclesiastes 9: 13-18

When I was a young Girl Guide I learned how to find directions using the sun and my wristwatch. I could light a fire with a minimal amount of dry material and one match. Much later, when I lived in rural Australia for a while, I learned how to use a plastic bag in a sandy hollow or attached to the end of a branch to catch the night-time dew, should I be stranded in dry terrain without water. These are simple, potentially life-saving, actions. Fortunately, I have not needed to put any of these survival skills to the test.

When times are tough, we often look for an elaborate or grand solution. The purchase of a lottery ticket carries with it the hope of a windfall of millions of dollars. In our loneliness we dream that the perfect partner or mate will simply appear beside us on the train or bus. When the doctor tells us we need to improve our fitness we quail at the thought of running marathons. The simplest advice – establish a budget, join a club or organisation, walk for 30 minutes a day – seems too simple or too slow when we want immediate results.

We do not need to be wealthy, beautiful or famous to possess a wisdom that is life giving, both for individuals and communities. Quiet wisdom is more effective than military or political power.

Spend a few moments thinking of those whose wisdom has been life saving for you.

May I see wisdom at work in the small daily steps I take.

Ask the aunties

1 Kings 4:29-34

Aunty Pari tells it how it is. She's been around for a long time. She's one of the kuia, wise older women in Te Haahi Weteriana o Aotearoa, the Methodist Church in New Zealand. She knows a lot of history, will tell you off if she thinks you need to pull up your socks, is quick to say so if she thinks you've got it right, has a twinkle in her eye and a hearty laugh, can sum up the politics of any situation.

I've lost count of the times I've been told to 'ask Aunty Pari' when I've had a question about something, or wanted to test out an idea about our bicultural church life and protocols. How often have you heard it said, in response to a question about why things are done a certain way, or how to resolve a difficult community matter 'go and ask the aunties'? The aunties, individually and collectively, are the repository of the wisdom of the community. They are in touch with people, rivers, mountains, forests, birds. They carry within them the memory and wisdom of the tipuna or ancestors.

Every community has its 'aunties' – the ones we go to for advice, for counsel, for reconnection, for healing. The aunties have their feet on the ground, their hands in the messiness of life, their hearts in the wellbeing of the people.

Give thanks for the wise elders in your family, your community.

First read the recipe

James 3:13-18

I enjoy cooking, and take some pride and pleasure in preparing food for family and friends. When I first acquired a crock-pot, or slow-cooker as it is now known, I didn't bother reading the instructions before I used it for the first time. I put everything in randomly – meat, vegetables, liquid, seasoning – and turned it on. When I got home from work, expecting a meal to be ready for the family, I discovered that the vegetables were barely cooked, and there was an excessive amount of liquid. As I belatedly read the instructions, I found out what I should have done to ensure that everything was cooked at the same time.

This chapter in James is about what one commentator describes as 'slow speaking' (C Freeman Sleeper, *James*, Abingdon New Testament Commentaries, Abingdon Press, 1998, pp.84–95). Instead of giving the instructions first, as did the manual that came with my kitchen appliance, James begins by describing the consequences of hasty speech. And then, at verse 13, comes a recipe, or set of instructions, for slow speaking. These ingredients are not plucked off the supermarket shelf, but are the gifts that come from wisdom.

Choosing the wrong ingredients or failing to follow the recipe can make the meal unappetising. A peaceable attitude, gentleness, willingness to yield, freedom from partiality or hypocrisy will result in a feast of peace.

May I show gentleness to my self and to those whom I encounter today.

Exiled in your own home

Daniel 2:20-23

When European imperial and missionary endeavour swept the world in the nineteenth century, it carried with it a view that the customs and religious beliefs of the indigenous peoples were to be supplanted by the 'superior' knowledge, wisdom and civilisation of the newcomers. For Maori in New Zealand, as for colonised peoples in other places, it meant that the land, mountains and rivers were renamed with English or European names, that the indigenous language was suppressed, that religious beliefs and practices, along with traditional healing arts, were ultimately legislated against. Maori who converted to the new religion were given 'Christian' names.

The tasks of decolonisation include reclaiming and valuing language and tradition, restoring place names, undoing unjust legislation.

Daniel and his friends were living in a period of foreign domination and power – colonisation – that was not dissimilar to what happened in New Zealand. They were, in effect, exiled at home. Foreign beliefs, customs and names were imposed upon them. Even so, Daniel was able to give thanks for the wisdom of his ancestors, to call on the old traditions and religion to sustain him in difficult times. He recognised that the gifts of wisdom and power were indeed divine gifts, and was thankful.

What traditional wisdom do you cherish, or need to reclaim?

May I be grateful for the wisdom of my forebears.

Wisdom

The acts of wisdom in creation and history

Proverbs 3:19-20

Notes based on the New Revised Standard Version of the Bible by
John Barnett

John Barnett is married with two grown-up daughters. He had been an Anglican priest in Birmingham for over thirty years before his current job as interfaith officer in the Wolverhampton part of the Lichfield Diocese, and minister of a small Black Country parish. He has been a member of the Traherne Association since 1997.

Burbling with delight

This week's passages lead us to praise God for creation, with human experience coming into special focus in some readings. The prayers are drawn from the writings of Thomas Traherne, the Herefordshire mystic, theologian and priest. All Traherne extracts are found in *Happiness and Holiness* by Denise Inge, Canterbury Press, 2008 (my modernised spelling).

Friends were recently telling us about their daughter's graduation. In one way it wasn't much of a story; we knew how it ended – the photograph was already on the mantelpiece – and any graduation ceremony has its langueurs. We still hung on to every word, encouraging them to tell us all the details, because we were reflecting and sharing in their pride, their hopes, their thankfulness and their love.

In a different way the beginning of things isn't much of a story either. We are at the edges of what we can meaningfully talk about in scientific or religious terms, and yet we stumble on. We try to express our understanding but also our thankfulness, our wonder and our love for the existence that surrounds us and of which we are part. In this short passage 'Wisdom', 'understanding' and 'knowledge' have their nuances, but in their near repetition they are a sort of holy burbling, expressing an inexpressible delight.

May we never grow tired of repeating your love and praise, creator God!

Who goes there?

Proverbs 8:22–26

'The Lord created me at the beginning of his work' (verse 22). Who is this prime creation, before the earth or the depths? The classic Jewish answer is Wisdom, a personified aspect of the one true God. For Christians – despite the word 'created' – it is the Spirit who moves on the face of the waters, or the Word who was in the beginning with God. These responses are exercises of inspired imagination, but there is a primal human experience involved too.

Sometimes, away from home, I have half woken in the dark and set out for the bathroom only to find utter confusion, my normal pathways blocked, the experience a disorienting blur, until I realise where I am. It takes more than raw sensation to make a world; we have to apply our own minds, our experience and judgement before chaos recedes.

In a way, the question 'who is this?' has at least four possible answers: wisdom, Spirit, Word … and me. Which of these is right? There is something to be said for trying to bring them into some sort of congruence, rather than choosing between them. If the Father, Word and Spirit are one, are we not also told that this divine Trinity dwells by grace in each of us? We are made both creatures and co-creators, joy upon joy. Traherne pleads in the following prayer for the gift of divine creativity, through a love that transforms those round him.

My Lord, I beseech Thee let my love unto all be regular like Thine …
I pray Thee for thy loving kindness' sake, supply my want in this particular.
And so make me love all that I may be a blessing to all …
And make all them that are round about me wise and holy as Thou art.

Thomas Traherne, *Centuries of Meditation* 1:79

Try tomorrow, as you wake, to think of your God-given role as co-creator. How are you called to affect the day?

The junior partner

Proverbs 8:27-31

One of our daughters sang in the City of Birmingham Symphony Youth Chorus, working with internationally acclaimed musicians. Over the years she came to appreciate classical music in a way we never have – from the inside, as it were. She also came to think of such people as Sir Simon Rattle as colleagues (albeit rather exalted ones!) with whom the chorus worked in shared creativity.

In this reading, the co-creators – Wisdom, Spirit, Word, us – have the great joy of working with the master craftsman, rejoicing in the world and its inhabitants as creative masterpieces and delighting in a bond of shared enterprise. If we take the bold step of applying this role to ourselves, our understanding and appreciation of both creation and creator deepen as we enter the apprentice's role, modelling ourselves on our master. Then, as we work alongside him, we make the awesome discovery that the delight is mutual: 'I was daily his delight' (verse 30). Again we have been drawn into the mutuality of the Trinity.

My Bible notes that 'master worker' in verse 30 can also be translated as 'a little child'. No crabby apprentice-master this, but one who both forms us in his own image and loves us as a tender father, expanding our divine potential and having mercy when we fall short.

Think of times you have perceived God acting. How might you imitate the things that come to mind?

Thy love itself is the godhead which I adore …
Fully manifested in all its operations;
In them and in itself ever to be enjoyed.
O make me feel how infinitely I am beloved,
And be the rest of my soul for ever.

Thomas Traherne, *Select Meditations*, IV, 39 (p.307)

What did the fish say?

Job 12:7-13

Beasts, birds, plants and fish are all chatting away, as Job the ventriloquist gives voice to the creatures round him. We might think that such a writer just says whatever he chooses, reflecting his own beliefs in giving a voice to dumb creatures.

Yet if we wait observantly on the created world, it does begin to speak to us, and with a voice that is not just our own but what seems like an Other in our midst. An indication of this is the oddity of meditation. You might expect that if you are anxious or depressed and try to meditate, to steer away from distracting thoughts and live in the moment, you would end up with pure anxiety or depression, yet meditation is often recommended as a way of addressing those feelings. It seems that when we simply attend to what is – to Being itself – freedom, lightness and vitality come. Sometimes such an awareness can also come unbidden, perhaps in the countryside or the garden, occasionally in a busy city street.

It may seem miraculous that creation can 'talk' to us like this, but we are creatures too, made of the same stuff. So when 'the ear test[s] words' (verse 12), it is part of the same physical and spiritual milieu as that to which it listens, and it is attuned to what harmonises with the Spirit within, 'God's counsel and understanding' (verse 13).

An ant is a great miracle in a little room:
A feeble creature made to be an ornament of the magnificent universe:
and no less a monument of eternal love, than almighty power...
An ant in its spiritual capacity is a symbol of [an] ... industrious man
And well resembles an orderly peaceful Christian.

Thomas Traherne, *Commentaries of Heaven* (p.75)

Spend a few minutes attending to an object, a picture, a view. That's all. Enjoy!

Getting ready to go

Job 28:23-28

Among the things we are co-creating are our own selves and our society, and this reading reminds us that order is essential. God weighs, apportions, measures, decrees, declares and establishes. Yes, but a word of warning. It is the oldest trick in the book for despots to justify oppressive measures as necessary to good order, something that has been trotted out again in the 'war against terror'. Religious institutions, too, can demand conformity, and scripture can be read so as to vindicate oppressive attitudes.

For some years I was chaplain to an apparently conformist bunch, a group of air cadets. They had to learn the fine points of navigation and had strict kit inspections, so that they sometimes seemed very regimented. But such strictness meant that in due course they could be turned out at night, on the wild Staffordshire heathland, to roam safely. What might have been oppressive was revealed as liberating; they knew where they were going and had with them what they needed.

In the Christian life, too, the call is not to security, but to adventure, a departure from the nullity and confusion of evil, alertly responding to the will of God. The call to good order is certainly there, but it is always subservient to the call to life.

O Lord, let the people's profaneness be healed
Not by … oppression of power,
But by an intelligent persuasion of inner holiness.
That in the midst of decency, order and beauty,
They may be spiritual and holy.

Thomas Traherne, *Church's Year-Book* (p.299)

Is there something you could tidy today? Think of re-organising it more usefully or beautifully, making orderliness creative.

Crash landing

Jeremiah 51: 15-19

I tried to water-ski this summer and, after a lot of trial and even more error, got the hang of it at last. It felt so easy I couldn't see why I had ever found it difficult. Just as I was thinking this, my legs shot out and, with a 'tumult of waters' (verse 16), I was submerged.

In this week's readings we have been challenged by the amazing dignity God gives us in allowing us to share in his creative work, but today we are brought low: 'Everyone is stupid and without knowledge' (verse 17). The difference between our creative activity and God's is made quite clear. Our products are shameful, false, lifeless, worthless, deluded and perishable.

If we are foolish enough to rely on our own devices the outlook is bleak, but the title the Lord takes, 'the portion of Jacob' (verse 19), opens another way. Jacob crashed, morally and socially, by stealing his brother's blessing, and had to flee from Esau, who was out to kill him in revenge. It was then the Lord came to him and promised amazing fruitfulness: 'your offspring [will be] like the dust of the earth' (Genesis 13:16), giving Jacob a share in the Lord's own life-creating potency. Many years later, Jacob faced God in the desert and wrestled through the night to make sure that blessing was renewed. We need that blessing equally urgently if we are to bear fruit that will last.

O my God revive my soul,
And refresh it with the streams of living waters!
Life, sense, affections, zeal: …
Replenish me with these,
And I shall no more be a stony well of dust,
But a spring and fountain of living waters,
Enriching and reviving all Thy works;…

Thomas Traherne, Select Meditations III, 62 (p.303)

God's rhythm of life

Psalm 104:23-30

In this psalm, human activity is represented only by ships, skimming over the surface of life – partly using but also greatly at the mercy of the rest of the created world. My wife has just returned from a tall ship voyage with the Guides, where she was amazed by the dolphins sporting alongside them day by day. We are reminded in this passage of the teeming superfluity of life. There is also a sense of its – of our – vulnerability, but instead of this being expressed as a threat and cause for anxiety, it is set in a context of dependence that speaks of grace and constant renewal.

The Lord is described as sending his Spirit, his breath, to his creation. Our daughter told us that when she went scuba diving (with the Guides again!), she had a great time – but first she had to learn to adjust her breathing to the rhythm of the equipment. So creation reverberates to the rhythm of the Lord in life, in death, in re-birth. As we bob about, tacking across the seas of life, we need consciously to adjust to that rhythm of grace and joy. It is a special Christian insight that not only should the created world adjust to the rhythm of the Lord, but also that by the incarnation God has adapted to his creatures – lover and beloved breathing in harmony.

Come Holy Ghost, eternal God,
Our hearts with life inspire.
Enkindle zeal in all our souls
And fill us with thy heavenly fire.

Send forth thy beams, and let thy grace
Upon my spirit shine:
That I may all thy works enjoy,
Revive, sing praises, be divine.

Thomas Traherne, *Church's Year-Book* (p.300)

Wisdom

The call of wisdom

Notes based on the New Revised Standard Version, by

Peter Fisher

Peter Fisher is a priest in the Church of England. Now retired from paid ministry, he has worked in different parts of England, both in parishes and in theological colleges (teaching systematic theology). He is married to Elizabeth and enjoys her baking, as well as playing the piano and digging the garden! He has been involved for many years in the Faith and Order movement, seeking Christian unity in the UK and the wider world.

Proverbs 1:20-33

Spoilt for choice

The streets are crowded. The shoppers who jostle in the market keep beaming with pre-Christmas cheer, but in their eyes is also a gleam of panic. There is too much to do, there are too many choices: choices at the food stalls, in the gift shops, in the purse. The noise level is high, too, so no wonder we hardly notice the woman on the corner, crying out to be heard. Who is it? She is God's superlative pesterer, Holy Wisdom – out looking for us, never content to sit passively in the temple or church. She aims to grab our attention when we are at our most mindless and preoccupied. She has little interest in our multiple choices, our panic, or the self-pity that being busy breeds. Wherever she pops up, she calls us back to the big choice. 'It is your life you are frittering away,' she seems to say; 'Stop, stop now, and listen to me.' And all through the coming week – this week above all – we will be stopped in our tracks by the big choice of God's Wisdom and Word.

Stop, stop now, and listen to me!

Learning what to want

Proverbs 8:1-11

Wisdom is out and about again, but in a different part of town. Now she is calling from the heights, by the crossroads, at the city gate. All public places, maybe places of decision, too: the kinds of places where election candidates canvass. Wisdom, now, as always, is calling us to make the big choice, even bigger than how to vote – the choice as to whom to follow and how to live. Thank God she is persistent! Because most of us are prepared to consider big choices only very occasionally, at moments when we are stopped in our tracks by brutal obstacles or astounding experiences. Such moments stay in the mind. We can remember the new determination they engendered. Recovering from a deep loss or disaster, or, equally, from a thrilling new experience of love or beauty, we make great resolutions! Then we are ready to listen to the call of Wisdom, to redirect our desires from trivialities to deep values. But gradually lazy, comfortable, habit reasserts itself, and our will to follow the call we once heard so clearly peters out.

Is this one reason why we cling to this time, the few minutes we carve out for reading the Bible and for prayer? Perhaps by its daily drip-feeding the time of quiet can be the school of our desires, God's gentle, practical way of teaching us what to keep wanting and working for.

O patient, persistent Wisdom from on high,
voice of the One who will not let me go;
keep calling and coaxing me, through the words of
scripture,
through the silence of the Spirit,
through the memory of my good turns,
and I will try to listen, with my mind, my heart and
my feet.

Hanging around hopefully

Proverbs 8:32-36

Was there once a time when you would go and lurk somewhere, maybe for half an hour at a time, just in the faint hope that one particular person would pass by? It might make you blush to think of it now, but that is just how we behave in the heat of infatuation or the first intense flush of love. And it is exactly how Wisdom envisages her true devotees: they 'watch daily' at her gates, 'waiting beside' her doors (verse 34). So strong is their desire to hear her voice that they will gladly spend time simply hanging around hopefully.

You may have noticed, in reading these passages about Wisdom's call to us, that we are seldom told much of the content of her teaching. At first this is puzzling and a bit frustrating. But on further reflection it makes sense. The all-important issue is not whether we agree with this or that particular insight which comes from the Word and Wisdom of God, or with each particular verse of scripture. The all-important thing is this: that it is this voice we long to hear. Like partisans in occupied territory, we will keep tuned in to Radio Free Europe, even when the signal is poor and we don't like the announcer's accent.

So today, as we hang around the Bible and watch at the gate of prayer, we rekindle our hope and longing to hear God's voice.

Here I am, waiting, Holy God
Now, for once, you are the one focus of my desire
and hope
and my heart is urging me to hang around a little while
longer.
Give me, I pray, a lover's determination, a lover's alertness,
so that even when I am no longer at your gate
and I seem to have forgotten you,
I remain truly tuned to your voice.

Grub's up!

Proverbs 9:1-6

Wisdom's invitation has taken on a new, enticing dimension. 'Come, eat ... my bread ... drink ... my wine' (verse 5). Here, at last, is that free lunch we always hankered after! But there is more to it than a free lunch. To start with, Wisdom has not just prepared a meal, she has taken far more trouble than that. She has built a house, even quarrying and carving her own pillars for the house. Why seven? We can't be sure, but the number sets the imagination going. Are these the pillars (like the seven days of Genesis 1) on which the creation is founded? Are we to surmise that divine Wisdom has framed the very structure of our world to afford a place of hospitality for us, somewhere for us to feast on God's generous provision? Or maybe the seven pillars simply indicate how grand a dining-hall has been prepared for us – assuming we are ready to answer the call.

Something clicks into place as we relish this scrumptious picture: it's all topsy-turvy. The queen is serving the beggars. The eternal resources of God are being put at the service of the feeblest of human beings – the 'simple'' and 'those without sense' (verse 4). Just picture the servant-girls of Wisdom, like industrious angels, scouring the world to get the invitation to us. Here in Proverbs we catch a glimpse of God's extravagance, and of that other feast, in the upper room.

O wise and kindly God,
you know that I become proud
when I forget how important I am to you;
may your gigantic love make me humble.

Well I never!

Matthew 5:1-12

A black activist, meeting Desmond Tutu for the first time, could not disguise his surprise. Having heard all about the great leader, he was amazed to see a gnome-like little man appear, laughing all the time (John Allen, *Rabble-Rouser for Peace: The Authorised Biography of Desmond Tutu*, Rider Books, 2006).

Greatness is seldom how we imagine it: neither, it seems, is Wisdom. As believers in the truth of the New Testament, we look to Jesus as the embodiment of God's Wisdom. But what we see and hear is both utterly compelling and quite unexpected. I once had an old poetry book; a previous owner had marked the most solemn passages with handwritten comments: 'O how true, how true!' I could see that reader sitting in a fireside armchair and nodding sagely. But no one who reads these words from Matthew 5 could react like that. Jesus' words take the wind out of our confident sails and shake our preconceptions as to what is wise and true.

How do you imagine Jesus speaking these words? Is he shouting, or do you have to strain to hear? Does the sound of his voice make you want to weep or to laugh – or both? Perhaps St Paul was thinking of the Beatitudes when he wrote, 'God's foolishness is wiser than human wisdom, and God's weakness is stronger than human strength' (1 Corinthians 1:25). Now we know what God's coming into the world means: the deepest comfort and hope ('blessing'), but not this side of utter dispossession.

A stranger once did bless the earth
who never caused a heart to mourn,
whose very voice gave sorrow mirth;
and how did earth his worth return?
it spurned him from its lowliest lot:
the meanest station owned him not.

John Clare, 'The Stranger'

Guest-workers?

Matthew 10:16-20, 24-26, 40-42

Wisdom's invitation has already taken on an unexpected tone of voice, now it is disclosing a whole new dimension. In Proverbs she invited us to be students, guests at a feast, or maybe even her devotees. But as the message of the Beatitudes unfolds through Matthew's Gospel we find our lives are becoming bound up with the one who calls us. It is a bit alarming. Jesus calls his friends, then sends them out to take the same risks he himself takes. He expects them to discover wisdom and innocence in the face of peril, and to be given the right words to say: all because they (we?) will receive the same Spirit from the Father that inspires Jesus. In fact they will stand in his place: 'Whoever welcomes you welcomes me' (verse 40).

God's wisdom is not to be learnt, or added to our stock of knowledge. Yes, we must attend thoughtfully to the words and watch the actions of Jesus, but it is those who make his words and actions their own who share in his wisdom.

Until the German occupation in the Second World War, Etty Hillesum seemed an unremarkable Dutch Jew. But as she followed her instinct to identify with the sufferings of her people and served them as a volunteer in a transit camp, she was transformed by a spirit of joy, forgiveness and love, ultimately out-facing death with acts and words of grace.

I shall promise you one thing, God, just one very small thing: I shall never burden my today with cares about my tomorrow, although that takes some practice. Each day is sufficient unto itself. I shall try to help You, God, to stop my strength ebbing away, though I cannot vouch for it in advance. ... You are sure to go through lean times with me now and then, when my faith weakens a little, but believe me, I shall always labour for You and remain faithful to You and I shall never drive You from my presence.

Etty Hillesum, *An Interrupted Life*,
Persephone Books, 1999, p.151

Energetic rest

Matthew 11: 25-30

Jesus echoes the ancient Jewish tradition of Wisdom more than ever in these verses. Yet, even as he speaks the language of Wisdom, he gives it a radical twist. Being infantile, 'simple', a bar to understanding in the Book of Proverbs, is for Jesus a condition of understanding. The earlier verses of chapter 11, before our passage, help to explain why: Jesus has seen his own ministry and John Baptist's rejected by the 'grown-ups' of Judea. It was usually the voiceless who recognised him and the none-too-bright who followed him. But Jesus does not complain about this, he rejoices. It fits in with what God wants, because God's will is 'gracious' – always looking to reward those who need it, not those who think they have earned it.

Near the end of the book of Ecclesiasticus, the 'uneducated' reader is urged to 'Put your neck under her [Wisdom's] yoke, and let your souls receive instruction' (Ecclesiasticus 51:26). Now Jesus readdresses the call. He calls the weary and burdened. His is no ordinary yoke, it is not a 'burden' at all. It is a means of rest. Can it be 'rest', when a chapter ago Jesus promised trouble and persecution to his followers? Perhaps it can. This deserves our Christmas meditations. By sharing his divine humility, may Jesus make his strenuous calling (even his suffering?) restful?

I have carried more yokes than some people have had
hot baths!
Dear God! You know I have tried to do my bit –
and not everyone has appreciated it.
Please can you show me what the 'rest' means?
Could it be that there's some part of being an infant that I
have forgotten about?

Wisdom

Jesus Christ, the wisdom of God

Notes based on the Revised Standard Version by

Elizabeth Fisher

Elizabeth Fisher has spent much of her life teaching the New Testament to adults and university students, most recently lecturing in an Anglican theological college. She has also worked for Christian unity, in the UK and Europe and in the synodical life of the Church of England. She is a lay canon of Birmingham Cathedral and now lives in a Pennine village in the North of England, where she enjoys fell-walking and baking.

Matthew 13:53-58

Knowing what really matters

Today's text comes at the heart of Matthew's Gospel. In a place where he should have been welcomed and the Word of God received, Jesus was rejected. Astonished at his ability, neighbours still saw only a local lad; they knew everything about him except what really mattered. Had over-familiarity blinded them to who he really was? Paul will call him a stumbling block for Jews.

Does over-familiarity blind us to the Bible's freshness, and its message? Jesus taught that the kingdom of heaven is like a scribe who brings out old and new (Matthew 13:52); perhaps all his neighbours could see was what was old. Matthew informs us that Jesus did not do new works there. John writes in his Gospel (1:11) 'that he came to what was his own, and his own people did not accept him'. By way of contrast, we find (in Matthew 12:50) that a new family is born when people do the will of their heavenly father. Those who see Jesus as God's wisdom of old will receive from him new acts of power.

Pray that we are kept from spiritual obtuseness and have open eyes to see the God of old in new ways.

An open secret

Ephesians 3:1-11

Three times in this passage Paul writes of the mystery that has been kept from earlier generations and recently revealed to him. God, in God's good time, has revealed that all people can be caught up into unity. Barriers that divide human beings have been broken down by the cross of Christ. The church, the body of Christ, has the particular and cosmic task of making this known. God's wisdom is unlike human wisdom; it is shown in what looks from the human perspective as weakness: a baby in a manger, a death on a cross. Jesus' death was the gateway to resurrection, and the means whereby Gentiles, alongside Jews, could be equal members within the Christian community. All this had been revealed on the Damascus road (see Ephesians 1:9), and is the core of the Christmas message.

Our society and that of Paul, on the surface, are very different. People today have had opportunities to hear the gospel. Then many people were involved in so-called mystery religions. Paul preached openly about the cross and resurrection of Jesus as the open mystery of God's wisdom for all with eyes to see. In Ephesians 1:17 he prayed that God would grant the Ephesians a spirit of wisdom and revelation for deeper knowledge of God. We ask that for ourselves and our world too today. Paul's message was new for the Ephesians, we ask that our generation may hear it afresh, this Christmastide.

In amongst everything else,
be here, Lord Jesus,
tonight and tomorrow.
Show me the rich mystery
of your new, reconciled, humanity
so that the mystery may
show through me.

God chooses to be a displaced person

Luke 2:1-7

Luke writes his account of the good news of Jesus' birth by linking it to the world's big events of the day. That imperial decision to have a census caused upheaval for those who had to return to their ancestral homes to be counted. Joseph and Mary were part of this movement. They travelled from Galilee in the north to Bethlehem in the south, and may have had to follow the longer route to avoid Samaritan territory that divided the two areas. When they arrived at their destination, there was no normal lodging place. This birth took place away from home, and in the last place any mother would wish.

For those with eyes to see, God's Wisdom came to earth in the right place: the city of David. Jesus, the Word and Wisdom of God, was also the Son of David. But maybe that birth which seems, humanly, so 'wrong', made it emphatically the right place. Because the gospel is good news for those in the wrong place, those in transit, those who feel that the big decisions are taken by others. Luke reminds us that God is in charge, always, and that God is 'working his purposes out' whatever human authorities might be scheming. But will the babe in the manger be given room in the world when he grows to manhood, or will he be left outside the city?

How can your church support Christians who are displaced from their homes and live in transit camps?

Heavenly Father, we thank you for the gift of life and the gift of your son, Jesus. We pray today for all who are giving birth, especially for any far from home, and in difficult circumstances. May they find themselves in the right place.

Crowning glory?

Acts 6:8-15

How strange that we move straight from the Christmas story to this event in the life of the early church. Stephen – one of the first followers of the risen Christ – emerged after the apostles preached, and was chosen to be one of seven deacons. His work was not limited to waiting at tables since, gifted with wisdom, he was a great preacher. He was originally a Greek-speaking Jew. His synagogue audience – Greek-speaking like him – were so challenged that they stirred up false accusations about him.

Like his master Jesus, Stephen had to submit himself to questioning. Like Jesus, he faced a martyr's death outside the city. Like Jesus, he forgave his persecutors (Acts 7:59-60). Stephen was the first martyr. Stephen's death was watched by Paul, who may have heard his message in that same synagogue. If the blood of the martyrs is the seedbed of the church, then Stephen's death had a rich harvest.

The gospel message at Christmas is not just a cosy story about a birth, but one that touches on all life and even death. Herod's slaughter of the little children (traditionally remembered on 28 December) reminds us that the good news is good in a wicked world. In Greek the name Stephen means 'crown': followers of Christ have found in suffering, and even death, a kind of crown (2 Timothy 4:8).

There are people in the world who face persecution for their faith. When one part of the Christian community suffers, in some way we all suffer.

Heavenly Father, we lift before you all those who, like Stephen, face persecution for their beliefs. Strengthen them in their trials, and bring good out of their troubles, for the sake of Jesus Christ our Saviour.

Light steps into darkness

John 1:1-14

John's Gospel begins, not with an emperor's plan, but with God's. John unfolds God's plan for the whole creation rather than telling a birth story. These hymn-like verses remind us that so much of scripture sounds God's praises. The human name of Jesus may not appear here, but the whole passage is about God's Wisdom, present at creation, powerful over all darkness, becoming human. John's Gospel is to be read, from start to finish, in that light. Jesus alone not only speaks God's wisdom: he embodies it. John's Gospel knows the power of darkness in the world – it will be night when Judas goes out to betray Jesus – but night never prevails, and can never extinguish the light.

A Jewish author, from the time just before Jesus, wrote, 'while gentle silence enveloped all things, and night in its swift course was now half gone, your all-powerful word leaped from heaven, from the royal throne' (Wisdom 18:14). John tells us that this Word 'was God', not just a messenger, but God dwelling ('pitching his tent') among us (verse 14). People could and can reject him. But those who accept him will find their status renewed in the image of God, redeemed; they will see and share his glory. Following him is following the way, the truth and life, and is destined to lead, ultimately, to sharing his unity in love with the Father.

Use this prayer at the lighting of a candle:

Blessed are you, Lord God, creator of day and night:
to you be praise and glory for ever …
By the light of Christ, your living Word,
dispel the darkness of our hearts
that we may walk as children of light
and sing your praise throughout the world.

Common Worship: Daily Prayer, The Archbishops' Council, London 2005, p.104

God chooses his messengers

Luke 2:8-20

Bethlehem today is a town in a barren environment. In the time of Jesus it was a tiny village; nearby, cosmopolitan Sepphoris was much larger. The barren hillside is a reminder of the past. It was to poor men caring for their flocks on that hillside outside the village that the Wisdom of God was revealed. The story emphasises that the shepherds did not expect a revelation, but they listened. The message was particularly good news for them. The angel says, 'I am bringing you good news' and, 'This will be a sign for you' (verses 10-12).

Many of us are not such good listeners. In a noisy, over-lit world, signs of hope can become invisible, inaudible. How many of us have eyes, ears and minds open to radically new messages, to divine wisdom? Luke tells us that the shepherds listened, reacted and ran to discover what had been announced to them, the baby in a manger. Then there were two different responses to this birth: Mary pondered; the shepherds proclaimed. These probably illiterate people are the first evangelists in Luke's Gospel!

It rings a bell, doesn't it? That God hides things from the 'intelligent' and reveals them to 'infants' (Matthew 11:25, from last Saturday's reading). Does God prefer addressing people in barren places, do they listen better and make better bearers of good tidings? And does God specialise in exalting 'the lowly' as Mary recognised (Luke 1:52)?

Heavenly Father, you chose shepherds to be messengers of your incarnation. Open our ears and eyes to receive your wisdom, and give us a ready tongue to speak boldly and sing clearly your good news, for the sake of your son, Jesus Christ, that the world may see in him the Saviour.

The wisdom of the aged

Luke 2:25-38

Luke's Gospel began with an angel visiting Zechariah in the temple and this story, which closes the birth narrative, also occurs in the temple. These stories act like bookends to the account of Jesus' birth.

As people who longed for the appearance of God's promised one, Simeon and Anna were waiting in the temple – where people expected the Messiah to appear. Anna had resisted the pressure on young widows in her day, to remarry. She chose to live out the words of the Psalm (27:4) 'One thing I asked of the Lord, that will I seek after: to live in the house of the Lord, all the days of my life, to behold the beauty of the Lord.' Like Simeon, she was in the right place at the right time to see in this baby 'the beauty of the Lord'. She responded by communicating her insight to everyone; he responded with his song. Both knew that their life's work had been fulfilled: Zechariah, earlier, had doubted. They needed no convincing.

Is it only old people who wait? Luke has already shown us watchful shepherds, so he probably didn't think so. And Anna must have made her decision to wait at an age when her friends were keeping busy. Were she and Simeon marked out by this, that they were people prepared to adjust to God's timescale, rather than expecting God to fit into theirs?

Heavens above!
Sometimes I fidget every moment through an egg-timer's worth of prayer.
Almost as if I didn't think there was anyone there seeking some time to address me,
and then to 'let me go in peace'.
Heavenly Wisdom,
implant in me a waiting gene, I pray –
and get a move on!

Down-to-earth wisdom

1 Corinthians 1: 18-24

Paul was writing to a church sharply divided – ethnically, politically, financially and in terms of power. Perhaps they shared one thing: confidence in their own opinions. Paul seems to have decided that there was no point in playing power games with them. Instead, he offered them a kind of slogan: 'Christ crucified'. That was and still is subversive, undercutting pride in our own gifts. To return to the centre of the gospel – the love of God offered to us in the one who empties himself in birth and death – is to be brought down to earth. It should bring an end to power struggles, too.

God has become incarnate: he is down to earth. God has thereby done what humans cannot do: in his wisdom he has shown what it is to be fully human. He has done it by starting at the opposite end to our normal starting-point, as if the key question were not 'what can I make of myself?' but 'what can I give of myself?' Elsewhere Paul calls Jesus the icon or image of the invisible God (Colossians 1:15). At the dawn of a new year, should we give his wise foolishness a try?

O God, you make all things new.
Let me be the same person, but new
with the freshness of your self-giving love.

Jesus, the wisdom of God

1 Corinthians 1: 25-31

Christians in Corinth were not only divided among themselves, they were also a mixed bag, and Paul let them know it. He was not very good at saying what people wanted to hear. Instead (in verse 26) he seems to tell them that they are a pretty undistinguished bunch. He didn't intend to belittle them, however. He wanted to build up their confidence, but to build it on a shared foundation (not 'my gifts are better than yours') and on confidence in God (not in brainpower or personal charisma). Whoever you are, Paul says, you belong to Christ. He has chosen you: now take pride in that.

Paul drew directly on the figure of Wisdom here, especially in verse 30. Wisdom was with God at creation. Wisdom showed us the right way to be in relation to God. Wisdom has come down to earth in Jesus. So here Paul is saying what the creed will later say. Jesus, the Word and Wisdom of God, is instrumental in creation and salvation.

It was not only love, but truth that came down at Christmas. And that truth is both humbling and uplifting; it tells us that God was willing to turn heaven upside down for us. And now, does God expect us to follow suit, and turn the world upside down?

At this time people often make 'New Year Resolutions', looking back on past failures and aiming to get better. How about doing something different this year? Spend some time thinking about the things you think are your 'weaknesses' – list them, if you can bear it. Then reflect carefully about each one and look for something really good hidden in that weakness. Finally, think or pray (or both) how God might like to use the good gifts hidden in your weaknesses in ways that help others.

All about IBRA

IBRA readings

The list of readings for the whole year is available to download from www.christianeducation.org.uk/ibra. You are welcome to make as many copies as you like.

IBRA books

Both extraordinary value at £8.75 each in the UK, with writers from around the world and many different Christian traditions.

IBRA samplers

From time to time IBRA publishes samplers using notes from *Light for our Path* and *Words for Today*, suitable for introducing new readers or for use with Bible study groups. Please contact us at the address below for availability.

IBRA Rep discount

If you live in the UK and purchase 6 or more copies of IBRA books, you can sign up as an IBRA Rep which entitles you to 10% discount off all your IBRA purchases. Just tick the IBRA Rep box on your order form and we'll do the rest.

IBRA International Fund

The IBRA International Fund enables the translation, printing and distribution of IBRA Bible notes and readings. For more details, see page 93. You can make a donation when ordering your books.

IBRA, 1020 Bristol Road, Selly Oak, Birmingham, B29 6LB.

International Bible Reading Association Partners

A worldwide service of Christian Education at work in five continents

HEADQUARTERS
1020 Bristol Road
Selly Oak
Birmingham
B29 6LB
United Kingdom

www.christianeducation.org.uk
ibra@christianeducation.org.uk

and the following agencies:

GHANA
IBRA Secretary
Box GP 919
Accra

asempa@iburstgh.com

INDIA
All India Sunday School Association
Plot No 8,
Threemurthy Colony
6th Cross, Mahendra Hills
PB no 2099
Secunderabad – 500 026
Andhra Pradesh

sundayschoolindia@yahoo.co.in

Fellowship of Professional Workers
Samanvay
Deepthi Chambers
Vijayapuri
Hyderabad – 500 017
Andhra Pradesh
fellowship2w@gmail.com

NEW ZEALAND AND AUSTRALIA
Epworth Bookshop
157B Karori Road
Marsden Village
Karori
Wellington 6012

Mailing address:
PO Box 17255
Karori
Wellington 6147

sales@epworthbooks.org.nz

NIGERIA
Hinderer House
The Cathedral Church of St David
Kudeti
PMB 5298 Dugbe
Ibadan
Oyo State

SOUTH AND CENTRAL AFRICA
IBRA South Africa
6 Roosmaryn Street
Durbanville 7550
biblereading@evmot.com

INTERNATIONAL BIBLE READING ASSOCIATION
1020 Bristol Road, Selly Oak, Birmingham B29 6LB, United Kingdom

You can order using this form or through your local IBRA rep, or online at http://shop.christianeducation.org.uk, or by email to sales@christianeducation.org.uk or by phone on 0121 472 4242

Please return this form to
IBRA, 1020 Bristol Road, Selly Oak, Birmingham B29 6LB

Order form for 2013 books

Name: ____________________

Address: ____________________

____

____

____________________ **Postcode:** ____________________

Telephone no: ____________________ **Email:** ____________________

Postage in the UK is free. Payments in pounds sterling, please. If you are ordering from overseas and require more than one copy please contact us for a discounted price.

Code		Quantity	Price	Total
UK customers				
AA120201	Light for our Path 2013		£8.75	
AA120202	Words for Today 2013		£8.75	
	I am an IBRA Rep (see page 192)		10% off	
	I am ordering 6+ books and would like to become an IBRA Rep		10% off	
Western Europe				
AA120201	Light for our Path 2013		£13.00	
AA120202	Words for Today 2013		£13.00	
Rest of the world				
AA120201	Light for our Path 2013		£15.00	
AA120202	Words for Today 2013		£15.00	
			Subtotal	
			Donation to the IBRA International Fund	
			Total	

☐ **I enclose a cheque (made payable to IBRA)**

☐ **Please charge my MASTERCARD/VISA/SWITCH** (delete as appropriate)

Card Number: ☐☐☐☐☐☐☐☐☐☐☐☐☐☐☐☐ **Issue Number:** ☐☐

Expiry Date: ☐☐ ☐☐

Security number (last three digits on back): ☐☐☐

Signature: ____________________

IBRA SCHEME OF READINGS 2013

New Year Manifesto
John proclaims Jesus
Jesus proclaims himself

Living Differently
But I say to you…
The new way
Hearing a different drummer
Living as children of light

Through Lent and Passiontide in Poetry
Temptations
Enemies and opposition
Suffering and distress
Being overwhelmed
Separation from God
Protection and deliverance
The passion of Christ

Readings in Luke
Resurrection and Ascension
Going up to Jerusalem
The last days

Hosea
Covenant and faithlessness
God's continued forgiveness

Fire
Fire in the Old Testament (1)
Fire in the Old Testament (2)
Fire in the New Testament

Acts 6–12: From Jerusalem to Antioch
Disciples increasing in number
Light dawns for Paul and then Peter
The church spreads

Questions in Job
My servant Job
Job's friends venture a few words
Job calls God to answer
A happy ending?

Mountains and Valleys
Mountains
And valleys

Paul for Today
A re-formed life: in Christ, of one Spirit & always thankful
Sharing good news: healing in Paul's divided world
Grace talk: God-walk - with a difference
Living letters: negotiating challenges of life together

Contested Sites
Promised or stolen land?
'… neither on this mountain nor in Jerusalem'
God's vineyard

Navigating Numbers
Taking stock, counting heads
Journeying on
Beyond the plains

Mothers
God at the birth
Mothering continues

Facing Death
Facing death in the Old Testament
Facing death in the New Testament
Facing death with God at our side
Facing death and beyond death

Readings in Luke
Jesus the Teacher
The kingdom is among you

Isaiah 56-66
Soon my salvation will come
Your sins have hidden his face
Good news to the oppressed
You are our father
They shall not labour in vain